ŚRĪMAD BHĀGAVATAM

Sixth Canto

"Prescribed Duties for Mankind"

(Part Two—Chapters 6-13)

With the Original Sanskrit Text, Its Roman Transliteration, Synonyms, Translation and Elaborate Purports by

His Divine Grace
A.C. Bhaktivedanta Swami Prabhupāda
Founder-*Ācārya* of the International Society for Krishna Consciousness

THE BHAKTIVEDANTA BOOK TRUST
New York · Los Angeles · London · Bombay

Readers interested in the subject matter of this book
are invited by the International Society for Krishna Consciousness
to correspond with its Secretary.

International Society for Krishna Consciousness
3764 Watseka Avenue
Los Angeles, California 90034

Library of Congress Catalogue Card Number: 73-169353
International Standard Book Number: 0-912776-82-x

First printing, 1975: 20,000 copies

Printed in the United States of America

ALL GLORY TO ŚRĪ GURU AND GAURĀṄGA

ŚRĪMAD BHĀGAVATAM

of

KṚṢṆA-DVAIPĀYANA VYĀSA

लोकाः सपाला यस्येमे श्वसन्ति विवशा वशे ।
द्विजा इव शिचा बद्धाः स काल इह कारणम् ॥ ८ ॥

lokāḥ sapālā yasyeme
śvasanti vivaśā vaśe
dvijā iva śicā baddhāḥ
sa kāla iha kāraṇam (p. 223)

BOOKS by
His Divine Grace A. C. Bhaktivedanta Swami Prabhupāda

Bhagavad-gītā As It Is
Śrīmad-Bhāgavatam, Cantos 1-6 (18 Vols.)
Śrī Caitanya-caritāmṛta (17 Vols.)
Teachings of Lord Caitanya
The Nectar of Devotion
The Nectar of Instruction
Śrī Īśopaniṣad
Easy Journey to Other Planets
Kṛṣṇa Consciousness: The Topmost Yoga System
Kṛṣṇa, the Supreme Personality of Godhead (3 Vols.)
Perfect Questions, Perfect Answers
Transcendental Teachings of Prahlad Mahārāja
Kṛṣṇa, the Reservoir of Pleasure
Life Comes from Life
The Perfection of Yoga
Beyond Birth and Death
On the Way to Kṛṣṇa
Rāja-vidyā: The King of Knowledge
Elevation to Kṛṣṇa Consciousness
Kṛṣṇa Consciousness: The Matchless Gift
Back to Godhead Magazine (Founder)

A complete catalogue is available upon request

The Bhaktivedanta Book Trust
3764 Watseka Avenue
Los Angeles, California 90034

Table of Contents

CHAPTER TWELVE
Vṛtrāsura's Glorious Death   215

CHAPTER THIRTEEN
King Indra Afflicted by Sinful Reaction   247

Appendixes

Preface

We must know the present need of human society. And what is that need? Human society is no longer bounded by geographical limits to particular countries or communities. Human society is broader than in the Middle Ages, and the world tendency is toward one state or one human society. The ideals of spiritual communism, according to *Śrīmad-Bhāgavatam*, are based more or less on the oneness of the entire human society, nay, on the entire energy of living beings. The need is felt by great thinkers to make this a successful ideology. *Śrīmad-Bhāgavatam* will fill this need in human society. It begins, therefore, with the aphorism of Vedānta philosophy (*janmādy asya yataḥ*) to establish the ideal of a common cause.

Human society, at the present moment, is not in the darkness of oblivion. It has made rapid progress in the field of material comforts, education and economic development throughout the entire world. But there is a pinprick somewhere in the social body at large, and therefore there are large-scale quarrels, even over less important issues. There is need of a clue as to how humanity can become one in peace, friendship and prosperity with a common cause. *Śrīmad-Bhāgavatam* will fill this need, for it is a cultural presentation for the re-spiritualization of the entire human society.

Śrīmad-Bhāgavatam should be introduced also in the schools and colleges, for it is recommended by the great student devotee Prahlāda Mahārāja in order to change the demonic face of society.

kaumāra ācaret prājño
dharmān bhāgavatān iha
durlabhaṁ mānuṣaṁ janma
tad apy adhruvam arthadam
(*Bhāg.* 7.6.1)

Disparity in human society is due to lack of principles in a godless civilization. There is God, or the Almighty One, from whom everything emanates, by whom everything is maintained and in whom everything is merged to rest. Material science has tried to find the ultimate source of creation very insufficiently, but it is a fact that there is one ultimate source of everything that be. This ultimate source is explained rationally and authoritatively in the beautiful *Bhāgavatam* or *Śrīmad-Bhāgavatam.*

Śrīmad-Bhāgavatam is the transcendental science not only for knowing the ultimate source of everything but also for knowing our relation with Him and our duty towards perfection of the human society on the basis of this perfect knowledge. It is powerful reading matter in the Sanskrit language, and it is now rendered into English elaborately so that simply by a careful reading one will know God perfectly well, so much so that the reader will be sufficiently educated to defend himself from the onslaught of atheists. Over and above this, the reader will be able to convert others to accept God as a concrete principle.

Śrīmad-Bhāgavatam begins with the definition of the ultimate source. It is a bona fide commentary on the *Vedānta-sūtra* by the same author, Śrīla Vyāsadeva, and gradually it develops into nine cantos up to the highest state of God realization. The only qualification one needs to study this great book of transcendental knowledge is to proceed step by step cautiously and not jump forward haphazardly as with an ordinary book. It should be gone through chapter by chapter, one after another. The reading matter is so arranged with its original Sanskrit text, its English transliteration, synonyms, translation and purports so that one is sure to become a God realized soul at the end of finishing the first nine cantos.

The Tenth Canto is distinct from the first nine cantos, because it deals directly with the transcendental activities of the Personality of Godhead Śrī Kṛṣṇa. One will be unable to capture the effects of the Tenth Canto without going through the first nine cantos. The book is complete in twelve cantos, each independent, but it is good for all to read them in small installments one after another.

I must admit my frailties in presenting *Śrīmad-Bhāgavatam,* but still I am hopeful of its good reception by the thinkers and leaders of society on the strength of the following statement of *Śrīmad-Bhāgavatam.*

tad vāg-visargo janatāgha-viplavo
yasmin pratiślokam abaddhavaty api

nāmāny anantasya yaśo 'nkitāni yac
chṛṇvanti gāyanti gṛṇanti sādhavaḥ
(*Bhāg.* 1.5.11)

"On the other hand, that literature which is full with descriptions of the transcendental glories of the name, fame, form and pastimes of the unlimited Supreme Lord is a transcendental creation meant to bring about a revolution in the impious life of a misdirected civilization. Such transcendental literatures, even though irregularly composed, are heard, sung and accepted by purified men who are thoroughly honest."

Oṁ tat sat

A. C. Bhaktivedanta Swami

Introduction

"This *Bhāgavata Purāṇa* is as brilliant as the sun, and it has arisen just after the departure of Lord Kṛṣṇa to His own abode, accompanied by religion, knowledge, etc. Persons who have lost their vision due to the dense darkness of ignorance in the age of Kali shall get light from this *Purāṇa*." (*Śrīmad-Bhāgavatam* 1.3.43)

The timeless wisdom of India is expressed in the *Vedas*, ancient Sanskrit texts that touch upon all fields of human knowledge. Originally preserved through oral tradition, the *Vedas* were first put into writing five thousand years ago by Śrīla Vyāsadeva, the "literary incarnation of God." After compiling the *Vedas*, Vyāsadeva set forth their essence in the aphorisms known as *Vedānta-sūtras*. *Śrīmad-Bhāgavatam* is Vyāsadeva's commentary on his own *Vedānta-sūtras*. It was written in the maturity of his spiritual life under the direction of Nārada Muni, his spiritual master. Referred to as "the ripened fruit of the tree of Vedic literature," *Śrīmad-Bhāgavatam* is the most complete and authoritative exposition of Vedic knowledge.

After compiling the *Bhāgavatam*, Vyāsa impressed the synopsis of it upon his son, the sage Śukadeva Gosvāmī. Śukadeva Gosvāmī subsequently recited the entire *Bhāgavatam* to Mahārāja Parīkṣit in an assembly of learned saints on the bank of the Ganges at Hastināpura (now Delhi). Mahārāja Parīkṣit was the emperor of the world and was a great *rājarṣi* (saintly king). Having received a warning that he would die within a week, he renounced his entire kingdom and retired to the bank of the Ganges to fast until death and receive spiritual enlightenment. The *Bhāgavatam* begins with Emperor Parīkṣit's sober inquiry to Śukadeva Gosvāmī:

> "You are the spiritual master of great saints and devotees. I am therefore begging you to show the way of perfection for all persons, and especially for one who is about to die. Please let me know what a man should hear, chant, remember and worship, and also what he should not do. Please explain all this to me."

Śukadeva Gosvāmī's answer to this question, and numerous other questions posed by Mahārāja Parīkṣit, concerning everything from the nature of the self to the origin of the universe, held the assembled sages in rapt attention continuously for the seven days leading to the King's death. The sage Sūta Gosvāmī, who was present on the bank of the Ganges when Śukadeva Gosvāmī first recited *Śrīmad-Bhāgavatam*, later repeated the *Bhāgavatam* before a gathering of sages in the forest of Naimiṣāraṇya. Those sages, concerned about the spiritual welfare of the people in general, had gathered to perform a long, continuous chain of sacrifices to counteract the degrading influence of the incipient age of Kali. In response to the sages' request that he speak the essence of Vedic wisdom, Sūta Gosvāmī repeated from memory the entire eighteen thousand verses of *Śrīmad-Bhāgavatam*, as spoken by Śukadeva Gosvāmī to Mahārāja Parīkṣit.

The reader of *Śrīmad-Bhāgavatam* hears Sūta Gosvāmī relate the questions of Mahārāja Parīkṣit and the answers of Śukadeva Gosvāmī. Also, Sūta Gosvāmī sometimes responds directly to questions put by Śaunaka Ṛṣi, the spokesman for the sages gathered at Naimiṣāraṇya. One therefore simultaneously hears two dialogues: one between Mahārāja Parīkṣit and Śukadeva Gosvāmī on the bank of the Ganges, and another at Naimiṣāraṇya between Sūta Gosvāmī and the sages at Naimiṣāraṇya Forest, headed by Śaunaka Ṛṣi. Furthermore, while instructing King Parīkṣit, Śukadeva Gosvāmī often relates historical episodes and gives accounts of lengthy philosophical discussions between such great souls as the saint Maitreya and his disciple Vidura. With this understanding of the history of the *Bhāgavatam*, the reader will easily be able to follow its intermingling of dialogues and events from various sources. Since philosophical wisdom, not chronological order, is most important in the text, one need only be attentive to the subject matter of *Śrīmad-Bhāgavatam* to appreciate fully its profound message.

It should also be noted that the volumes of the *Bhāgavatam* need not be read consecutively, starting with the first and proceeding to the last. The translator of this edition compares the *Bhāgavatam* to sugar candy—wherever you taste it, you will find it equally sweet and relishable.

This edition of the *Bhāgavatam* is the first complete English translation of this important text with an elaborate commentary, and it is the first widely available to the English-speaking public. It is the product of the scholarly and devotional effort of His Divine Grace A. C. Bhaktivedanta Swami Prabhupāda, the world's most distinguished teacher of Indian religious and philosophical thought. His consummate Sanskrit scholarship and intimate familiarity with Vedic culture and thought as well as the modern way of life combine to reveal to the West a magnificent exposition of this important classic.

Readers will find this work of value for many reasons. For those interested in the classical roots of Indian civilization, it serves as a vast reservoir of detailed information on virtually every one of its aspects. For students of comparative philosophy and religion, the *Bhāgavatam* offers a penetrating view into the meaning of India's profound spiritual heritage. To sociologists and anthropologists, the *Bhāgavatam* reveals the practical workings of a peaceful and scientifically organized Vedic culture, whose institutions were integrated on the basis of a highly developed spiritual world view. Students of literature will discover the *Bhāgavatam* to be a masterpiece of majestic poetry. For students of psychology, the text provides important perspectives on the nature of consciousness, human behavior and the philosophical study of identity. Finally, to those seeking spiritual insight, the *Bhāgavatam* offers simple and practical guidance for attainment of the highest self-knowledge and realization of the Absolute Truth. The entire multivolume text, presented by the Bhaktivedanta Book Trust, promises to occupy a significant place in the intellectual, cultural and spiritual life of modern man for a long time to come.

—The Publishers

His Divine Grace
A. C. Bhaktivedanta Swami Prabhupāda
Founder-Ācārya of the International Society for Krishna Consciousness

PLATE ONE

"After King Indra insulted his spiritual master Bṛhaspati, the demons equipped themselves with weapons and declared war against the demigods. As a result of their misbehavior toward Bṛhaspati, the demigods' heads, thighs and arms and the other parts of their bodies were injured by the sharp arrows of the demons. The demigods, headed by Indra, saw no other course than to immediately approach Lord Brahmā, the first living being in charge of material creation, with bowed heads for shelter and proper instruction. When the most powerful Lord Brahmā saw the demigods coming toward him, their bodies gravely injured by the arrows of the demons, he pacified and instructed them by his great causeless mercy." *(pp. 41–43)*

PLATE TWO

Viśvarūpa, who was engaged by the demigods as their priest, instructed King Indra about the Nārāyaṇa armor, which enabled him to conquer the leaders of the demons. After chanting various *mantras*, Viśvarūpa began to chant the following protective prayer to Lord Nārāyaṇa. "The Supreme Lord, who sits on the back of the bird Garuḍa, touching him with His lotus feet, holds eight weapons—the conchshell, disc, shield, sword, club, arrows, bow and ropes. May that Supreme Personality of Godhead protect me at all times with His eight arms. He is all-powerful because he fully possesses the eight mystic powers." Next he offered prayers to the Lord's personal expansions, to the Supreme Lord Kṛṣṇa, and to the weapons of Lord Nārāyaṇa. He thus taught King Indra how to take shelter of the mystic armor. *(pp. 65–92)*

PLATE THREE

"After Viśvarūpa was killed by King Indra, Viśvarūpa's father, Tvaṣṭā, performed ritualistic ceremonies to kill Indra by offering oblations in the sacrificial fire. Thereafter, from the southern side of the sacrificial fire came a fearful personality who looked like the destroyer of the entire creation at the end of the millennium. Like arrows released in the four directions, the demon's body grew, day after day. Tall and blackish, he appeared like a burnt hill and was as lustrous as a bright array of clouds in the evening. The hair on the demon's body and his beard and mustache were the color of melted copper, and his eyes were piercing like the midday sun. He appeared unconquerable, as if holding the three worlds on the point of his blazing trident. Dancing and shouting with a loud voice, he made the entire surface of the earth tremble as if from an earthquake. As he yawned again and again, he seemed to be trying to swallow the whole sky with his mouth, which was as deep as a cave. He seemed to be licking up all the stars in the sky with his tongue and eating the entire universe with his long, sharp teeth. Seeing this gigantic demon, everyone, in great fear, ran here and there in all directions." *(pp. 108–110)*

PLATE FOUR

"The shower of various weapons and arrows released by the demons to kill the soldiers of the demigods did not reach them because the demigods, acting quickly, cut the weapons into thousands of pieces in the sky. As their weapons and *mantras* decreased, the demons began showering mountain peaks, trees and stones upon the demigod soldiers, but the demigods were so powerful and expert that they nullified all these weapons by breaking them to pieces in the sky as before. When the soldiers of the demons, commanded by Vṛtrāsura, saw that the soldiers of King Indra were quite well, having not been injured at all by their volleys of weapons, not even by the trees, stones and mountain peaks, the demons were very much afraid. Leaving aside their leader even in the very beginning of the fight, they decided to flee because all their prowess had been taken away by the enemy." *(pp. 180–183)*

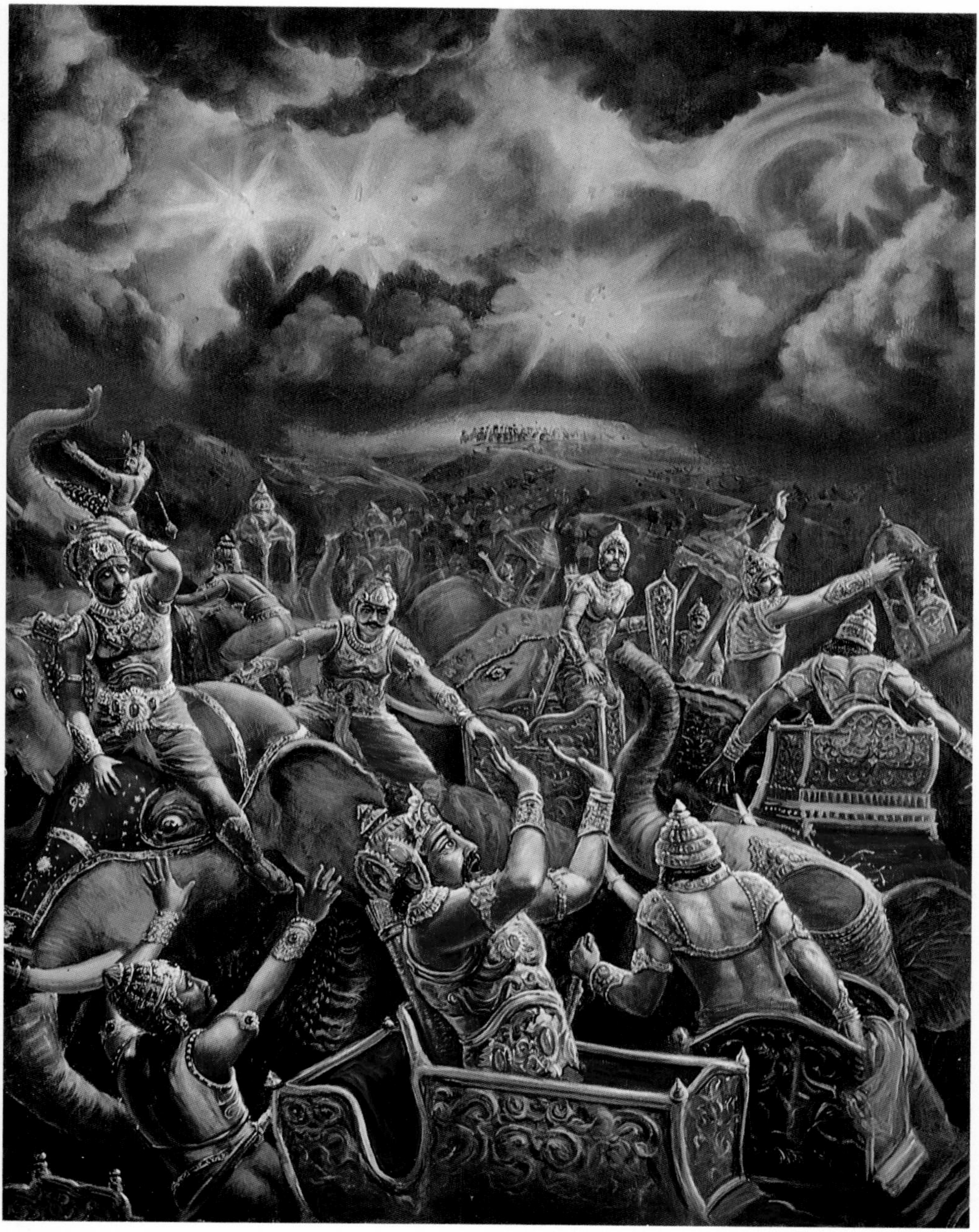

PLATE FIVE

"When all the demigods heard Vṛtrāsura's tumultuous roar, which resembled that of a lion, they fainted and fell to the ground as if struck by thunderbolts. As the demigods closed their eyes in fear, Vṛtrāsura, taking up his trident and making the earth tremble with his great strength, trampled the demigods beneath his feet on the battlefield the way a mad elephant tramples hollow bamboo in the forest. Seeing Vṛtrāsura's disposition, Indra, the King of heaven, became intolerant and threw at him one of his great clubs, which are extremely difficult to counteract. However, as the club flew toward him, Vṛtrāsura easily caught it with his left hand. The powerful Vṛtrāsura angrily struck the head of Indra's elephant with that club, making a tumultuous sound on the battlefield. Struck with the club by Vṛtrāsura like a mountain struck by a thunderbolt, the elephant Airāvata, feeling great pain and spitting blood from its broken mouth, was pushed back fourteen yards. In great distress, the elephant fell, with Indra on its back." *(pp. 192–195)*

PLATE SIX

"After Indra cut off his two arms, Vṛtrāsura, bleeding profusely, assumed a gigantic body which shook even the mountains and began crushing the surface of the earth with his legs. He came before Indra and swallowed him and Airāvata, his carrier, just as a big python might swallow an elephant. The Nārāyaṇa armor protected King Indra, and with his thunderbolt he pierced through Vṛtrāsura's abdomen and came out. Indra, the killer of the demon Bala, then cut off Vṛtrāsura's head, which was as high as the peak of a mountain. At that time, the living spark came forth from Vṛtrāsura's body and returned home, back to Godhead. While all the demigods looked on, he entered the transcendental world to become an associate of Lord Saṅkarṣaṇa." *(pp. 240–246)*

PLATE SEVEN

"After killing the *brāhmaṇa* Vṛtrāsura, King Indra suffered because of this sinful killing. Indra saw personified sinful reaction chasing him, appearing like a *caṇḍāla* woman, a woman of the lowest class. She seemed very old, and all the limbs of her body trembled. Because she was afflicted with tuberculosis, her body and garments were covered with blood. Breathing an unbearable fishy odor that polluted the entire street, she called to Indra, 'Wait! Wait!' Indra first fled to the sky, but there also he saw the woman of personified sin chasing him. This witch followed him wherever he went. At last he very quickly went to the northeast and entered the Mānasa-sarovara Lake." *(pp. 258–260)*

CHAPTER SIX

The Progeny of the Daughters of Dakṣa

As described in this chapter, Prajāpati Dakṣa begot sixty daughters in the womb of his wife Asiknī. These daughters were given in charity to various persons to increase the population. Since these offspring of Dakṣa were women, Nārada Muni did not try to lead them toward the renounced order of life. Thus the daughters were saved from Nārada Muni. Ten of the daughters were given in marriage to Dharmarāja, thirteen to Kaśyapa Muni, and twenty-seven to the moon-god, Candra. In this way fifty daughters were distributed, and of the other ten daughters, four were given to Kaśyapa and two each to Bhūta, Aṅgirā and Kṛśāśva. One should know that it is because of the union of these sixty daughters with various exalted personalities that the entire universe was filled with various kinds of living entities, such as human beings, demigods, demons, beasts, birds and serpents.

TEXT 1

श्रीशुक उवाच
ततः प्राचेतसोऽसिक्न्यामनुनीतः स्वयम्भुवा ।
षष्टिं सञ्जनयामास दुहितॄः पितृवत्सलाः ॥ १ ॥

śrī-śuka uvāca
tataḥ prācetaso 'siknyām
anunītaḥ svayambhuvā
ṣaṣṭiṁ sañjanayām āsa
duhitṝḥ pitṛ-vatsalāḥ

śrī-śukaḥ uvāca—Śrī Śukadeva Gosvāmī said; *tataḥ*—after that incident; *prācetasaḥ*—Dakṣa; *asiknyām*—in his wife named Asiknī; *anunītaḥ*—pacified; *svayambhuvā*—by Lord Brahmā; *ṣaṣṭim*—sixty;

sañjanayām āsa—begot; *duhitṝḥ*—daughters; *pitṛ-vatsalāḥ*—all very affectionate to their father.

TRANSLATION

Śrī Śukadeva Gosvāmī said: My dear King, thereafter, at the request of Lord Brahmā, Prajāpati Dakṣa, who is known as Prācetasa, begot sixty daughters in the womb of his wife Asiknī. All the daughters were very affectionate toward their father.

PURPORT

After the incidents concerning the loss of his many sons, Dakṣa repented his misunderstanding with Nārada Muni. Lord Brahmā then saw Dakṣa and instructed him to beget children again. This time Dakṣa was very cautious to beget female children instead of male children so that Nārada Muni would not disturb them by urging them to accept the renounced order. Females are not meant for the renounced order of life; they should be faithful to their good husbands, for if a husband is competent for liberation, his wife will also achieve liberation with him. As stated in the *śāstra*, the results of a husband's pious activities are shared by his wife. Therefore a woman's duty is to be very chaste and faithful to her husband. Then without separate endeavor she will share in all the profit the husband earns.

TEXT 2

दश धर्माय कायादाद्द्विषट् त्रिणव चेन्दवे ।
भूताङ्गिरःकृशाश्वेभ्यो द्वे द्वे तार्क्ष्याय चापराः ॥ २ ॥

daśa dharmāya kāyādād
dvi-ṣaṭ tri-ṇava cendave
bhūtāṅgiraḥ-kṛśāśvebhyo
dve dve tārkṣyāya cāparāḥ

daśa—ten; *dharmāya*—unto King Dharma, Yamarāja; *kāya*—unto Kaśyapa; *adāt*—gave; *dvi-ṣaṭ*—twice six and one (thirteen); *tri-nava*—thrice nine (twenty-seven); *ca*—also; *indave*—unto the moon-god; *bhūta-aṅgiraḥ-kṛśāśvebhyaḥ*—unto Bhūta, Aṅgirā and Kṛśāśva; *dve*

dve—two each; *tārkṣyāya*—again unto Kaśyapa; *ca*—and; *aparāḥ*—the balance.

TRANSLATION

He gave ten daughters in charity to Dharmarāja [Yamarāja], thirteen to Kaśyapa [first twelve and then one more], twenty-seven to the moon-god, and two each to Aṅgirā, Kṛśāśva and Bhūta. The other four daughters were given to Kaśyapa. [Thus Kaśyapa received seventeen daughters in all.]

TEXT 3

नामधेयान्यमूषां त्वं सापत्यानां च मे शृणु ।
यासां प्रसूतिप्रसवैर्लोका आपूरितास्त्रयः ॥ ३ ॥

nāmadheyāny amūṣāṁ tvaṁ
sāpatyānāṁ ca me śṛṇu
yāsāṁ prasūti-prasavair
lokā āpūritās trayaḥ

nāmadheyāni—the different names; *amūṣām*—of them; *tvam*—you; *sa-apatyānām*—with their offspring; *ca*—and; *me*—from me; *śṛṇu*—please hear; *yāsām*—of all of whom; *prasūti-prasavaiḥ*—by so many children and descendants; *lokāḥ*—the worlds; *āpūritāḥ*—populated; *trayaḥ*—three (the upper, middle and lower worlds).

TRANSLATION

Now please hear from me the names of all these daughters and their descendants, who filled all the three worlds.

TEXT 4

भानुर्लम्बा ककुद्यामिर्विश्वा साध्या मरुत्वती ।
वसुर्मुहूर्ता सङ्कल्पा धर्मपत्न्यः सुताञ् शृणु ॥ ४ ॥

bhānur lambā kakud yāmir
viśvā sādhyā marutvatī

vasur muhūrtā saṅkalpā
dharma-patnyaḥ sutāñ śṛṇu

bhānuḥ—Bhānu; *lambā*—Lambā; *kakut*—Kakud; *yāmiḥ*—Yāmi; *viśvā*—Viśvā; *sādhyā*—Sādhyā; *marutvatī*—Marutvatī; *vasuḥ*—Vasu; *muhūrtā*—Muhūrtā; *saṅkalpā*—Saṅkalpā; *dharma-patnyaḥ*—the wives of Yamarāja; *sutān*—their sons; *śṛṇu*—now hear of.

TRANSLATION

The ten daughters given to Yamarāja were named Bhānu, Lambā, Kakud, Yāmi, Viśvā, Sādhyā, Marutvatī, Vasu, Muhūrtā and Saṅkalpā. Now hear the names of their sons.

TEXT 5

भानोस्तु देवऋषभ इन्द्रसेनस्ततो नृप ।
विद्योत आसील्लम्बायास्ततश्च स्तनयित्नवः ॥ ५ ॥

bhānos tu deva-ṛṣabha
indrasenas tato nṛpa
vidyota āsīl lambāyās
tataś ca stanayitnavaḥ

bhānoḥ—from the womb of Bhānu; *tu*—of course; *deva-ṛṣabhaḥ*—Deva-ṛṣabha; *indrasenaḥ*—Indrasena; *tataḥ*—from him (Deva-ṛṣabha); *nṛpa*—O King; *vidyotaḥ*—Vidyota; *āsīt*—appeared; *lambāyāḥ*—from the womb of Lambā; *tataḥ*—from him; *ca*—and; *stanayitnavaḥ*—all the clouds.

TRANSLATION

O King, a son named Deva-ṛṣabha was born from the womb of Bhānu, and from him came a son named Indrasena. From the womb of Lambā came a son named Vidyota, who generated all the clouds.

TEXT 6

ककुदः सङ्कटस्तस्य कीकटस्तनयो यतः ।
भुवो दुर्गाणि यामेयः स्वर्गो नन्दिस्ततोऽभवत् ॥ ६ ॥

kakudaḥ saṅkaṭas tasya
kīkaṭas tanayo yataḥ
bhuvo durgāṇi yāmeyaḥ
svargo nandis tato 'bhavat

kakudaḥ—from the womb of Kakud; *saṅkaṭaḥ*—Saṅkaṭa; *tasya*—from him; *kīkaṭaḥ*—Kīkaṭa; *tanayaḥ*—son; *yataḥ*—from whom; *bhuvaḥ*—of the earth; *durgāṇi*—many demigods, protectors of this universe (which is called Durgā); *yāmeyaḥ*—of Yāmi; *svargaḥ*—Svarga; *nandiḥ*—Nandi; *tataḥ*—from him (Svarga); *abhavat*—was born.

TRANSLATION

From the womb of Kakud came the son named Saṅkaṭa, whose son was named Kīkaṭa. From Kīkaṭa came the demigods named Durga. From Yāmi came the son named Svarga, whose son was named Nandi.

TEXT 7

विश्वेदेवास्तु विश्वाया अप्रजांस्तान् प्रचक्षते ।
साध्योगणश्च साध्याया अर्थसिद्धिस्तु तत्सुतः॥ ७॥

viśve-devās tu viśvāyā
aprajāṁs tān pracakṣate
sādhyo-gaṇaś ca sādhyāyā
arthasiddhis tu tat-sutaḥ

viśve-devāḥ—the demigods named the Viśvadevas; *tu*—but; *viśvāyāḥ*—from Viśvā; *aprajān*—without sons; *tān*—them; *pracakṣate*—it is said; *sādhyaḥ-gaṇaḥ*—the demigods named the Sādhyas; *ca*—and; *sādhyāyāḥ*—from the womb of Sādhyā; *arthasiddhiḥ*—Arthasiddhi; *tu*—but; *tat-sutaḥ*—the son of the Sādhyas.

TRANSLATION

The sons of Viśvā were the Viśvadevas, who had no progeny. From the womb of Sādhyā came the Sādhyas, who had a son named Arthasiddhi.

TEXT 8

मरुत्वांश्च जयन्तश्च मरुत्वत्या बभूवतुः ।
जयन्तो वासुदेवांश उपेन्द्र इति यं विदुः ॥ ८ ॥

marutvāṁś ca jayantaś ca
marutvatyā babhūvatuḥ
jayanto vāsudevāṁśa
upendra iti yaṁ viduḥ

marutvān—Marutvān; *ca*—also; *jayantaḥ*—Jayanta; *ca*—and; *marutvatyāḥ*—from Marutvatī; *babhūvatuḥ*—took birth; *jayantaḥ*—Jayanta; *vāsudeva-aṁśaḥ*—an expansion of Vāsudeva; *upendraḥ*—Upendra; *iti*—thus; *yam*—whom; *viduḥ*—they know.

TRANSLATION

The two sons who took birth from the womb of Marutvatī were Marutvān and Jayanta. Jayanta, who is an expansion of Lord Vāsudeva, is known as Upendra.

TEXT 9

मौहूर्तिका देवगणा मुहूर्तायाश्च जज्ञिरे ।
ये वै फलं प्रयच्छन्ति भूतानां स्वस्वकालजम् ॥ ९ ॥

mauhūrtikā deva-gaṇā
muhūrtāyāś ca jajñire
ye vai phalaṁ prayacchanti
bhūtānāṁ sva-sva-kālajam

mauhūrtikāḥ—Mauhūrtikas; *deva-gaṇāḥ*—the demigods; *muhūrtāyāḥ*—from the womb of Muhūrtā; *ca*—and; *jajñire*—took birth; *ye*—all of whom; *vai*—indeed; *phalam*—result; *prayacchanti*—deliver; *bhūtānām*—of the living entities; *sva-sva*—their own; *kāla-jam*—born of time.

TRANSLATION

The demigods named the Mauhūrtikas took birth from the womb of Muhūrtā. These demigods deliver the results of actions to the living entities of their respective times.

TEXTS 10–11

सङ्कल्पायास्तु सङ्कल्पः कामः सङ्कल्पजः स्मृतः।
वसवोऽष्टौ वसोः पुत्रास्तेषां नामानि मे शृणु ॥१०॥
द्रोणः प्राणो ध्रुवोऽर्कोऽग्निर्दोषो वास्तुर्विभावसुः।
द्रोणस्याभिमतेः पत्न्या हर्षशोकभयादयः ॥११॥

saṅkalpāyās tu saṅkalpaḥ
kāmaḥ saṅkalpajaḥ smṛtaḥ
vasavo 'ṣṭau vasoḥ putrās
teṣāṁ nāmāni me śṛṇu

droṇaḥ prāṇo dhruvo 'rko 'gnir
doṣo vāstur vibhāvasuḥ
droṇasyābhimateḥ patnyā
harṣa-śoka-bhayādayaḥ

saṅkalpāyāḥ—from the womb of Saṅkalpā; *tu*—but; *saṅkalpaḥ*—Saṅkalpa; *kāmaḥ*—Kāma; *saṅkalpa-jaḥ*—the son of Saṅkalpa; *smṛtaḥ*—known; *vasavaḥ aṣṭau*—the eight Vasus; *vasoḥ*—of Vasu; *putrāḥ*—the sons; *teṣām*—of them; *nāmāni*—the names; *me*—from me; *śṛṇu*—just hear; *droṇaḥ*—Droṇa; *prāṇaḥ*—Prāṇa; *dhruvaḥ*—Dhruva; *arkaḥ*—Arka; *agniḥ*—Agni; *doṣaḥ*—Doṣa; *vāstuḥ*—Vāstu; *vibhāvasuḥ*—Vibhāvasu; *droṇasya*—of Droṇa; *abhimateḥ*—from Abhimati; *patnyāḥ*—the wife; *harṣa-śoka-bhaya-ādayaḥ*—the sons named Harṣa, Śoka, Bhaya and so on.

TRANSLATION

The son of Saṅkalpā was known as Saṅkalpa, and from him lust was born. The sons of Vasu were known as the eight Vasus. Just

hear their names from me: Droṇa, Prāṇa, Dhruva, Arka, Agni, Doṣa, Vāstu and Vibhāvasu. From Abhimati, the wife of the Vasu named Droṇa, were generated the sons named Harṣa, Śoka, Bhaya and so on.

TEXT 12

प्राणस्योर्जस्वती भार्या सह आयुः पुरोजवः ।
ध्रुवस्य भार्या धरणिरसूत विविधाः पुरः ॥१२॥

prāṇasyorjasvatī bhāryā
saha āyuḥ purojavaḥ
dhruvasya bhāryā dharaṇir
asūta vividhāḥ puraḥ

prāṇasya—of Prāṇa; *ūrjasvatī*—Ūrjasvatī; *bhāryā*—the wife; *sahaḥ*—Saha; *āyuḥ*—Āyus; *purojavaḥ*—Purojava; *dhruvasya*—of Dhruva; *bhāryā*—the wife; *dharaṇiḥ*—Dharaṇi; *asūta*—gave birth to; *vividhāḥ*—the various; *puraḥ*—cities and towns.

TRANSLATION

Ūrjasvatī, the wife of Prāṇa, gave birth to three sons, named Saha, Āyus and Purojava. The wife of Dhruva was known as Dharaṇi, and from her womb various cities took birth.

TEXT 13

अर्कस्य वासना भार्या पुत्रास्तर्षादयः स्मृताः ।
अग्नेर्भार्या वसोर्धारा पुत्रा द्रविणकादयः ॥१३॥

arkasya vāsanā bhāryā
putrās tarṣādayaḥ smṛtāḥ
agner bhāryā vasor dhārā
putrā draviṇakādayaḥ

arkasya—of Arka; *vāsanā*—Vāsanā; *bhāryā*—the wife; *putrāḥ*—the sons; *tarṣa-ādayaḥ*—named Tarṣa and so on; *smṛtāḥ*—celebrated;

agneḥ—of Agni; *bhāryā*—wife; *vasoḥ*—the Vasu; *dhārā*—Dhārā; *putrāḥ*—the sons; *draviṇaka-ādayaḥ*—known as Draviṇaka and so on.

TRANSLATION

From the womb of Vāsanā, the wife of Arka, came many sons, headed by Tarṣa. Dhārā, the wife of the Vasu named Agni, gave birth to many sons, headed by Draviṇaka.

TEXT 14

स्कन्दश्च कृत्तिकापुत्रो ये विशाखादयस्ततः ।
दोषस्य शर्वरीपुत्रः शिशुमारो हरेः कला ॥१४॥

skandaś ca kṛttikā-putro
ye viśākhādayas tataḥ
doṣasya śarvarī-putraḥ
śiśumāro hareḥ kalā

skandaḥ—Skanda; *ca*—also; *kṛttikā-putraḥ*—the son of Kṛttikā; *ye*—all of whom; *viśākha-ādayaḥ*—headed by Viśākha; *tataḥ*—from him (Skanda); *doṣasya*—of Doṣa; *śarvarī-putraḥ*—the son of his wife Śarvarī; *śiśumāraḥ*—Śiśumāra; *hareḥ kalā*—an expansion of the Supreme Personality of Godhead.

TRANSLATION

From Kṛttikā, another wife of Agni, came the son named Skanda, Kārttikeya, whose sons were headed by Viśākha. From the womb of Śarvarī, the wife of the Vasu named Doṣa, came the son named Śiśumāra, who was an expansion of the Supreme Personality of Godhead.

TEXT 15

वास्तोराङ्गिरसीपुत्रो विश्वकर्माकृतीपतिः ।
ततो मनुश्चाक्षुषोऽभूद् विश्वे साध्या मनोः सुताः॥१५॥

vāstor āṅgirasī-putro
viśvakarmākṛtī-patiḥ

tato manuś cākṣuṣo 'bhūd
viśve sādhyā manoḥ sutāḥ

vāstoḥ—of Vāstu; *āṅgirasī*—of his wife named Āṅgirasī; *putraḥ*—the son; *viśvakarmā*—Viśvakarmā; *ākṛtī-patiḥ*—the husband of Ākṛtī; *tataḥ*—from them; *manuḥ cākṣuṣaḥ*—the Manu named Cākṣuṣa; *abhūt*—was born; *viśve*—the Viśvadevas; *sādhyāḥ*—the Sādhyas; *manoḥ*—of Manu; *sutāḥ*—the sons.

TRANSLATION

From Āṅgirasī, the wife of the Vasu named Vāstu, was born the great architect Viśvakarmā. Viśvakarmā became the husband of Ākṛtī, from whom the Manu named Cākṣuṣa was born. The sons of Manu were known as the Viśvadevas and Sādhyas.

TEXT 16

विभावसोरसूतोषा व्युष्टं रोचिषमातपम् ।
पञ्चयामोऽथ भूतानि येन जाग्रति कर्मसु ॥१६॥

vibhāvasor asūtoṣā
vyuṣṭaṁ rociṣam ātapam
pañcayāmo 'tha bhūtāni
yena jāgrati karmasu

vibhāvasoḥ—of Vibhāvasu; *asūta*—gave birth to; *ūṣā*—named Ūṣā; *vyuṣṭam*—Vyuṣṭa; *rociṣam*—Rociṣa; *ātapam*—Ātapa; *pañcayāmaḥ*—Pañcayāma; *atha*—thereafter; *bhūtāni*—the living entities; *yena*—by whom; *jāgrati*—are awakened; *karmasu*—in material activities.

TRANSLATION

Ūṣā, the wife of Vibhāvasu, gave birth to three sons—Vyuṣṭa, Rociṣa and Ātapa. From Ātapa came Pañcayāma, the span of day, who awakens all living entities to material activities.

TEXTS 17–18

सरूपासूत भूतस्य भार्या रुद्रांश्च कोटिशः ।
रैवतोऽजो भवो भीमो वाम उग्रो वृषाकपिः ॥१७॥
अजैकपादहिर्ब्रध्नो बहुरूपो महानिति ।
रुद्रस्य पार्षदाश्चान्ये घोराः प्रेतविनायकाः ॥१८॥

sarūpāsūta bhūtasya
bhāryā rudrāṁś ca koṭiśaḥ
raivato 'jo bhavo bhīmo
vāma ugro vṛṣākapiḥ

ajaikapād ahirbradhno
bahurūpo mahān iti
rudrasya pārṣadāś cānye
ghorāḥ preta-vināyakāḥ

sarūpā—Sarūpā; *asūta*—gave birth; *bhūtasya*—of Bhūta; *bhāryā*—the wife; *rudrān*—Rudras; *ca*—and; *koṭiśaḥ*—ten million; *raivataḥ*—Raivata; *ajaḥ*—Aja; *bhavaḥ*—Bhava; *bhīmaḥ*—Bhīma; *vāmaḥ*—Vāma; *ugraḥ*—Ugra; *vṛṣākapiḥ*—Vṛṣākapi; *ajaikapāt*—Ajaikapāt; *ahirbradhnaḥ*—Ahirbradhna; *bahurūpaḥ*—Bahurūpa; *mahān*—Mahān; *iti*—thus; *rudrasya*—of these Rudras; *pārṣadāḥ*—their associates; *ca*—and; *anye*—other; *ghorāḥ*—very fearful; *preta*—ghosts; *vināyakāḥ*—and hobgoblins.

TRANSLATION

Sarūpā, the wife of Bhūta, gave birth to the ten million Rudras, of whom the eleven principal Rudras were Raivata, Aja, Bhava, Bhīma, Vāma, Ugra, Vṛṣākapi, Ajaikapāt, Ahirbradhna, Bahurūpa and Mahān. Their associates, the ghosts and goblins, who are very fearful, were born of the other wife of Bhūta.

PURPORT

Śrīla Viśvanātha Cakravartī Ṭhākura comments that Bhūta had two wives. One of them, Sarūpā, gave birth to the eleven Rudras, and the other wife gave birth to the associates of the Rudras known as the ghosts and hobgoblins.

TEXT 19

प्रजापतेरङ्गिरसः स्वधा पत्नी पितॄनथ ।
अथर्वाङ्गिरसं वेदं पुत्रत्वे चाकरोत् सती ॥१९॥

prajāpater aṅgirasaḥ
svadhā patnī pitṝn atha
atharvāṅgirasaṁ vedaṁ
putratve cākarot satī

prajāpateḥ aṅgirasaḥ—of another *prajāpati,* known as Aṅgirā; *svadhā*—Svadhā; *patnī*—his wife; *pitṝn*—the Pitās; *atha*—thereafter; *atharva-āṅgirasam*—Atharvāṅgirasa; *vedam*—the personified *Veda; putratve*—as the son; *ca*—and; *akarot*—accepted; *satī*—Satī.

TRANSLATION

The prajāpati Aṅgirā had two wives, named Svadhā and Satī. The wife named Svadhā accepted all the Pitās as her sons, and Satī accepted the Atharvāṅgirasa Veda as her son.

TEXT 20

कृशाश्वोऽर्चिषि भार्यायां धूमकेतुमजीजनत् ।
धिषणायां वेदशिरो देवलं वयुनं मनुम् ॥२०॥

kṛśāśvo 'rciṣi bhāryāyāṁ
dhūmaketum ajījanat
dhiṣaṇāyāṁ vedaśiro
devalaṁ vayunaṁ manum

kṛśāśvaḥ—Kṛśāśva; *arciṣi*—Arcis; *bhāryāyām*—in his wife; *dhūmaketum*—to Dhūmaketu; *ajījanat*—gave birth; *dhiṣaṇāyām*—in the wife known as Dhiṣaṇā; *vedaśiraḥ*—Vedaśirā; *devalam*—Devala; *vayunam*—Vayuna; *manum*—Manu.

TRANSLATION

Kṛśāśva had two wives, named Arcis and Dhiṣaṇā. In the wife named Arcis he begot Dhūmaketu and in Dhiṣaṇā he begot four sons, named Vedaśirā, Devala, Vayuna and Manu.

TEXTS 21–22

ताक्ष्र्यस्य विनता कद्रूः पतङ्गी यामिनीति च ।
पतङ्गयसूत पतगान् यामिनी शलभानथ ॥२१॥
सुपर्णासूत गरुडं साक्षाद् यज्ञेशवाहनम् ।
सूर्यसूतमनूरुं च कद्रूर्नागाननेकशः ॥२२॥

tārkṣyasya vinatā kadrūḥ
pataṅgī yāminīti ca
pataṅgy asūta patagān
yāminī śalabhān atha

suparṇāsūta garuḍaṁ
sākṣād yajñeśa-vāhanam
sūrya-sūtam anūruṁ ca
kadrūr nāgān anekaśaḥ

tārkṣyasya—of Kaśyapa, whose other name is Tārkṣya; *vinatā*—Vinatā; *kadrūḥ*—Kadrū; *pataṅgī*—Pataṅgī; *yāminī*—Yāminī; *iti*—thus; *ca*—and; *pataṅgī*—Pataṅgī; *asūta*—gave birth; *patagān*—to birds of different varieties; *yāminī*—Yāminī; *śalabhān*—(gave birth to) locusts; *atha*—thereafter; *suparṇā*—the wife named Vinatā; *asūta*—gave birth; *garuḍam*—to the celebrated bird known as Garuḍa; *sākṣāt*—directly; *yajñeśa-vāhanam*—the carrier of the Supreme Personality of Godhead, Viṣṇu; *sūrya-sūtam*—the chariot driver of the sun-god; *anūrum*—Anūru; *ca*—and; *kadrūḥ*—Kadrū; *nāgān*—serpents; *anekaśaḥ*—in varieties.

TRANSLATION

Kaśyapa, who is also named Tārkṣya, had four wives—Vinatā [Suparṇā], Kadrū, Pataṅgī and Yāminī. Pataṅgī gave birth to many

kinds of birds, and Yāminī gave birth to locusts. Vinatā [Suparṇā] gave birth to Garuḍa, the carrier of Lord Viṣṇu, and to Anūru, or Aruṇa, the chariot driver of the sun-god. Kadrū gave birth to different varieties of serpents.

TEXT 23

कृत्तिकादीनि नक्षत्राणीन्दोः पत्न्यस्तु भारत ।
दक्षशापात् सोऽनपत्यस्तासु यक्ष्मग्रहार्दितः ॥२३॥

kṛttikādīni nakṣatrāṇ-
īndoḥ patnyas tu bhārata
dakṣa-śāpāt so 'napatyas
tāsu yakṣma-grahārditaḥ

kṛttikā-ādīni—headed by Kṛttikā; *nakṣatrāṇi*—the constellations; *indoḥ*—of the moon-god; *patnyaḥ*—the wives; *tu*—but; *bhārata*—O Mahārāja Parīkṣit, descendant of the dynasty of Bharata; *dakṣa-śāpāt*—because of being cursed by Dakṣa; *saḥ*—the moon-god; *anapatyaḥ*—without children; *tāsu*—in so many wives; *yakṣma-graha-arditaḥ*—being oppressed by a disease that brings about gradual destruction.

TRANSLATION

O Mahārāja Parīkṣit, best of the Bhāratas, the constellations named Kṛttikā were all wives of the moon-god. However, because Prajāpati Dakṣa had cursed him to suffer from a disease causing gradual destruction, the moon-god could not beget children in any of his wives.

PURPORT

Because the moon-god was very much attached to Rohiṇī, he neglected all his other wives. Therefore, seeing the bereavement of these daughters, Prajāpati Dakṣa became angry and cursed him.

TEXTS 24–26

पुनः प्रसाद्य तं सोमः कला लेभे क्षये दिताः ।
शृणु नामानि लोकानां मातॄणां शङ्कराणि च ॥२४॥

अथ कश्यपपत्नीनां यत्प्रसूतमिदं जगत् ।
अदितिर्दितिर्दनुः काष्ठा अरिष्टा सुरसा इला ॥२५॥
मुनिः क्रोधवशा ताम्रा सुरभिः सरमा तिमिः ।
तिमेर्यादोगणा आसन् श्वापदाः सरमासुताः ॥२६॥

punaḥ prasādya taṁ somaḥ
kalā lebhe kṣaye ditāḥ
śṛṇu nāmāni lokānāṁ
mātṝṇāṁ śaṅkarāṇi ca

atha kaśyapa-patnīnāṁ
yat-prasūtam idaṁ jagat
aditir ditir danuḥ kāṣṭhā
ariṣṭā surasā ilā

muniḥ krodhavaśā tāmrā
surabhiḥ saramā timiḥ
timer yādo-gaṇā āsan
śvāpadāḥ saramā-sutāḥ

punaḥ—again; *prasādya*—pacifying; *tam*—him (Prajāpati Dakṣa); *somaḥ*—the moon-god; *kalāḥ*—portions of light; *lebhe*—achieved; *kṣaye*—in gradual destruction (the dark fortnight); *ditāḥ*—removed; *śṛṇu*—please hear; *nāmāni*—all the names; *lokānām*—of the planets; *mātṝṇām*—of the mothers; *śaṅkarāṇi*—pleasing; *ca*—also; *atha*—now; *kaśyapa-patnīnām*—of the wives of Kaśyapa; *yat-prasūtam*—from whom was born; *idam*—this; *jagat*—whole universe; *aditiḥ*—Aditi; *ditiḥ*—Diti; *danuḥ*—Danu; *kāṣṭhā*—Kāṣṭhā; *ariṣṭā*—Ariṣṭā; *surasā*—Surasā; *ilā*—Ilā; *muniḥ*—Muni; *krodhavaśā*—Krodhavaśā; *tāmrā*—Tāmrā; *surabhiḥ*—Surabhi; *saramā*—Saramā; *timiḥ*—Timi; *timeḥ*—from Timi; *yādaḥ-gaṇāḥ*—the aquatics; *āsan*—appeared; *śvāpadāḥ*—the ferocious animals like the lions and tigers; *saramā-sutāḥ*—the children of Saramā.

TRANSLATION

Thereafter the King of the moon pacified Prajāpati Dakṣa with courteous words and thus regained the portions of light he had

lost during his disease. Nevertheless he could not beget children. The moon loses his shining power during the dark fortnight, and in the bright fortnight it is manifest again. O King Parīkṣit, now please hear from me the names of Kaśyapa's wives, from whose wombs the population of the entire universe has come. They are the mothers of almost all the population of the entire universe, and their names are very auspicious to hear. They are Aditi, Diti, Danu, Kāṣṭhā, Ariṣṭā, Surasā, Ilā, Muni, Krodhavaśā, Tāmrā, Surabhi, Saramā and Timi. From the womb of Timi all the aquatics took birth, and from the womb of Saramā the ferocious animals like the tigers and lions took birth.

TEXT 27

सुरभेर्महिषागावो ये चान्ये द्विशफा नृप ।
ताम्रायाः श्येनगृध्राद्या मुनेरप्सरसां गणाः ॥२७॥

surabher mahiṣā gāvo
ye cānye dviśaphā nṛpa
tāmrāyāḥ śyena-gṛdhrādyā
muner apsarasāṁ gaṇāḥ

surabheḥ—from the womb of Surabhi; *mahiṣāḥ*—buffalo; *gāvaḥ*—cows; *ye*—who; *ca*—also; *anye*—others; *dvi-śaphāḥ*—having cloven hooves; *nṛpa*—O King; *tāmrāyāḥ*—from Tāmrā; *śyena*—eagles; *gṛdhra-ādyāḥ*—vultures and so on; *muneḥ*—from Muni; *apsarasām*—of angels; *gaṇāḥ*—the groups.

TRANSLATION

My dear King Parīkṣit, from the womb of Surabhi the buffalo, cow and other animals with cloven hooves took birth, from the womb of Tāmrā the eagles, vultures and other large birds of prey took birth, and from the womb of Muni the angels took birth.

TEXT 28

दन्दशूकादयः सर्पा राजन् क्रोधवशात्मजाः ।
इलाया भूरुहाः सर्वे यातुधानाश्च सौरसाः ॥२८॥

dandaśūkādayaḥ sarpā
rājan krodhavaśātmajāḥ
ilāyā bhūruhāḥ sarve
yātudhānāś ca saurasāḥ

dandaśūka-ādayaḥ—headed by the *dandaśūka* snakes; *sarpāḥ*—reptiles; *rājan*—O King; *krodhavaśā-ātma-jāḥ*—born from Krodhavaśā; *ilāyāḥ*—from the womb of Ilā; *bhūruhāḥ*—the creepers and trees; *sarve*—all; *yātudhānāḥ*—the cannibals (Rākṣasas); *ca*—also; *saurasāḥ*—from the womb of Surasā.

TRANSLATION

The sons born of Krodhavaśā were the serpents known as dandaśūka, as well as other serpents and the mosquitoes. All the various creepers and trees were born from the womb of Ilā. The Rākṣasas, bad spirits, were born from the womb of Surasā.

TEXTS 29–31

अरिष्टायास्तु गन्धर्वाः काष्ठाया द्विशफेतराः ।
सुता दनोरेकषष्टिस्तेषां प्राधानिकाञ् शृणु ॥२९॥
द्विमूर्धा शम्बरोऽरिष्टो हयग्रीवो विभावसुः ।
अयोमुखः शङ्कुशिराः स्वर्भानुः कपिलोऽरुणः ॥३०॥
पुलोमा वृषपर्वा च एकचक्रोऽनुतापनः ।
धूम्रकेशो विरूपाक्षो विप्रचित्तिश्च दुर्जयः ॥३१॥

ariṣṭāyās tu gandharvāḥ
kāṣṭhāyā dviśaphetarāḥ
sutā danor eka-ṣaṣṭis
teṣāṁ prādhānikāñ śṛṇu

dvimūrdhā śambaro 'riṣṭo
hayagrīvo vibhāvasuḥ
ayomukhaḥ śaṅkuśirāḥ
svarbhānuḥ kapilo 'ruṇaḥ

pulomā vṛṣaparvā ca
ekacakro 'nutāpanaḥ
dhūmrakeśo virūpākṣo
vipracittiś ca durjayaḥ

ariṣṭāyāḥ—from the womb of Ariṣṭā; *tu*—but; *gandharvāḥ*—the Gandharvas; *kāṣṭhāyāḥ*—from the womb of Kāṣṭhā; *dvi-śapha-itarāḥ*—animals such as horses, which do not have cloven hooves; *sutāḥ*—sons; *danoḥ*—from the womb of Danu; *eka-ṣaṣṭiḥ*—sixty-one; *teṣām*—of them; *prādhānikān*—the important ones; *śṛṇu*—hear; *dvimūrdhā*—Dvimūrdhā; *śambaraḥ*—Śambara; *ariṣṭaḥ*—Ariṣṭa; *hayagrīvaḥ*—Hayagrīva; *vibhāvasuḥ*—Vibhāvasu; *ayomukhaḥ*—Ayomukha; *śaṅkuśirāḥ*—Śaṅkuśirā; *svarbhānuḥ*—Svarbhānu; *kapilaḥ*—Kapila; *aruṇaḥ*—Aruṇa; *pulomā*—Pulomā; *vṛṣaparvā*—Vṛṣaparvā; *ca*—also; *ekacakraḥ*—Ekacakra; *anutāpanaḥ*—Anutāpana; *dhūmrakeśaḥ*—Dhūmrakeśa; *virūpākṣaḥ*—Virūpākṣa; *vipracittiḥ*—Vipracitti; *ca*—and; *durjayaḥ*—Durjaya.

TRANSLATION

The Gandharvas were born from the womb of Ariṣṭā, and animals whose hooves are not split, such as the horse, were born from the womb of Kāṣṭhā. O King, from the womb of Danu came sixty-one sons, of whom these eighteen were very important: Dvimūrdhā, Śambara, Ariṣṭa, Hayagrīva, Vibhāvasu, Ayomukha, Śaṅkuśirā, Svarbhānu, Kapila, Aruṇa, Pulomā, Vṛṣaparvā, Ekacakra, Anutāpana, Dhūmrakeśa, Virūpākṣa, Vipracitti and Durjaya.

TEXT 32

स्वर्भानोः सुप्रभां कन्यामुवाह नमुचिः किल ।
वृषपर्वणस्तु शर्मिष्ठां ययातिर्नाहुषो बली ॥३२॥

svarbhānoḥ suprabhāṁ kanyām
uvāha namuciḥ kila
vṛṣaparvaṇas tu śarmiṣṭhāṁ
yayātir nāhuṣo balī

svarbhānoḥ—of Svarbhānu; *suprabhām*—Suprabhā; *kanyām*—the daughter; *uvāha*—married; *namuciḥ*—Namuci; *kila*—indeed; *vṛṣaparvaṇaḥ*—of Vṛṣaparvā; *tu*—but; *śarmiṣṭhām*—Śarmiṣṭhā; *yayātiḥ*—King Yayāti; *nāhuṣaḥ*—the son of Nahuṣa; *balī*—very powerful.

TRANSLATION

The daughter of Svarbhānu named Suprabhā was married by Namuci. The daughter of Vṛṣaparvā named Śarmiṣṭhā was given to the powerful King Yayāti, the son of Nahuṣa.

TEXTS 33–36

वैश्वानरसुता याश्च चतस्रश्चारुदर्शनाः ।
उपदानवी हयशिरा पुलोमा कालका तथा ॥३३॥
उपदानवीं हिरण्याक्षः क्रतुर्हयशिरां नृप ।
पुलोमां कालकां च द्वे वैश्वानरसुते तु कः ॥३४॥
उपयेमेऽथ भगवान् कश्यपो ब्रह्मचोदितः ।
पौलोमाः कालकेयाश्च दानवा युद्धशालिनः ॥३५॥
तयोः षष्टिसहस्राणि यज्ञघ्नांस्ते पितुः पिता ।
जघान स्वर्गतो राजन्नेक इन्द्रप्रियङ्करः ॥३६॥

vaiśvānara-sutā yāś ca
catasraś cāru-darśanāḥ
upadānavī hayaśirā
pulomā kālakā tathā

upadānavīṁ hiraṇyākṣaḥ
kratur hayaśirāṁ nṛpa
pulomāṁ kālakāṁ ca dve
vaiśvānara-sute tu kaḥ

upayeme 'tha bhagavān
kaśyapo brahma-coditaḥ
paulomāḥ kālakeyāś ca
dānavā yuddha-śālinaḥ

tayoḥ ṣaṣṭi-sahasrāṇi
yajña-ghnāṁs te pituḥ pitā
jaghāna svar-gato rājann
eka indra-priyaṅkaraḥ

vaiśvānara-sutāḥ—the daughters of Vaiśvānara; *yāḥ*—who; *ca*—and; *catasraḥ*—four; *cāru-darśanāḥ*—very, very beautiful; *upadānavī*—Upadānavī; *hayaśirā*—Hayaśirā; *pulomā*—Pulomā; *kālakā*—Kālakā; *tathā*—as well; *upadānavīm*—Upadānavī; *hiraṇyākṣaḥ*—the demon Hiraṇyākṣa; *kratuḥ*—Kratu; *hayaśirām*—Hayaśirā; *nṛpa*—O King; *pulomām kālakām ca*—Pulomā and Kālakā; *dve*—the two; *vaiśvānara-sute*—daughters of Vaiśvānara; *tu*—but; *kaḥ*—the *prajāpati; upayeme*—married; *atha*—then; *bhagavān*—the most powerful; *kaśyapaḥ*—Kaśyapa Muni; *brahma-coditaḥ*—requested by Lord Brahmā; *paulomāḥ kālakeyāḥ ca*—the Paulomas and Kālakeyas; *dānavāḥ*—demons; *yuddha-śālinaḥ*—very fond of fighting; *tayoḥ*—of them; *ṣaṣṭi-sahasrāṇi*—sixty thousand; *yajña-ghnān*—who were disturbing sacrifices; *te*—your; *pituḥ*—of the father; *pitā*—the father; *jaghāna*—killed; *svaḥ-gataḥ*—in the heavenly planets; *rājan*—O King; *ekaḥ*—alone; *indra-priyam-karaḥ*—to please King Indra.

TRANSLATION

Vaiśvānara, the son of Danu, had four beautiful daughters, named Upadānavī, Hayaśirā, Pulomā and Kālakā. Hiraṇyākṣa married Upadānavī, and Kratu married Hayaśirā. Thereafter, at the request of Lord Brahmā, Prajāpati Kaśyapa married Pulomā and Kālakā, the other two daughters of Vaiśvānara. From the wombs of these two wives of Kaśyapa came sixty thousand sons, headed by Nivātakavaca, who are known as the Paulomas and the Kālakeyas. They were physically very strong and expert in fighting, and their aim was to disturb the sacrifices performed by the great sages. My dear King, when your grandfather Arjuna went to the heavenly planets, he alone killed all these demons, and thus King Indra became extremely affectionate toward him.

TEXT 37

विप्रचित्तिः सिंहिकायां शतं चैकमजीजनत् ।
राहुज्येष्ठं केतुशतं ग्रहत्वं य उपागताः ॥३७॥

vipracittiḥ siṁhikāyāṁ
śataṁ caikam ajījanat
rāhu-jyeṣṭhaṁ ketu-śataṁ
grahatvaṁ ya upāgatāḥ

vipracittiḥ—Vipracitti; *siṁhikāyām*—in the womb of his wife Siṁhikā; *śatam*—to one hundred; *ca*—and; *ekam*—one; *ajījanat*—gave birth; *rāhu-jyeṣṭham*—among whom Rāhu is the oldest; *ketu-śatam*—one hundred Ketus; *grahatvam*—planethood; *ye*—all of whom; *upāgatāḥ*—obtained.

TRANSLATION

In his wife Siṁhikā, Vipracitti begot one hundred and one sons, of whom the eldest is Rāhu and the others are the one hundred Ketus. All of them attained positions in the influential planets.

TEXTS 38–39

अथातः श्रूयतां वंशो योऽदितेरनुपूर्वशः ।
यत्र नारायणो देवः स्वांशेनावातरद्विभुः ॥३८॥
विवस्वानर्यमा पूषा त्वष्टाथ सविता भगः ।
धाता विधाता वरुणो मित्रः शत्रु उरुक्रमः ॥३९॥

athātaḥ śrūyatāṁ vaṁśo
yo 'diter anupūrvaśaḥ
yatra nārāyaṇo devaḥ
svāṁśenāvātarad vibhuḥ

vivasvān aryamā pūṣā
tvaṣṭātha savitā bhagaḥ

dhātā vidhātā varuṇo
mitraḥ śatru urukramaḥ

atha—thereafter; *ataḥ*—now; *śrūyatām*—let it be heard; *vaṁśaḥ*—the dynasty; *yaḥ*—which; *aditeḥ*—from Aditi; *anupūrvaśaḥ*—in chronological order; *yatra*—wherein; *nārāyaṇaḥ*—the Supreme Personality of Godhead; *devaḥ*—the Lord; *sva-aṁśena*—by His own plenary expansion; *avātarat*—descended; *vibhuḥ*—the Supreme; *vivasvān*—Vivasvān; *aryamā*—Aryamā; *pūṣā*—Pūṣā; *tvaṣṭā*—Tvaṣṭā; *atha*—thereafter; *savitā*—Savitā; *bhagaḥ*—Bhaga; *dhātā*—Dhātā; *vidhātā*—Vidhātā; *varuṇaḥ*—Varuṇa; *mitraḥ*—Mitra; *śatruḥ*—Śatru; *urukramaḥ*—Urukrama.

TRANSLATION

Now please hear me as I describe the descendants of Aditi in chronological order. In this dynasty the Supreme Personality of Godhead Nārāyaṇa descended by His plenary expansion. The names of the sons of Aditi are as follows: Vivasvān, Aryamā, Pūṣā, Tvaṣṭā, Savitā, Bhaga, Dhātā, Vidhātā, Varuṇa, Mitra, Śatru and Urukrama.

TEXT 40

विवस्वतः श्राद्धदेवं संज्ञासूयत वै मनुम् ।
मिथुनं च महाभागा यमं देवं यमीं तथा ।
सैव भूत्वाथ वडवा नासत्यौ सुषुवे भुवि ॥४०॥

vivasvataḥ śrāddhadevaṁ
saṁjñāsūyata vai manum
mithunaṁ ca mahā-bhāgā
yamaṁ devaṁ yamīṁ tathā
saiva bhūtvātha vaḍavā
nāsatyau suṣuve bhuvi

vivasvataḥ—of the sun-god; *śrāddhadevam*—named Śrāddhadeva; *saṁjñā*—Saṁjñā; *asūyata*—gave birth; *vai*—indeed; *manum*—to Manu; *mithunam*—twins; *ca*—and; *mahā-bhāgā*—the fortunate

Saṁjñā; *yamam*—to Yamarāja; *devam*—the demigod; *yamīm*—to his sister named Yamī; *tathā*—as well as; *sā*—she; *eva*—also; *bhūtvā*—becoming; *atha*—then; *vaḍavā*—a mare; *nāsatyau*—to the Aśvinī-kumāras; *suṣuve*—gave birth; *bhuvi*—on this earth.

TRANSLATION

Saṁjñā, the wife of Vivasvān, the sun-god, gave birth to the Manu named Śrāddhadeva, and the same fortunate wife also gave birth to the twins Yamarāja and the River Yamunā. Then Yamī, while wandering on the earth in the form of a mare, gave birth to the Aśvinī-kumāras.

TEXT 41

छाया शनैश्चरं लेभे सावर्णिं च मनुं ततः ।
कन्यां च तपतीं या वै वव्रे संवरणं पतिम् ॥४१॥

chāyā śanaiścaraṁ lebhe
sāvarṇiṁ ca manuṁ tataḥ
kanyāṁ ca tapatīṁ yā vai
vavre saṁvaraṇaṁ patim

chāyā—Chāyā, another wife of the sun-god; *śanaiścaram*—Saturn; *lebhe*—begot; *sāvarṇim*—Sāvarṇi; *ca*—and; *manum*—the Manu; *tataḥ*—from him (Vivasvān); *kanyām*—one daughter; *ca*—as well as; *tapatīm*—named Tapatī; *yā*—who; *vai*—indeed; *vavre*—married; *saṁvaraṇam*—Saṁvaraṇa; *patim*—husband.

TRANSLATION

Chāyā, another wife of the sun-god, begot two sons named Śanaiścara and Sāvarṇi Manu, and one daughter, Tapatī, who married Saṁvaraṇa.

TEXT 42

अर्यम्णो मातृका पत्नी तयोश्चर्षणयः सुताः ।
यत्र वै मानुषी जातिर्ब्रह्मणा चोपकल्पिता ॥४२॥

aryamṇo mātṛkā patnī
tayoś carṣaṇayaḥ sutāḥ
yatra vai mānuṣī jātir
brahmaṇā copakalpitā

aryamṇaḥ—of Aryamā; *mātṛkā*—Mātṛkā; *patnī*—the wife; *tayoḥ*—by their union; *carṣaṇayaḥ sutāḥ*—many sons who were learned scholars; *yatra*—wherein; *vai*—indeed; *mānuṣī*—human; *jātiḥ*—species; *brahmaṇā*—by Lord Brahmā; *ca*—and; *upakalpitā*—was created.

TRANSLATION

From the womb of Mātṛkā, the wife of Aryamā, were born many learned scholars. Among them Lord Brahmā created the human species, which are endowed with an aptitude for self-examination.

TEXT 43

पूषानपत्यः पिष्टादो भग्नदन्तोऽभवत् पुरा ।
योऽसौ दक्षाय कुपितं जहास विवृतद्विजः ॥४३॥

pūṣānapatyaḥ piṣṭādo
bhagna-danto 'bhavat purā
yo 'sau dakṣāya kupitaṁ
jahāsa vivṛta-dvijaḥ

pūṣā—Pūṣā; *anapatyaḥ*—without children; *piṣṭa-adaḥ*—who lives by eating flour; *bhagna-dantaḥ*—with broken teeth; *abhavat*—became; *purā*—formerly; *yaḥ*—who; *asau*—that; *dakṣāya*—at Dakṣa; *kupitam*—very angry; *jahāsa*—laughed; *vivṛta-dvijaḥ*—uncovering his teeth.

TRANSLATION

Pūṣā had no sons. When Lord Śiva was angry at Dakṣa, Pūṣā had laughed at Lord Śiva and shown his teeth. Therefore he lost his teeth and had to live by eating only ground flour.

TEXT 44

त्वष्टुर्दैत्यात्मजा भार्या रचना नाम कन्यका ।
संनिवेशस्तयोर्जज्ञे विश्वरूपश्च वीर्यवान् ॥४४॥

tvaṣṭur daityātmajā bhāryā
racanā nāma kanyakā
sanniveśas tayor jajñe
viśvarūpaś ca vīryavān

tvaṣṭuḥ—of Tvaṣṭā; *daitya-ātma-jā*—the daughter of a demon; *bhāryā*—wife; *racanā*—Racanā; *nāma*—named; *kanyakā*—a maiden; *sanniveśaḥ*—Sanniveśa; *tayoḥ*—of those two; *jajñe*—was born; *viśvarūpaḥ*—Viśvarūpa; *ca*—and; *vīryavān*—very powerful in bodily strength.

TRANSLATION

Racanā, the daughter of the Daityas, became the wife of Prajāpati Tvaṣṭā. By his semina he begot in her womb two very powerful sons named Sanniveśa and Viśvarūpa.

TEXT 45

तं वव्रिरे सुरगणा स्वस्रीयं द्विषतामपि ।
विमतेन परित्यक्ता गुरुणाङ्गिरसेन यत् ॥४५॥

taṁ vavrire sura-gaṇā
svasrīyaṁ dviṣatām api
vimatena parityaktā
guruṇāṅgirasena yat

tam—him (Viśvarūpa); *vavrire*—accepted as a priest; *sura-gaṇāḥ*—the demigods; *svasrīyam*—the son of a daughter; *dviṣatām*—of the inimical demons; *api*—although; *vimatena*—being disrespected; *parityaktāḥ*—who were given up; *guruṇā*—by their spiritual master; *āṅgirasena*—Bṛhaspati; *yat*—since.

TRANSLATION

Although Viśvarūpa was the son of the daughter of their eternal enemies the demons, the demigods accepted him as their priest in accordance with the order of Brahmā when they were abandoned by their spiritual master, Bṛhaspati, whom they had disrespected.

Thus end the Bhaktivedanta purports to the Sixth Canto, Sixth Chapter, of the Śrīmad-Bhāgavatam, *entitled "The Progeny of the Daughters of Dakṣa."*

CHAPTER SEVEN

Indra Offends His Spiritual Master, Bṛhaspati

As related in this chapter, Indra, the King of heaven, committed an offense at the feet of his spiritual master, Bṛhaspati. Bṛhaspati therefore left the demigods, who then had no priest. However, at the request of the demigods, Viśvarūpa, the son of the *brāhmaṇa* Tvaṣṭā, became their priest.

Once upon a time, Indra, the King of the demigods, was sitting with his wife Śacīdevī and being praised by various demigods like the Siddhas, Cāraṇas and Gandharvas when Bṛhaspati, the spiritual master of the demigods, entered the assembly. Indra, being too absorbed in material opulence, forgot himself and did not respect Bṛhaspati, who thus became aware of Indra's pride in his material opulence and immediately disappeared from the assembly to teach him a lesson. Indra became most repentant, understanding that because of his opulence he had forgotten to respect his spiritual master. He left the palace to beg pardon from his spiritual master, but could not find Bṛhaspati anywhere.

Because of his disrespectful behavior toward his spiritual master, Indra lost all his opulence and was conquered by the demons, who defeated the demigods in a great fight and occupied Indra's throne. King Indra, along with the other demigods, later took shelter of Lord Brahmā. Understanding the situation, Lord Brahmā chastised the demigods for their offense to their spiritual master. Following Lord Brahmā's orders, the demigods accepted Viśvarūpa, who was a *brāhmaṇa* and the son of Tvaṣṭā, as their priest. Then they performed *yajñas* under the priesthood of Viśvarūpa and were able to conquer the demons.

TEXT 1

श्रीराजोवाच

कस्य हेतोः परित्यक्ता आचार्येणात्मनः सुराः ।
एतदाचक्ष्व भगवञ्छिष्याणामक्रमं गुरौ ॥ १ ॥

śrī-rājovāca
kasya hetoḥ parityaktā
ācāryeṇātmanaḥ surāḥ
etad ācakṣva bhagavañ
chiṣyāṇāṁ akramaṁ gurau

śrī-rājā uvāca—the King inquired; *kasya hetoḥ*—for what reason; *parityaktāḥ*—rejected; *ācāryeṇa*—by the spiritual master, Bṛhaspati; *ātmanaḥ*—of himself; *surāḥ*—all the demigods; *etat*—this; *ācakṣva*—kindly describe; *bhagavan*—O great sage (Śukadeva Gosvāmī); *śiṣyāṇām*—of the disciples; *akramam*—the offense; *gurau*—unto the spiritual master.

TRANSLATION

Mahārāja Parīkṣit inquired from Śukadeva Gosvāmī: O great sage, why did the spiritual master of the demigods, Bṛhaspati, reject the demigods, who were his own disciples? What offense did the demigods commit against their spiritual master? Please describe to me this incident.

PURPORT

Śrīla Viśvanātha Cakravartī Ṭhākura comments:

saptame guruṇā tyaktair
devair daitya-parājitaiḥ
viśvarūpo gurutvena
vṛto brahmopadeśataḥ

"This Seventh Chapter describes how Bṛhaspati was offended by the demigods, how he left them and the demigods were defeated, and how the demigods, following the instructions of Lord Brahmā, accepted Viśvarūpa as the priest to perform their sacrifice."

TEXTS 2–8

श्रीबादरायणिरुवाच
इन्द्रस्त्रिभुवनैश्वर्यमदोल्लङ्घितसत्पथः ।
मरुद्भिर्वसुभी रुद्रैरादित्यैरृभुभिर्नृप ॥ २ ॥

विश्वेदेवैश्च साध्यैश्च नासत्याभ्यां परिश्रितः ।
सिद्धचारणगन्धर्वैर्मुनिभिर्ब्रह्मवादिभिः ॥ ३ ॥
विद्याधराप्सरोभिश्च किन्नरैः पतगोरगैः ।
निषेव्यमाणो मघवान् स्तूयमानश्च भारत ॥ ४ ॥
उपगीयमानो ललितमास्थानाध्यासनाश्रितः ।
पाण्डुरेणातपत्रेण चन्द्रमण्डलचारुणा ॥ ५ ॥
युक्तश्चान्यैः पारमेष्ठ्यैश्चामरव्यजनादिभिः ।
विराजमानः पौलम्या सहार्धासनया भृशम् ॥ ६ ॥
स यदा परमाचार्यं देवानामात्मनश्च ह ।
नाभ्यनन्दत संप्राप्तं प्रत्युत्थानासनादिभिः ॥ ७ ॥
वाचस्पतिं मुनिवरं सुरासुरनमस्कृतम् ।
नोच्चचालासनादिन्द्रः पश्यन्नपि सभागतम् ॥ ८ ॥

śrī-bādarāyaṇir uvāca
indras tribhuvanaiśvarya-
madollaṅghita-satpathaḥ
marudbhir vasubhī rudrair
ādityair ṛbhubhir nṛpa

viśvedevaiś ca sādhyaiś ca
nāsatyābhyāṁ pariśritaḥ
siddha-cāraṇa-gandharvair
munibhir brahmavādibhiḥ

vidyādharāpsarobhiś ca
kinnaraiḥ patagoragaiḥ
niṣevyamāṇo maghavān
stūyamānaś ca bhārata

upagīyamāno lalitam
āsthānādhyāsanāśritaḥ
pāṇḍureṇātapatreṇa
candra-maṇḍala-cāruṇā

yuktaś cānyaiḥ pārameṣṭhyaiś
cāmara-vyajanādibhiḥ
virājamānaḥ paulamyā
sahārdhāsanayā bhṛśam

sa yadā paramācāryaṁ
devānām ātmanaś ca ha
nābhyanandata samprāptaṁ
pratyutthānāsanādibhiḥ

vācaspatiṁ muni-varaṁ
surāsura-namaskṛtam
noccacālāsanād indraḥ
paśyann api sabhāgatam

śrī-bādarāyaṇiḥ uvāca—Śrī Śukadeva Gosvāmī replied; *indraḥ*—King Indra; *tri-bhuvana-aiśvarya*—because of possessing all the material opulences of the three worlds; *mada*—due to pride; *ullaṅghita*—who has transgressed; *sat-pathaḥ*—the path of Vedic civilization; *marudbhiḥ*—by the wind demigods, known as the Maruts; *vasubhiḥ*—by the eight Vasus; *rudraiḥ*—by the eleven Rudras; *ādityaiḥ*—by the Ādityas; *ṛbhubhiḥ*—by the Ṛbhus; *nṛpa*—O King; *viśvedevaiḥ ca*—and by the Viśvadevas; *sādhyaiḥ*—by the Sādhyas; *ca*—also; *nāsatyā-bhyām*—by the two Aśvinī-kumāras; *pariśritaḥ*—surrounded; *siddha*—by the inhabitants of Siddhaloka; *cāraṇa*—the Cāraṇas; *gandharvaiḥ*—and the Gandharvas; *munibhiḥ*—by the great sages; *brahma-vādibhiḥ*—by greatly learned impersonalist scholars; *vidyādhara-ap-sarobhiḥ ca*—and by the Vidyādharas and Apsarās; *kinnaraiḥ*—by the Kinnaras; *pataga-uragaiḥ*—by the Patagas (birds) and Uragas (snakes); *niṣevyamāṇaḥ*—being served; *maghavān*—King Indra; *stūyamānaḥ ca*—and being offered prayers; *bhārata*—O Mahārāja Parīkṣit; *upagīyamānaḥ*—being sung before; *lalitam*—very sweetly; *āsthāna*—in his assembly; *adhyāsana-āśritaḥ*—situated on the throne; *pāṇ-ḍureṇa*—white; *ātapatreṇa*—with an umbrella over the head; *candra-maṇḍala-cāruṇā*—as beautiful as the circle of the moon; *yuktaḥ*—endowed; *ca anyaiḥ*—and by other; *pārameṣṭhyaiḥ*—symptoms of an exalted king; *cāmara*—by yak-tail; *vyajana-ādibhiḥ*—fans and other paraphernalia; *virājamānaḥ*—shining; *paulamyā*—his wife, Śacī; *saha*—with; *ardha-āsanayā*—who occupied half the throne; *bhṛśam*—greatly; *saḥ*—he (Indra); *yadā*—when; *parama-ācāryam*—the most exalted *ācārya*, spiritual master; *devānām*—of all the demigods; *ātmanaḥ*—of himself; *ca*—and; *ha*—indeed; *na*—not; *abhyanandata*—welcomed; *samprāptam*—having appeared in the assembly; *pratyutthāna*—by getting up from the throne; *āsana-ādibhiḥ*—and by a seat and other greetings; *vācaspatim*—the priest of the demigods, Bṛhaspati; *muni-varam*—the best of all the sages; *sura-asura-namaskṛtam*—who is respected by both the demigods and the *asuras*; *na*—not; *uccacāla*—did get up; *āsanāt*—from the throne; *indraḥ*—Indra; *paśyan api*—although seeing; *sabhā-āgatam*—entering the assembly.

TRANSLATION

Śukadeva Gosvāmī said: O King, once upon a time, the King of heaven, Indra, being extremely proud because of his great opulence of the three worlds, transgressed the law of Vedic etiquette. Seated on his throne, he was surrounded by the Maruts, Vasus, Rudras, Ādityas, Ṛbhus, Viśvadevas, Sādhyas, Aśvinī-kumāras, Siddhas, Cāraṇas and Gandharvas and by great saintly persons. Also surrounding him were the Vidyādharas, Apsarās, Kinnaras, Patagas [birds] and Uragas [snakes]. All of them were offering Indra their respects and services, and the Apsarās and Gandharvas were dancing and singing with very sweet musical instruments. Over Indra's head was a white umbrella as effulgent as the full moon. Fanned by yak-tail whisks and served with all the paraphernalia of a great king, Indra was sitting with his wife, Śacīdevī, who occupied half the throne, when the great sage Bṛhaspati appeared in that assembly. Bṛhaspati, the best of the sages, was the spiritual master of Indra and the demigods and was respected by the demigods and demons alike. Nevertheless, although Indra saw his spiritual master before him, he did not rise from his own seat or offer a seat to his spiritual master, nor did Indra offer him a respectful welcome. Indra did nothing to show him respect.

TEXT 9

ततो निर्गत्य सहसा कविराङ्गिरसः प्रभुः ।
आययौ स्वगृहं तूष्णीं विद्वान् श्रीमदविक्रियाम् ॥ ९ ॥

tato nirgatya sahasā
kavir āṅgirasaḥ prabhuḥ
āyayau sva-gṛhaṁ tūṣṇīṁ
vidvān śrī-mada-vikriyām

tataḥ—thereafter; *nirgatya*—going out; *sahasā*—suddenly; *kaviḥ*—the great learned sage; *āṅgirasaḥ*—Bṛhaspati; *prabhuḥ*—the master of the demigods; *āyayau*—returned; *sva-gṛham*—to his home; *tūṣṇīm*—being silent; *vidvān*—having known; *śrī-mada-vikriyām*—deterioration because of madness due to opulence.

TRANSLATION

Bṛhaspati knew everything that would happen in the future. Seeing Indra's transgression of etiquette, he completely understood that Indra was puffed up by his material opulence. Although able to curse Indra, he did not do so. Instead, he left the assembly and in silence returned to his home.

TEXT 10

तर्ह्येव प्रतिबुध्येन्द्रो गुरुहेलनमात्मनः ।
गर्हयामास सदसि स्वयमात्मानमात्मना ॥ १० ॥

tarhy eva pratibudhyendro
guru-helanam ātmanaḥ
garhayām āsa sadasi
svayam ātmānam ātmanā

tarhi—then, immediately; *eva*—indeed; *pratibudhya*—realizing; *indraḥ*—King Indra; *guru-helanam*—disrespect to the spiritual master; *ātmanaḥ*—his own; *garhayām āsa*—reproached; *sadasi*—in that assembly; *svayam*—personally; *ātmānam*—himself; *ātmanā*—by himself.

TRANSLATION

Indra, the King of heaven, could immediately understand his mistake. Realizing he had disrespected his spiritual master, he condemned himself in the presence of all the members of the assembly.

TEXT 11

अहो बत मयासाधु कृतं वै दभ्रबुद्धिना ।
यन्मयैश्वर्यमत्तेन गुरुः सदसि कात्कृतः ॥११॥

aho bata mayāsādhu
kṛtaṁ vai dabhra-buddhinā
yan mayaiśvarya-mattena
guruḥ sadasi kātkṛtaḥ

aho—alas; *bata*—indeed; *mayā*—by me; *asādhu*—disrespectful; *kṛtam*—the action done; *vai*—certainly; *dabhra-buddhinā*—being of less intelligence; *yat*—because; *mayā*—by me; *aiśvarya-mattena*—being very proud of material opulence; *guruḥ*—the spiritual master; *sadasi*—in this assembly; *kāt-kṛtaḥ*—mistreated.

TRANSLATION

Alas, what a regrettable deed I have committed because of my lack of intelligence and my pride in my material opulences. I failed to show respect to my spiritual master when he entered this assembly, and thus I have insulted him.

TEXT 12

को गृध्येत् पण्डितो लक्ष्मीं त्रिपिष्टपपतेरपि ।
ययाहमासुरं भावं नीतोऽद्य विबुधेश्वरः ॥१२॥

ko gṛdhyet paṇḍito lakṣmīṁ
tripiṣṭapa-pater api
yayāham āsuraṁ bhāvaṁ
nīto 'dya vibudheśvaraḥ

kaḥ—who; *gṛdhyet*—would accept; *paṇḍitaḥ*—a learned man; *lakṣmīm*—opulences; *tri-piṣṭa-pa-pateḥ api*—although I am the King of the demigods; *yayā*—by which; *aham*—I; *āsuram*—demoniac; *bhāvam*—mentality; *nītaḥ*—carried to; *adya*—now; *vibudha*—of the demigods, who are in the mode of goodness; *īśvaraḥ*—the King.

TRANSLATION

Although I am King of the demigods, who are situated in the mode of goodness, I was proud of a little opulence and polluted by false ego. Under the circumstances, who in this world would accept such riches at the risk of falling down? Alas! I condemn my wealth and opulence.

PURPORT

Śrī Caitanya Mahāprabhu prayed to the Supreme Personality of Godhead, *na dhanaṁ na janaṁ na sundarīṁ kavitāṁ vā jagad-īśa kāmaye:* "O my Lord, I do not aspire for material opulence or wealth, nor do I want a great number of followers to accept me as their leader, nor do I want a very beautiful wife to please me." *Mama janmani janmanīśvare bhavatād bhaktir ahaitukī tvayi:* "I do not even want liberation. All I want, life after life, is to be a faithful servant of Your Lordship." According to the laws of nature, when one is extremely opulent one becomes degraded, and this is true both individually and collectively. The demigods are situated in the mode of goodness, but sometimes even one who is situated in such an exalted position as King Indra, the king of all the demigods, falls down because of material opulence. We are now actually seeing this in America. The entire American nation has tried to advance in material opulence without striving to produce ideal human beings. The result is that Americans are now regretting the wholesale criminality of American society and are wondering how America has become so lawless and unmanageable. As stated in *Śrīmad-Bhāgavatam* (7.5.31), *na te viduḥ svārtha-gatiṁ hi viṣṇum:* persons who are unenlightened do not know the aim of life, which is to return home, back to Godhead. Therefore, both individually and collectively, they try to enjoy so-called material comforts, and they become addicted to wine and women. The men produced in such a society are less than fourth class.

They are the unwanted population known as *varṇa-saṅkara*, and as stated in *Bhagavad-gītā*, an increase of *varṇa-saṅkara* population creates a hellish society. This is the society in which Americans now find themselves.

Fortunately, however, the Hare Kṛṣṇa movement has come to America, and many fortunate young men are giving serious attention to this movement, which is creating ideal men of first-class character, men who completely refrain from meat-eating, illicit sex, intoxication and gambling. If the American people are serious about curbing the degraded criminal life of their nation, they must take to the Kṛṣṇa consciousness movement and try to create the kind of human society advised in *Bhagavad-gītā* (*cātur-varṇyaṁ mayā sṛṣṭaṁ guṇa-karma-vibhāgaśaḥ*). They must divide their society into first-class men, second-class men, third-class men and fourth-class men. Since they are now creating only men who are less than fourth class, how can they avoid the dangers of a criminal society? Long, long ago, Lord Indra regretted his disrespect to his spiritual master, Bṛhaspati. Similarly, it is advised that the American people regret their mistaken advancement in civilization. They should take advice from the spiritual master, the representative of Kṛṣṇa. If they do so, they will be happy, and theirs will be an ideal nation to lead the entire world.

TEXT 13

यः पारमेष्ठ्यं धिषणमधितिष्ठन् न कञ्चन ।
प्रत्युत्तिष्ठेदिति ब्रूयुर्धर्मं ते न परं विदुः ॥१३॥

yaḥ pārameṣṭhyaṁ dhiṣaṇam
adhitiṣṭhan na kañcana
pratyuttiṣṭhed iti brūyur
dharmaṁ te na paraṁ viduḥ

yaḥ—anyone who; *pārameṣṭhyam*—royal; *dhiṣaṇam*—throne; *adhitiṣṭhan*—sitting on; *na*—not; *kañcana*—anyone; *pratyuttiṣṭhet*—should rise before; *iti*—thus; *brūyuḥ*—those who say; *dharmam*—the codes of religion; *te*—they; *na*—not; *param*—higher; *viduḥ*—know.

TRANSLATION

If a person says, "One who is situated on the exalted throne of a king should not stand up to show respect to another king or a brāhmaṇa," it is to be understood that he does not know the superior religious principles.

PURPORT

Śrīla Viśvanātha Cakravartī Ṭhākura says in this regard that when a president or king is sitting on his throne, he does not need to show respect to everyone who comes within his assembly, but he must show respect to superiors like his spiritual master, *brāhmaṇas* and Vaiṣṇavas. There are many examples of how he should act. When Lord Kṛṣṇa was sitting on His throne and Nārada fortunately entered His assembly, even Lord Kṛṣṇa immediately stood up with His officers and ministers to offer respectful obeisances to Nārada. Nārada knew that Kṛṣṇa is the Supreme Personality of Godhead, and Kṛṣṇa knew that Nārada was His devotee, but although Kṛṣṇa is the Supreme Lord and Nārada is the Lord's devotee, the Lord observed the religious etiquette. Since Nārada was a *brahmacārī*, a *brāhmaṇa* and an exalted devotee, even Kṛṣṇa, while acting as a king, offered His respectful obeisances unto Nārada. Such is the conduct visible in the Vedic civilization. A civilization in which the people do not know how the representative of Nārada and Kṛṣṇa should be respected, how society should be formed and how one should advance in Kṛṣṇa consciousness—a society concerned only with manufacturing new cars and new skyscrapers every year and then breaking them to pieces and making new ones—may be technologically advanced, but it is not a human civilization. A human civilization is advanced when its people follow the *cātur-varṇya* system, the system of four orders of life. There must be ideal, first-class men to act as advisors, second-class men to act as administrators, third-class men to produce food and protect cows, and fourth-class men who obey the three higher classes of society. One who does not follow the standard system of society should be considered a fifth-class man. A society without Vedic laws and regulations will not be very helpful to humanity. As stated in this verse, *dharmaṁ te na paraṁ viduḥ:* such a society does not know the aim of life and the highest principle of religion.

TEXT 14

तेषां कुपथदेष्टॄणां पततां तमसि ह्यधः ।
ये श्रद्दध्युर्वचस्ते वै मज्जन्त्यश्मप्लवा इव ॥१४॥

teṣāṁ kupatha-deṣṭṝṇāṁ
patatāṁ tamasi hy adhaḥ
ye śraddadhyur vacas te vai
majjanty aśma-plavā iva

teṣām—of them (the misleaders); *ku-patha-deṣṭṝṇām*—who show the path of danger; *patatām*—themselves falling; *tamasi*—in darkness; *hi*—indeed; *adhaḥ*—down; *ye*—anyone who; *śraddadhyuḥ*—place faith in; *vacaḥ*—the words; *te*—they; *vai*—indeed; *majjanti*—sink; *aśma-plavāḥ*—boats made of stone; *iva*—like.

TRANSLATION

Leaders who have fallen into ignorance and who mislead people by directing them to the path of destruction [as described in the previous verse] are, in effect, boarding a stone boat, and so too are those who blindly follow them. A stone boat would be unable to float and would sink in the water with its passengers. Similarly, those who mislead people go to hell, and their followers go with them.

PURPORT

As stated in the Vedic literature (*Bhāg.* 11.20.17):

nṛ-deham ādyaṁ sulabhaṁ sudurlabhaṁ
plavaṁ sukalpaṁ guru-karṇa-dhāram

We, the conditioned souls, have fallen in the ocean of nescience, but the human body fortunately provides us a good opportunity to cross the ocean because the human body is like a very good boat. When directed by a spiritual master acting as the captain, the boat can very easily cross the ocean. Furthermore, the boat is helped across by favorable winds, which are the instructions of Vedic knowledge. If one does not take advantage of all these facilities to cross the ocean of nescience, he is certainly committing suicide.

One who boards a boat made of stone is doomed. To be elevated to the stage of perfection, humanity must first give up false leaders who present boats of stone. All of human society is in such a dangerous position that to be rescued it must abide by the standard instructions of the *Vedas.* The cream of these instructions appears in the form of *Bhagavad-gītā.* One should not take shelter of any other instructions, for *Bhagavad-gītā* gives direct instructions on how to fulfill the aim of human life. Lord Śrī Kṛṣṇa therefore says, *sarva-dharmān parityajya mām ekaṁ śaraṇaṁ vraja:* "Give up all other processes of religion and simply surrender to Me." Even if one does not accept Lord Kṛṣṇa as the Supreme Personality of Godhead, His instructions are so exalted and beneficial for humanity that if one follows His instructions one will be saved. Otherwise one will be cheated by unauthorized meditation and gymnastic methods of *yoga.* Thus one will board a boat of stone, which will sink and drown all its passengers. Unfortunately, although the American people are extremely eager to get out of materialistic chaos, they are sometimes found to patronize the makers of stone boats. That will not help them. They must take the proper boat offered by Kṛṣṇa in the form of the Kṛṣṇa consciousness movement. Then they will be easily saved. In this regard Śrīla Viśvanātha Cakravartī Ṭhākura comments: *aśmamayaḥ plavo yeṣāṁ te yathā majjantaṁ plavam anumajjanti tatheti rāja-nīty-upadeṣṭṛṣu sva-sabhyeṣu kopo vyañjitaḥ.* If society is guided by political diplomacy, with one nation maneuvering against another, it will certainly sink like a stone boat. Political maneuvering and diplomacy will not save human society. People must take to Kṛṣṇa consciousness to understand the aim of life, to understand God, and to fulfill the human mission.

TEXT 15

अथाहममराचार्यमगाधधिषणं द्विजम् ।
प्रसादयिष्ये निशठः शीर्ष्णा तच्चरणं स्पृशन् ॥१५॥

athāham amarācāryam
agādha-dhiṣaṇaṁ dvijam

prasādayiṣye niśaṭhaḥ
śīrṣṇā tac-caraṇaṁ spṛśan

atha—therefore; *aham*—I; *amara-ācāryam*—the spiritual master of the demigods; *agādha-dhiṣaṇam*—whose spiritual knowledge is deep; *dvijam*—the perfect *brāhmaṇa; prasādayiṣye*—I shall please; *niśaṭhaḥ*—without duplicity; *śīrṣṇā*—with my head; *tat-caraṇam*—his lotus feet; *spṛśan*—touching.

TRANSLATION

King Indra said: Therefore with great frankness and without duplicity I shall now bow my head at the lotus feet of Bṛhaspati, the spiritual master of the demigods. Because he is in the mode of goodness, he is fully aware of all knowledge and is the best of the brāhmaṇas. Now I shall touch his lotus feet and offer my obeisances unto him to try to satisfy him.

PURPORT

Coming to his senses, King Indra realized that he was not a very sincere disciple of his spiritual master, Bṛhaspati. Therefore he decided that henceforward he would be *niśaṭha*, nonduplicitous. *Niśaṭhaḥ śīrṣṇā tac-caraṇaṁ spṛśan:* he decided to touch his head to the feet of his spiritual master. From this example, we should learn this principle enunciated by Viśvanātha Cakravartī Ṭhākura:

yasya prasādād bhagavat-prasādo
yasyāprasādān na gatiḥ kuto 'pi

"By the mercy of the spiritual master one is benedicted by the mercy of Kṛṣṇa. Without the grace of the spiritual master, one cannot make any advancement." A disciple should never be a hypocrite or be unfaithful to his spiritual master. In *Śrīmad-Bhāgavatam* (11.17.27), the spiritual master is also called *ācārya. Ācāryaṁ māṁ vijānīyān:* the Supreme Personality of Godhead says that one should respect the spiritual master, accepting him as the Lord Himself. *Nāvamanyeta karhicit:* one should not disrespect the *ācārya* at any time. *Na martya-buddhyāsūyeta:* one should never think the *ācārya* an ordinary person. Familiarity sometimes breeds contempt, but one should be very careful in one's dealings with the *ācārya. Agādha-dhiṣaṇaṁ dvijam:* the *ācārya* is a perfect *brāhmaṇa* and has unlimited intelligence in guiding the activities of his disciple. Therefore Kṛṣṇa advises in *Bhagavad-gītā* (4.34):

tad viddhi praṇipātena
paripraśnena sevayā
upadekṣyanti te jñānaṁ
jñāninas tattva-darśinaḥ

"Just try to learn the truth by approaching a spiritual master. Inquire from him submissively and render service unto him. The self-realized soul can impart knowledge unto you because he has seen the truth." One should fully surrender unto the spiritual master, and with service (*sevayā*) one should approach him for further spiritual enlightenment.

TEXT 16

एवं चिन्तयतस्तस्य मघोनो भगवान् गृहात् ।
बृहस्पतिर्गतोऽदृष्टां गतिमध्यात्ममायया ॥१६॥

evaṁ cintayatas tasya
maghono bhagavān gṛhāt
bṛhaspatir gato 'dṛṣṭāṁ
gatim adhyātma-māyayā

evam—thus; *cintayataḥ*—while thinking very seriously; *tasya*—he; *maghonaḥ*—Indra; *bhagavān*—the most powerful; *gṛhāt*—from his home; *bṛhaspatiḥ*—Bṛhaspati; *gataḥ*—went; *adṛṣṭām*—invisible; *gatim*—to a state; *adhyātma*—due to being highly elevated in spiritual consciousness; *māyayā*—by his potency.

TRANSLATION

While Indra, the King of the demigods, thought in this way and repented in his own assembly, Bṛhaspati, the most powerful

spiritual master, understood his mind. Thus he became invisible to Indra and left home, for Bṛhaspati was spiritually more powerful than King Indra.

TEXT 17

गुरोर्नाधिगतः संज्ञां परीक्षन् भगवान् स्वराट् ।
ध्यायन् धिया सुरैर्युक्तः शर्म नालभतात्मनः ॥१७॥

guror nādhigataḥ saṁjñāṁ
parīkṣan bhagavān svarāṭ
dhyāyan dhiyā surair yuktaḥ
śarma nālabhatātmanaḥ

guroḥ—of his spiritual master; *na*—not; *adhigataḥ*—finding; *saṁjñām*—trace; *parīkṣan*—searching vigorously all around; *bhagavān*—the most powerful Indra; *svarāṭ*—independent; *dhyāyan*—meditating; *dhiyā*—by wisdom; *suraiḥ*—by the demigods; *yuktaḥ*—surrounded; *śarma*—peace; *na*—not; *alabhata*—obtained; *ātmanaḥ*—of the mind.

TRANSLATION

Although Indra searched vigorously with the assistance of the other demigods, he could not find Bṛhaspati. Then Indra thought, "Alas, my spiritual master has become dissatisfied with me, and now I have no means of achieving good fortune." Although Indra was surrounded by demigods, he could not find peace of mind.

TEXT 18

तच्छ्रुत्वैवासुराः सर्व आश्रित्यौशनसं मतम् ।
देवान् प्रत्युद्यमं चक्रुर्दुर्मदा आततायिनः ॥१८॥

tac chrutvaivāsurāḥ sarva
āśrityauśanasaṁ matam
devān pratyudyamaṁ cakrur
durmadā ātatāyinaḥ

tat śrutvā—hearing that news; *eva*—indeed; *asurāḥ*—the demons; *sarve*—all; *āśritya*—taking shelter of; *auśanasam*—of Śukrācārya; *matam*—the instruction; *devān*—the demigods; *pratyudyamam*—action against; *cakruḥ*—performed; *durmadāḥ*—not very intelligent; *ātatāyinaḥ*—equipped with arms for fighting.

TRANSLATION

Hearing of the pitiable condition of King Indra, the demons, following the instructions of their guru, Śukrācārya, equipped themselves with weapons and declared war against the demigods.

TEXT 19

तैर्विसृष्टेषुभिस्तीक्ष्णैर्निर्भिन्नाङ्गोरुबाहवः ।
ब्रह्माणं शरणं जग्मुः सहेन्द्रा नतकन्धराः ॥१९॥

tair visṛṣṭeṣubhis tīkṣṇair
nirbhinnāṅgoru-bāhavaḥ
brahmāṇaṁ śaraṇaṁ jagmuḥ
sahendrā nata-kandharāḥ

taiḥ—by them (the demons); *visṛṣṭa*—thrown; *iṣubhiḥ*—by the arrows; *tīkṣṇaiḥ*—very sharp; *nirbhinna*—pierced all over; *aṅga*—bodies; *uru*—thighs; *bāhavaḥ*—and arms; *brahmāṇam*—of Lord Brahmā; *śaraṇam*—the shelter; *jagmuḥ*—approached; *saha-indrāḥ*—with King Indra; *nata-kandharāḥ*—their heads bent downward.

TRANSLATION

The demigods' heads, thighs and arms and the other parts of their bodies were injured by the sharp arrows of the demons. The demigods, headed by Indra, saw no other course than to immediately approach Lord Brahmā with bowed heads for shelter and proper instruction.

TEXT 20

तांस्तथाभ्यर्दितान् वीक्ष्य भगवानात्मभूरजः ।
कृपया परया देव उवाच परिसान्त्वयन् ॥२०॥

tāṁs tathābhyarditān vīkṣya
bhagavān ātmabhūr ajaḥ
kṛpayā parayā deva
uvāca parisāntvayan

tān—them (the demigods); *tathā*—in that way; *abhyarditān*—afflicted by the weapons of the demons; *vīkṣya*—seeing; *bhagavān*—the most powerful; *ātma-bhūḥ*—Lord Brahmā; *ajaḥ*—who was not born like an ordinary human being; *kṛpayā*—out of causeless mercy; *parayā*—great; *devaḥ*—Lord Brahmā; *uvāca*—said; *parisāntvayan*—pacifying them.

TRANSLATION

When the most powerful Lord Brahmā saw the demigods coming toward him, their bodies gravely injured by the arrows of the demons, he pacified them by his great causeless mercy and spoke as follows.

TEXT 21

श्रीब्रह्मोवाच
अहो बत सुरश्रेष्ठा ह्यभद्रं वः कृतं महत् ।
ब्रह्मिष्ठं ब्राह्मणं दान्तमैश्वर्यान्नाभ्यनन्दत ॥२१॥

śrī-brahmovāca
aho bata sura-śreṣṭhā
hy abhadraṁ vaḥ kṛtaṁ mahat
brahmiṣṭhaṁ brāhmaṇaṁ dāntam
aiśvaryān nābhyanandata

śrī-brahmā uvāca—Lord Brahmā said; *aho*—alas; *bata*—it is very astonishing; *sura-śreṣṭhāḥ*—O best of the demigods; *hi*—indeed; *abhadram*—injustice; *vaḥ*—by you; *kṛtam*—done; *mahat*—great; *brahmiṣṭham*—a person fully obedient to the Supreme Brahman; *brāhmaṇam*—a *brāhmaṇa; dāntam*—who has fully controlled the mind and senses; *aiśvaryāt*—because of your material opulence; *na*—not; *abhyanandata*—welcomed properly.

TRANSLATION

Lord Brahmā said: O best of the demigods, unfortunately, because of madness resulting from your material opulence, you failed to receive Bṛhaspati properly when he came to your assembly. Because he is aware of the Supreme Brahman and fully in control of his senses, he is the best of the brāhmaṇas. Therefore it is very astonishing that you have acted impudently toward him.

PURPORT

Lord Brahmā recognized the brahminical qualifications of Bṛhaspati, who was the spiritual master of the demigods because of his awareness of the Supreme Brahman. Bṛhaspati was very much in control of his senses and mind, and therefore he was a most qualified *brāhmaṇa*. Lord Brahmā chastised the demigods for not properly respecting this *brāhmaṇa*, who was their *guru*. Lord Brahmā wanted to impress upon the demigods that one's *guru* should not be disrespected under any circumstances. When Bṛhaspati entered the assembly of the demigods, they and their king, Indra, took him for granted. Since he came every day, they thought, they did not need to show him special respect. As it is said, familiarity breeds contempt. Being very much displeased, Bṛhaspati immediately left Indra's palace. Thus all the demigods, headed by Indra, became offenders at the lotus feet of Bṛhaspati, and Lord Brahmā, being aware of this, condemned their neglect. In a song we sing every day, Narottama dāsa Ṭhākura says, *cakṣu-dāna dila yei, janme janme prabhu sei:* the *guru* gives spiritual insight to the disciple, and therefore the *guru* should be considered his master, life after life. Under no circumstances should the *guru* be disrespected, but the demigods, being puffed up by their material possessions, were disrespectful to their *guru.* Therefore *Śrīmad-Bhāgavatam* (11.17.27) advises, *ācāryaṁ māṁ vijānīyān nāvamanyeta karhicit/ na martya-buddhyāsūyeta:* the *ācārya* should always be offered respectful obeisances; one should never envy the *ācārya*, considering him an ordinary human being.

TEXT 22

तस्यायमनयस्यासीत् परेभ्यो वः पराभवः ।
प्रक्षीणेभ्यः स्ववैरिभ्यः समृद्धानां च यत् सुराः ॥२२॥

tasyāyam anayasyāsīt
parebhyo vaḥ parābhavaḥ
prakṣīṇebhyaḥ sva-vairibhyaḥ
samṛddhānāṁ ca yat surāḥ

tasya—that; *ayam*—this; *anayasya*—of your ungrateful activity; *āsīt*—was; *parebhyaḥ*—by others; *vaḥ*—of all of you; *parābhavaḥ*—the defeat; *prakṣīṇebhyaḥ*—although they were weak; *sva-vairibhyaḥ*—by your own enemies, who were previously defeated by you; *samṛddhānām*—being yourselves very opulent; *ca*—and; *yat*—which; *surāḥ*—O demigods.

TRANSLATION

Because of your misbehavior toward Bṛhaspati, you have been defeated by the demons. My dear demigods, since the demons were weak, having been defeated by you several times, how else could you, who were so advanced in opulence, be defeated by them?

PURPORT

The *devas* are celebrated for fighting with the *asuras* perpetually. In such fights the *asuras* were always defeated, but this time the demigods were defeated. Why? The reason, as stated here, was that they had offended their spiritual master. Their impudent disrespect of their spiritual master was the cause of their defeat by the demons. As stated in the *śāstras*, when one disrespects a respectable superior, one loses his longevity and the results of his pious activities, and in this way one is degraded.

TEXT 23

मघवन् द्विषतः पश्य प्रक्षीणान् गुर्वतिक्रमात् ।
सम्प्रत्युपचितान् भूयः काव्यमाराध्य भक्तितः ।
आददीरन् निलयनं ममापि भृगुदेवताः ॥२३॥

maghavan dviṣataḥ paśya
prakṣīṇān gurv-atikramāt
sampraty upacitān bhūyaḥ

kāvyam ārādhya bhaktitaḥ
ādadīran nilayanaṁ
mamāpi bhṛgu-devatāḥ

maghavan—O Indra; *dviṣataḥ*—your enemies; *paśya*—just see; *prakṣīṇān*—being very weak (formerly); *guru-atikramāt*—because of disrespecting their *guru*, Śukrācārya; *samprati*—at the present moment; *upacitān*—powerful; *bhūyaḥ*—again; *kāvyam*—their spiritual master, Śukrācārya; *ārādhya*—worshiping; *bhaktitaḥ*—with great devotion; *ādadīran*—may take away; *nilayanam*—the abode, Satyaloka; *mama*—my; *api*—even; *bhṛgu-devatāḥ*—who are now strong devotees of Śukrācārya, the disciple of Bhṛgu.

TRANSLATION

O Indra, your enemies, the demons, were extremely weak because of their disrespect toward Śukrācārya, but since they have now worshiped Śukrācārya with great devotion, they have again become powerful. By their devotion to Śukrācārya, they have increased their strength so much that now they are even able to easily seize my abode from me.

PURPORT

Lord Brahmā wanted to point out to the demigods that by the strength of the *guru* one can become most powerful within this world, and by the displeasure of the *guru* one can lose everything. This is confirmed by the song of Viśvanātha Cakravartī Ṭhākura:

yasya prasādād bhagavat-prasādo
yasyāprasādān na gatiḥ kuto 'pi

"By the mercy of the spiritual master one is benedicted by the mercy of Kṛṣṇa. Without the grace of the spiritual master, one cannot make any advancement." Although the demons are insignificant in comparison to Lord Brahmā, because of the strength of their *guru* they were so powerful that they could even seize Brahmaloka from Lord Brahmā. We therefore pray to the spiritual master:

mūkaṁ karoti vācālaṁ
paṅguṁ laṅghayate girim
yat-kṛpā tam ahaṁ vande
śrī-guruṁ dīna-tāraṇam

By the mercy of the *guru,* even a dumb man can become the greatest orator, and even a lame man can cross mountains. As advised by Lord Brahmā, one should remember this śāstric injunction if one desires success in his life.

TEXT 24

त्रिपिष्टपं किं गणयन्त्यभेद्य-
मन्त्रा भृगूणामनुशिक्षितार्थाः ।
न विप्रगोविन्दगवीश्वराणां
भवन्त्यभद्राणि नरेश्वराणाम् ॥२४॥

tripiṣṭapaṁ kiṁ gaṇayanty abhedya-
mantrā bhṛgūṇām anuśikṣitārthāḥ
na vipra-govinda-gav-īśvarāṇāṁ
bhavanty abhadrāṇi nareśvarāṇām

tri-piṣṭa-pam—all the demigods, including Lord Brahmā; *kim*—what; *gaṇayanti*—they care for; *abhedya-mantrāḥ*—whose determination to carry out the orders of the spiritual master is unbreakable; *bhṛgūṇām*—of the disciples of Bhṛgu Muni like Śukrācārya; *anuśikṣita-arthāḥ*—deciding to follow the instructions; *na*—not; *vipra*—the *brāhmaṇas; govinda*—the Supreme Personality of Godhead, Kṛṣṇa; *go*—the cows; *īśvarāṇām*—of persons favoring or considering worshipable; *bhavanti*—are; *abhadrāṇi*—any misfortunes; *nara-īśvarāṇām*—or of kings who follow this principle.

TRANSLATION

Because of their firm determination to follow the instructions of Śukrācārya, his disciples, the demons, are now unconcerned about the demigods. In fact, kings or others who have determined faith

in the mercy of brāhmaṇas, cows and the Supreme Personality of Godhead, Kṛṣṇa, and who always worship these three are always strong in their position.

PURPORT

From the instructions of Lord Brahmā it is understood that everyone should very faithfully worship the *brāhmaṇas*, the Supreme Personality of Godhead and the cows. The Supreme Personality of Godhead is *go-brāhmaṇa-hitāya ca:* He is always very kind to cows and *brāhmaṇas.* Therefore one who worships Govinda must satisfy Him by worshiping the *brāhmaṇas* and cows. If a government worships the *brāhmaṇas*, the cows and Kṛṣṇa, Govinda, it is never defeated anywhere; otherwise it must always be defeated and condemned everywhere. At the present moment, all over the world, governments have no respect for *brāhmaṇas*, cows and Govinda, and consequently there are chaotic conditions all over the world. In summary, although the demigods were very powerful in material opulence, the demons defeated them in battle because the demigods had behaved disrespectfully toward a *brāhmaṇa*, Bṛhaspati, who was their spiritual master.

TEXT 25

तद् विश्वरूपं भजताशु विप्रं
तपस्विनं त्वाष्ट्रमथात्मवन्तम् ।
सभाजितोऽर्थान् स विधास्यते वो
यदि क्षमिष्यध्वमुतास्य कर्म ॥२५॥

tad viśvarūpaṁ bhajatāśu vipraṁ
tapasvinaṁ tvāṣṭram athātmavantam
sabhājito 'rthān sa vidhāsyate vo
yadi kṣamiṣyadhvam utāsya karma

tat—therefore; *viśvarūpam*—Viśvarūpa; *bhajata*—just worship as *guru; āśu*—immediately; *vipram*—who is a perfect *brāhmaṇa; tapasvinam*—undergoing great austerities and penances; *tvāṣṭram*—the son of Tvaṣṭā; *atha*—as well as; *ātma-vantam*—very independent; *sabhājitaḥ*—being worshiped; *arthān*—the interests; *saḥ*—he; *vidhāsyate*—

will execute; *vaḥ*—of all of you; *yadi*—if; *kṣamiṣyadhvam*—you tolerate; *uta*—indeed; *asya*—his; *karma*—activities (to support the Daityas).

TRANSLATION

O demigods, I instruct you to approach Viśvarūpa, the son of Tvaṣṭā, and accept him as your guru. He is a pure and very powerful brāhmaṇa undergoing austerity and penances. Pleased by your worship, he will fulfill your desires, provided that you tolerate his being inclined to side with the demons.

PURPORT

Lord Brahmā advised the demigods to accept the son of Tvaṣṭā as their spiritual master although he was always inclined toward the benefit of the *asuras.*

TEXT 26

श्रीशुक उवाच
त एवमुदिता राजन् ब्रह्मणा विगतज्वराः ।
ऋषिं त्वाष्ट्रमुपव्रज्य परिष्वज्येदमब्रुवन् ॥२६॥

śrī-śuka uvāca
ta evam uditā rājan
brahmaṇā vigata-jvarāḥ
ṛṣiṁ tvāṣṭram upavrajya
pariṣvajyedam abruvan

śrī-śukaḥ uvāca—Śukadeva Gosvāmī said; *te*—all the demigods; *evam*—thus; *uditāḥ*—being advised; *rājan*—O King Parīkṣit; *brahmaṇā*—by Lord Brahmā; *vigata-jvarāḥ*—being relieved from the aggrievement caused by the demons; *ṛṣim*—the great sage; *tvāṣṭram*—to the son of Tvaṣṭā; *upavrajya*—going; *pariṣvajya*—embracing; *idam*—this; *abruvan*—spoke.

TRANSLATION

Śrīla Śukadeva Gosvāmī continued: Thus advised by Lord Brahmā and relieved of their anxiety, all the demigods went to the

sage Viśvarūpa, the son of Tvaṣṭā. My dear King, they embraced him and spoke as follows.

TEXT 27

श्रीदेवा ऊचुः
वयं तेऽतिथयः प्राप्ता आश्रमं भद्रमस्तु ते ।
कामः सम्पाद्यतां तात पितॄणां समयोचितः ॥२७॥

śrī-devā ūcuḥ
vayaṁ te 'tithayaḥ prāptā
āśramaṁ bhadram astu te
kāmaḥ sampādyatāṁ tāta
pitṝṇāṁ samayocitaḥ

śrī-devāḥ ūcuḥ—the demigods said; *vayam*—we; *te*—your; *atithayaḥ*—guests; *prāptāḥ*—arrived at; *āśramam*—your abode; *bhadram*—good fortune; *astu*—let there be; *te*—unto you; *kāmaḥ*—the desire; *sampādyatām*—let it be executed; *tāta*—O darling; *pitṝṇām*—of us, who are just like your fathers; *samayocitaḥ*—suitable to the present time.

TRANSLATION

The demigods said: Beloved Viśvarūpa, may there be all good fortune for you. We, the demigods, have come to your āśrama as your guests. Please try to fulfill our desires according to the time, since we are on the level of your parents.

TEXT 28

पुत्राणां हि परो धर्मः पितृशुश्रूषणं सताम् ।
अपि पुत्रवतां ब्रह्मन् किमुत ब्रह्मचारिणाम् ॥२८॥

putrāṇāṁ hi paro dharmaḥ
pitṛ-śuśrūṣaṇaṁ satām
api putravatāṁ brahman
kim uta brahmacāriṇām

putrāṇām—of sons; *hi*—indeed; *paraḥ*—superior; *dharmaḥ*—religious principle; *pitṛ-śuśrūṣaṇam*—the service of the parents; *satām*—good; *api*—even; *putra-vatām*—of those who have sons; *brahman*—O dear *brāhmaṇa; kim uta*—what to speak; *brahmacāriṇām*—of *brahmacārīs.*

TRANSLATION

O brāhmaṇa, the highest duty of a son, even though he has sons of his own, is to serve his parents, and what to speak of a son who is a brahmacārī?

TEXTS 29–30

आचार्यो ब्रह्मणो मूर्तिः पिता मूर्तिः प्रजापतेः ।
भ्राता मरुत्पतेर्मूर्तिर्माता साक्षात् क्षितेस्तनुः ॥२९॥
दयाया भगिनी मूर्तिर्धर्मस्यात्मातिथिः स्वयम् ।
अग्नेरभ्यागतो मूर्तिः सर्वभूतानि चात्मनः ॥३०॥

ācāryo brahmaṇo mūrtiḥ
pitā mūrtiḥ prajāpateḥ
bhrātā marutpater mūrtir
mātā sākṣāt kṣites tanuḥ

dayāyā bhaginī mūrtir
dharmasyātmātithiḥ svayam
agner abhyāgato mūrtiḥ
sarva-bhūtāni cātmanaḥ

ācāryaḥ—the teacher or spiritual master who instructs Vedic knowledge by his personal behavior; *brahmaṇaḥ*—of all the *Vedas; mūrtiḥ*—the personification; *pitā*—the father; *mūrtiḥ*—the personification; *prajāpateḥ*—of Lord Brahmā; *bhrātā*—the brother; *marut-pateḥ mūrtiḥ*—the personification of Indra; *mātā*—the mother; *sākṣāt*—directly; *kṣiteḥ*—of the earth; *tanuḥ*—the body; *dayāyāḥ*—of mercy; *bhaginī*—the sister; *mūrtiḥ*—the personification; *dharmasya*—of religious principles; *ātma*—the self; *atithiḥ*—the guest; *svayam*—personally;

agneḥ—of the fire-god; *abhyāgataḥ*—the invited guest; *mūrtiḥ*—the personification; *sarva-bhūtāni*—all living entities; *ca*—and; *ātmanaḥ*—of the Supreme Lord Viṣṇu.

TRANSLATION

The ācārya, the spiritual master who teaches all the Vedic knowledge and gives initiation by offering the sacred thread, is the personification of all the Vedas. Similarly, a father personifies Lord Brahmā; a brother, King Indra; a mother, the planet earth; and a sister, mercy. A guest personifies religious principles, an invited guest personifies the demigod Agni, and all living entities personify Lord Viṣṇu, the Supreme Personality of Godhead.

PURPORT

According to the moral instructions of Cāṇakya Paṇḍita, *ātmavat sarva-bhūteṣu:* one should observe all living entities to be on the same level as oneself. This means that no one should be neglected as inferior; because Paramātmā is seated in everyone's body, everyone should be respected as a temple of the Supreme Personality of Godhead. This verse describes the different ways in which one should respect a *guru*, a father, a brother, a sister, a guest and so on.

TEXT 31

तस्मात् पितॄणामार्तानामार्तिं परपराभवम् ।
तपसापनयंस्तात सन्देशं कर्तुमर्हसि ॥३१॥

tasmāt pitṝṇām ārtānām
ārtiṁ para-parābhavam
tapasāpanayaṁs tāta
sandeśaṁ kartum arhasi

tasmāt—therefore; *pitṝṇām*—of the parents; *ārtānām*—who are in distress; *ārtim*—the grief; *para-parābhavam*—being defeated by the enemies; *tapasā*—by the strength of your austerities; *apanayan*—taking away; *tāta*—O dear son; *sandeśam*—our desire; *kartum arhasi*—you deserve to execute.

TRANSLATION

Dear son, we have been defeated by our enemies, and therefore we are very much aggrieved. Please mercifully fulfill our desires by relieving our distress through the strength of your austerities. Please fulfill our prayers.

TEXT 32

वृणीमहे त्वोपाध्यायं ब्रह्मिष्ठं ब्राह्मणं गुरुम् ।
यथाञ्जसा विजेष्यामः सपत्नांस्तव तेजसा ॥३२॥

vṛṇīmahe tvopādhyāyaṁ
brahmiṣṭhaṁ brāhmaṇaṁ gurum
yathāñjasā vijeṣyāmaḥ
sapatnāṁs tava tejasā

vṛṇīmahe—we choose; *tvā*—you; *upādhyāyam*—as teacher and spiritual master; *brahmiṣṭham*—being perfectly aware of the Supreme Brahman; *brāhmaṇam*—a qualified *brāhmaṇa; gurum*—the perfect spiritual master; *yathā*—so that; *añjasā*—very easily; *vijeṣyāmaḥ*—we shall defeat; *sapatnān*—our rivals; *tava*—your; *tejasā*—by the power of austerity.

TRANSLATION

Since you are completely aware of the Supreme Brahman, you are a perfect brāhmaṇa, and therefore you are the spiritual master of all orders of life. We accept you as our spiritual master and director so that by the power of your austerity we may easily defeat the enemies who have conquered us.

PURPORT

One must approach a particular type of *guru* to execute a particular type of duty. Therefore although Viśvarūpa was inferior to the demigods, the demigods accepted him as their *guru* to conquer the demons.

TEXT 33

न गर्हयन्ति ह्यर्थेषु यविष्ठाङ्घ्र्यभिवादनम् ।
छन्दोभ्योऽन्यत्र न ब्रह्मन् वयो ज्यैष्ठ्यस्य कारणम् ॥३३॥

na garhayanti hy artheṣu
yaviṣṭhāṅghry-abhivādanam
chandobhyo 'nyatra na brahman
vayo jyaiṣṭhyasya kāraṇam

na—not; *garhayanti*—forbid; *hi*—indeed; *artheṣu*—in acquiring interests; *yaviṣṭha-aṅghri*—at the lotus feet of a junior; *abhivādanam*—offering obeisances; *chandobhyaḥ*—the Vedic *mantras; anyatra*—apart from; *na*—not; *brahman*—O *brāhmaṇa; vayaḥ*—age; *jyaiṣṭhyasya*—of seniority; *kāraṇam*—the cause.

TRANSLATION

The demigods continued: Do not fear criticism for being younger than us. Such etiquette does not apply in regard to Vedic mantras. Except in relationship to Vedic mantras, seniority is determined by age, but one may offer respectful obeisances even to a younger person who is advanced in chanting Vedic mantras. Therefore although you are junior in relationship to us, you may become our priest without hesitation.

PURPORT

It is said, *vṛddhatvaṁ vayasā vinā:* one may be senior without being advanced in age. Even if one is not old, one gains seniority if he is senior in knowledge. Viśvarūpa was junior in relationship to the demigods because he was their nephew, but the demigods wanted to accept him as their priest, and therefore he would have to accept obeisances from them. The demigods explained that this should not be a cause for hesitation; he could become their priest because he was advanced in Vedic knowledge. Similarly, Cāṇakya Paṇḍita advises, *nīcād apy uttamaṁ jñānam:* one may accept education from a member of a lower social order. The *brāhmaṇas*, the members of the most elevated *varṇa*, are teachers, but a person in a lower family, such as a family of *kṣatriyas, vaiśyas* or even *śūdras*, may be accepted as a teacher if he has knowledge. Śrī Caitanya Mahāprabhu approved of this when He expressed this opinion before Rāmānanda Rāya (Cc. *Madhya* 8.128):

kibā vipra, kibā nyāsī, śūdra kene naya
yei kṛṣṇa-tattva-vettā, sei 'guru' haya

It does not matter whether one is a *brāhmaṇa, śūdra, gṛhastha* or *sannyāsī.* These are all material designations. A spiritually advanced person has nothing to do with such designations. Therefore, if one is advanced in the science of Kṛṣṇa consciousness, regardless of his position in human society, he may become a spiritual master.

TEXT 34

श्रीऋषिरुवाच
अभ्यर्थितः सुरगणैः पौरहित्ये महातपाः ।
स विश्वरूपस्तानाह प्रसन्नः श्लक्ष्णया गिरा ॥३४॥

śrī-ṛṣir uvāca
abhyarthitaḥ sura-gaṇaiḥ
paurahitye mahā-tapāḥ
sa viśvarūpas tān āha
prasannaḥ ślakṣṇayā girā

śrī-ṛṣiḥ uvāca—Śukadeva Gosvāmī continued to speak; *abhyarthitaḥ*—being requested; *sura-gaṇaiḥ*—by the demigods; *paurahitye*—in accepting the priesthood; *mahā-tapāḥ*—highly advanced in austerity and penances; *saḥ*—he; *viśvarūpaḥ*—Viśvarūpa; *tān*—to the demigods; *āha*—spoke; *prasannaḥ*—being satisfied; *ślakṣṇayā*—sweet; *girā*—with words.

TRANSLATION

Śukadeva Gosvāmī continued: When all the demigods requested the great Viśvarūpa to be their priest, Viśvarūpa, who was advanced in austerities, was very pleased. He replied to them as follows.

TEXT 35

श्रीविश्वरूप उवाच
विगर्हितं धर्मशीलैर्ब्रह्मवर्चउपव्ययम् ।
कथं नु मद्विधो नाथा लोकेशैरभियाचितम् ।
प्रत्याख्यास्यति तच्छिष्यः स एव स्वार्थ उच्यते ॥३५॥

śrī-viśvarūpa uvāca
vigarhitaṁ dharma-śīlair
brahmavarca-upavyayam
kathaṁ nu mad-vidho nāthā
lokeśair abhiyācitam
pratyākhyāsyati tac-chiṣyaḥ
sa eva svārtha ucyate

śrī-viśvarūpaḥ uvāca—Śrī Viśvarūpa said; *vigarhitam*—condemned; *dharma-śīlaiḥ*—by persons respectful to the religious principles; *brahma-varcaḥ*—of brahminical strength or power; *upavyayam*—causes loss; *katham*—how; *nu*—indeed; *mat-vidhaḥ*—a person like me; *nāthāḥ*—O lords; *loka-īśaiḥ*—by the ruling powers of different planets; *abhiyācitam*—request; *pratyākhyāsyati*—will refuse; *tat-śiṣyaḥ*—who is on the level of their disciple; *saḥ*—that; *eva*—indeed; *sva-arthaḥ*—real interest; *ucyate*—is described as.

TRANSLATION

Śrī Viśvarūpa said: O demigods, although the acceptance of priesthood is decried as causing the loss of previously acquired brahminical power, how can someone like me refuse to accept your personal request? You are all exalted commanders of the entire universe. I am your disciple and must take many lessons from you. Therefore I cannot refuse you. I must agree for my own benefit.

PURPORT

The professions of a qualified *brāhmaṇa* are *paṭhana*, *pāṭhana*, *yajana*, *yājana*, *dāna* and *pratigraha*. The words *yajana* and *yājana* mean that a *brāhmaṇa* becomes the priest of the populace for the sake of their elevation. One who accepts the post of spiritual master neutralizes the sinful reactions of the *yajamāna*, the one on whose behalf he performs *yajña*. Thus the results of the pious acts previously performed by the priest or spiritual master are diminished. Therefore priesthood is not accepted by learned *brāhmaṇas*. Nevertheless, the greatly learned *brāhmaṇa* Viśvarūpa became the priest of the demigods because of his profound respect for them.

TEXT 36

अकिञ्चनानां हि धनं शिलोञ्छनं
तेनेह निर्वर्तितसाधुसत्क्रियः ।
कथं विगर्ह्यं नु करोम्यधीश्वराः
पौरोधसं हृष्यति येन दुर्मतिः ॥३६॥

akiñcanānāṁ hi dhanaṁ śiloñchanaṁ
teneha nirvartita-sādhu-satkriyaḥ
kathaṁ vigarhyaṁ nu karomy adhīśvarāḥ
paurodhasaṁ hṛṣyati yena durmatiḥ

akiñcanānām—of persons who have taken to austerities and penances to become detached from worldly possessions; *hi*—certainly; *dhanam*—the wealth; *śila*—the collecting of grains left in the field; *uñchanam*—and the collecting of grains left in the wholesale marketplace; *tena*—by that means; *iha*—here; *nirvartita*—accomplishing; *sādhu*—of the exalted devotees; *sat-kriyaḥ*—all the pious activities; *katham*—how; *vigarhyam*—reproachable; *nu*—indeed; *karomi*—I shall execute; *adhīśvarāḥ*—O great governors of the planetary systems; *paurodhasam*—the duty of priesthood; *hṛṣyati*—is pleased; *yena*—by which; *durmatiḥ*—one who is less intelligent.

TRANSLATION

O exalted governors of various planets, the true brāhmaṇa, who has no material possessions, maintains himself by the profession of accepting śiloñchana. In other words, he picks up grains left in the field and on the ground in the wholesale marketplace. By this means, householder brāhmaṇas who actually abide by the principles of austerity and penance maintain themselves and their families and perform all necessary pious activities. A brāhmaṇa who desires to achieve happiness by gaining wealth through professional priesthood must certainly have a very low mind. How shall I accept such priesthood?

PURPORT

A first-class *brāhmaṇa* does not accept any rewards from his disciples or *yajamānas*. Practicing austerities and penances, he instead goes to the agricultural field and collects food grains left by the agriculturalists to be collected by *brāhmaṇas*. Similarly, such *brāhmaṇas* go to marketplaces where grains are purchased and sold wholesale, and there they collect grains left by the merchants. In this way, such exalted *brāhmaṇas* maintain their bodies and families. Such priests never demand anything from their disciples to live in opulence, imitating *kṣatriyas* or *vaiśyas*. In other words, a pure *brāhmaṇa* voluntarily accepts a life of poverty and lives in complete dependence on the mercy of the Lord. Not very many years ago, a *brāhmaṇa* in Kṛṣṇanagara, near Navadvīpa, was offered some help from the local Zamindar, Vraja Kṛṣṇacandra. The *brāhmaṇa* refused to accept the help. He said that since he was very happy in his householder life, taking rice given by his disciples and cooking vegetables of tamarind leaves, there was no question of taking help from the Zamindar. The conclusion is that although a *brāhmaṇa* may receive much opulence from his disciples, he should not utilize the rewards of his priesthood for his personal benefit; he must use them for the service of the Supreme Personality of Godhead.

TEXT 37

तथापि न प्रतिब्रूयां गुरुभिः प्रार्थितं कियत् ।
भवतां प्रार्थितं सर्वं प्राणैरर्थैश्च साधये ॥३७॥

tathāpi na pratibrūyāṁ
gurubhiḥ prārthitaṁ kiyat
bhavatāṁ prārthitaṁ sarvaṁ
prāṇair arthaiś ca sādhaye

tathā api—still; *na*—not; *pratibrūyām*—I may refuse; *gurubhiḥ*—by persons on the level of my spiritual master; *prārthitam*—request; *kiyat*—of small value; *bhavatām*—of all of you; *prārthitam*—the desire; *sarvam*—whole; *prāṇaiḥ*—by my life; *arthaiḥ*—by my possessions; *ca*—also; *sādhaye*—I shall execute.

TRANSLATION

All of you are my superiors. Therefore although accepting priesthood is sometimes reproachable, I cannot refuse even a small request from you. I agree to be your priest. I shall fulfill your request by dedicating my life and possessions.

TEXT 38

श्रीबादरायणिरुवाच
तेभ्य एवं प्रतिश्रुत्य विश्वरूपो महातपाः ।
पौरहित्यं वृतश्चक्रे परमेण समाधिना ॥३८॥

śrī-bādarāyaṇir uvāca
tebhya evaṁ pratiśrutya
viśvarūpo mahā-tapāḥ
paurahityaṁ vṛtaś cakre
parameṇa samādhinā

śrī-bādarāyaṇiḥ uvāca—Śrī Śukadeva Gosvāmī said; *tebhyaḥ*—unto them (the demigods); *evam*—thus; *pratiśrutya*—promising; *viśvarūpaḥ*—Viśvarūpa; *mahā-tapāḥ*—the most exalted personality; *paurahityam*—the priesthood; *vṛtaḥ*—surrounded by them; *cakre*—executed; *parameṇa*—supreme; *samādhinā*—with attention.

TRANSLATION

Śrī Śukadeva Gosvāmī continued: O King, after making this promise to the demigods, the exalted Viśvarūpa, surrounded by the demigods, performed the necessary priestly activities with great enthusiasm and attention.

PURPORT

The word *samādhinā* is very important. *Samādhi* means complete absorption with an undiverted mind. Viśvarūpa, who was a most learned *brāhmaṇa*, not only accepted the request of the demigods, but took their request seriously and performed the activities of priesthood with an undiverted mind. In other words, he accepted the priesthood not for material gain, but to profit the demigods. Such is the duty of a priest. The word *puraḥ* means "family," and *hita* means "benefit." Thus the word *purohita* indicates that the priest is the well-wisher of the family. Another meaning of the word *puraḥ* is "first." A priest's first duty is to see that his disciples benefit spiritually and materially by all means. Then he is satisfied. A priest should never be interested in performing Vedic rituals for his personal benefit.

TEXT 39

सुरद्विषां श्रियं गुप्तामौशनस्यापि विद्यया ।
आच्छिद्यादान्महेन्द्राय वैष्णव्या विद्यया विभुः॥३९॥

sura-dviṣāṁ śriyaṁ guptām
auśanasyāpi vidyayā
ācchidyādān mahendrāya
vaiṣṇavyā vidyayā vibhuḥ

sura-dviṣām—of the enemies of the demigods; *śriyam*—the opulence; *guptām*—protected; *auśanasya*—of Śukrācārya; *api*—although; *vidyayā*—by the talents; *ācchidya*—collecting; *adāt*—delivered; *mahā-indrāya*—unto King Indra; *vaiṣṇavyā*—of Lord Viṣṇu; *vidyayā*—by a prayer; *vibhuḥ*—the most powerful Viśvarūpa.

TRANSLATION

The opulence of the demons, who are generally known as the enemies of the demigods, was protected by the talents and tactics of Śukrācārya, but Viśvarūpa, who was most powerful, composed a protective prayer known as the Nārāyaṇa-kavaca. By this intelligent mantra, he took away the opulence of the demons and gave it to Mahendra, the King of heaven.

PURPORT

The distinction between the demigods (*devas*) and demons (*asuras*) is that the demigods are all devotees of Lord Viṣṇu whereas the demons are devotees of demigods like Lord Śiva, Goddess Kālī and Goddess Durgā. Sometimes the demons are also devotees of Lord Brahmā. For example, Hiraṇyakaśipu was a devotee of Lord Brahmā, Rāvaṇa was a devotee of

Lord Śiva, and Mahiṣāsura was a devotee of Goddess Durgā. The demigods are devotees of Lord Viṣṇu (*viṣṇu-bhaktaḥ smṛto daiva*), whereas the demons (*āsuras tad-viparyayaḥ*) are always against the *viṣṇu-bhaktas*, or Vaiṣṇavas. To oppose the Vaiṣṇavas, the demons become devotees of Lord Śiva, Lord Brahmā, Kālī, Durgā, and so on. In the days of yore, many long years ago, there was animosity between the *devas* and the *asuras*, and the same spirit still continues, for the devotees of Lord Śiva and Goddess Durgā are always envious of Vaiṣṇavas, who are devotees of Lord Viṣṇu. This strain between the devotees of Lord Śiva and Lord Viṣṇu has always existed. In the higher planetary systems, fights between the demons and the demigods continue for a long, long time.

Herein we see that Viśvarūpa made for the demigods a protective covering, saturated with a Viṣṇu *mantra*. Sometimes the Viṣṇu *mantra* is called Viṣṇu-jvara, and the Śiva *mantra* is called Śiva-jvara. We find in the *śāstras* that sometimes the Śiva-jvara and Viṣṇu-jvara are employed in the fights between the demons and the demigods.

The word *sura-dviṣām*, which in this verse means "of the enemies of the demigods," also refers to the atheists. *Śrīmad-Bhāgavatam* elsewhere says that Lord Buddha appeared for the purpose of bewildering the demons or atheists. The Supreme Personality of Godhead always awards His benediction to devotees. The Lord Himself confirms this in *Bhagavad-gītā* (9.31):

kaunteya pratijānīhi
na me bhaktaḥ praṇaśyati

"O son of Kuntī, declare it boldly that My devotee never perishes."

TEXT 40

यया गुप्तः सहस्राक्षो जिग्येऽसुरचमूर्विभुः ।
तां प्राह स महेन्द्राय विश्वरूप उदारधीः ॥४०॥

yayā guptaḥ sahasrākṣo
jigye 'sura-camūr vibhuḥ
tāṁ prāha sa mahendrāya
viśvarūpa udāra-dhīḥ

yayā—by which; *guptaḥ*—protected; *sahasra-akṣaḥ*—the thousand-eyed demigod, Indra; *jigye*—conquered; *asura*—of the demons; *camūḥ*—military power; *vibhuḥ*—becoming very powerful; *tām*—that; *prāha*—spoke; *saḥ*—he; *mahendrāya*—unto the King of heaven, Mahendra; *viśvarūpaḥ*—Viśvarūpa; *udāra-dhīḥ*—very broad-minded.

TRANSLATION

Viśvarūpa, who was most liberal, spoke to King Indra [Sahasrākṣa] the secret hymn that protected Indra and conquered the military power of the demons.

Thus end the Bhaktivedanta purports to the Sixth Canto, Seventh Chapter, of the Śrīmad-Bhāgavatam, *entitled "Indra Offends His Spiritual Master, Bṛhaspati."*

CHAPTER EIGHT

The Nārāyaṇa-kavaca Shield

This chapter describes how Indra, the King of heaven, was victorious over the soldiers of the demons, and it also describes the shield of the Viṣṇu *mantra.*

To take protection from this shield, one must first touch *kuśa* grass and wash one's mouth with *ācamana-mantras.* One should observe silence and then place the eight-syllable Viṣṇu *mantra* on the parts of his body and place the twelve-syllable *mantra* on his hands. The eight-syllable *mantra* is *oṁ namo nārāyaṇāya.* This *mantra* should be distributed all over the front and back of the body. The twelve-syllable *mantra,* which begins with the *praṇava, oṁkāra,* is *oṁ namo bhagavate vāsudevāya.* One syllable should be placed on each of the fingers and should be preceded by the *praṇava, oṁkāra.* Thereafter, one must chant *oṁ viṣṇave namaḥ,* which is a six-syllable *mantra.* One must progressively place the syllables of the *mantra* on the heart, the head, between the two eyebrows, on the *śikhā* and between the eyes, and then one should chant *maḥ astrāya phaṭ* and with this *mantra* protect himself from all directions. *Nādevo devam arcayet:* one who has not risen to the level of a *deva* cannot chant this *mantra.* According to this direction of the *śāstra,* one must think himself qualitatively nondifferent from the Supreme.

After finishing this dedication, one must offer a prayer to the eight-armed Lord Viṣṇu, who sits on the shoulders of Garuḍadeva. One also has to think of the fish incarnation, Vāmana, Kūrma, Nṛsiṁha, Varāha, Paraśurāma, Rāmacandra (the elder brother of Lakṣmaṇa), Nara-Nārāyaṇa, Dattātreya (an empowered incarnation), Kapila, Sanat-kumāra, Hayagrīva, Nāradadeva (the incarnation of a devotee), Dhanvantari, Ṛṣabhadeva, Yajña, Balarāma, Vyāsadeva, Buddhadeva and Keśava. One should also think of Govinda, the master of Vṛndāvana, and one should think of Nārāyaṇa, the master of the spiritual sky. One should think of Madhusūdana, Tridhāmā, Mādhava, Hṛṣīkeśa, Padmanābha, Janārdana, Dāmodara and Viśveśvara, as well as the Supreme

Personality of Godhead Kṛṣṇa Himself. After offering prayers to the Lord's personal expansions known as the *svāṁśa* and *śaktyāveśa-avatāras,* one should pray to the weapons of Lord Nārāyaṇa, such as the Sudarśana, *gadā, śaṅkha, khaḍga* and bow.

After explaining this process, Śukadeva Gosvāmī told Mahārāja Parīkṣit how Viśvarūpa, the brother of Vṛtrāsura, described the glories of the Nārāyaṇa-kavaca to Indra.

TEXTS 1–2

श्रीराजोवाच

यया गुप्तः सहस्राक्षः सवाहान् रिपुसैनिकान् ।
क्रीडन्निव विनिर्जित्य त्रिलोक्या बुभुजे श्रियम् ॥१॥
भगवंस्तन्ममाख्याहि वर्म नारायणात्मकम् ।
यथाततायिनः शत्रून् येन गुप्तोऽजयन्मृधे ॥ २ ॥

śrī-rājovāca
yayā guptaḥ sahasrākṣaḥ
savāhān ripu-sainikān
krīḍann iva vinirjitya
tri-lokyā bubhuje śriyam

bhagavaṁs tan mamākhyāhi
varma nārāyaṇātmakam
yathātatāyinaḥ śatrūn
yena gupto 'jayan mṛdhe

śrī-rājā uvāca—King Parīkṣit said; *yayā*—by which (the spiritual armor); *guptaḥ*—protected; *sahasra-akṣaḥ*—the thousand-eyed King Indra; *sa-vāhān*—with their carriers; *ripu-sainikān*—the soldiers and commanders of the enemies; *krīḍan iva*—just like playing; *vinirjitya*—conquering; *tri-lokyāḥ*—of the three worlds (the higher, middle and lower planetary systems); *bubhuje*—enjoyed; *śriyam*—the opulence; *bhagavan*—O great sage; *tat*—that; *mama*—unto me; *ākhyāhi*—please explain; *varma*—defensive armor made of a *mantra; nārāyaṇa-āt-*

makam—consisting of the mercy of Nārāyaṇa; *yathā*—in which way; *ātatāyinaḥ*—who were endeavoring to kill him; *śatrūn*—enemies; *yena*—by which; *guptaḥ*—being protected; *ajayat*—conquered; *mṛdhe*—in the fight.

TRANSLATION

King Parīkṣit inquired from Śukadeva Gosvāmī: My lord, kindly explain the Viṣṇu mantra armor that protected King Indra and enabled him to conquer his enemies, along with their carriers, and enjoy the opulence of the three worlds. Please explain to me that Nārāyaṇa armor, by which King Indra achieved success in battle, conquering the enemies who were endeavoring to kill him.

TEXT 3

श्रीबादरायणिरुवाच
वृतः पुरोहितस्त्वाष्ट्रो महेन्द्रायानुपृच्छते ।
नारायणाख्यं वर्माह तदिहैकमनाः शृणु ॥ ३ ॥

śrī-bādarāyaṇir uvāca
vṛtaḥ purohitas tvāṣṭro
mahendrāyānupṛcchate
nārāyaṇākhyaṁ varmāha
tad ihaika-manāḥ śṛṇu

śrī-bādarāyaṇiḥ uvāca—Śrī Śukadeva Gosvāmī said; *vṛtaḥ*—the chosen; *purohitaḥ*—priest; *tvāṣṭraḥ*—the son of Tvaṣṭā; *mahendrāya*—unto King Indra; *anupṛcchate*—after he (Indra) inquired; *nārāyaṇa-ākhyam*—named Nārāyaṇa-kavaca; *varma*—defensive armor made of a *mantra; āha*—he said; *tat*—that; *iha*—this; *eka-manāḥ*—with great attention; *śṛṇu*—hear from me.

TRANSLATION

Śrī Śukadeva Gosvāmī said: King Indra, the leader of the demigods, inquired about the armor known as Nārāyaṇa-kavaca from Viśvarūpa, who was engaged by the demigods as their priest. Please hear Viśvarūpa's reply with great attention.

TEXTS 4–6

श्रीविश्वरूप उवाच
धौताङ्घ्रिपाणिराचम्य सपवित्र उदङ्मुखः ।
कृतस्वाङ्गकरन्यासो मन्त्राभ्यां वाग्यतः शुचिः॥ ४ ॥
नारायणपरं वर्म सन्नह्येद् भय आगते ।
पादयोर्जानुनोरूर्वोरुदरे हृद्यथोरसि ॥ ५ ॥
मुखे शिरस्यानुपूर्व्यादोङ्कारादीनि विन्यसेत् ।
ॐ नमो नारायणायेति विपर्ययमथापि वा ॥ ६ ॥

śrī-viśvarūpa uvāca
dhautāṅghri-pāṇir ācamya
sapavitra udaṅ-mukhaḥ
kṛta-svāṅga-kara-nyāso
mantrābhyāṁ vāg-yataḥ śuciḥ

nārāyaṇa-paraṁ varma
sannahyed bhaya āgate
pādayor jānunor ūrvor
udare hṛdy athorasi

mukhe śirasy ānupūrvyād
oṁkārādīni vinyaset
oṁ namo nārāyaṇāyeti
viparyayam athāpi vā

śrī-viśvarūpaḥ uvāca—Śrī Viśvarūpa said; *dhauta*—having completely washed; *aṅghri*—feet; *pāṇiḥ*—hands; *ācamya*—performing *ācamana* (sipping a little water three times after chanting the prescribed *mantra*); *sa-pavitraḥ*—wearing rings made of *kuśa* grass (on the ring finger of each hand); *udak-mukhaḥ*—sitting facing the north; *kṛta*—making; *sva-aṅga-kara-nyāsaḥ*—mental assignment of the eight parts of the body and twelve parts of the hands; *mantrābhyām*—with the two *mantras* (*oṁ namo bhagavate vāsudevāya* and *oṁ namo nārāyaṇāya*); *vāk-yataḥ*—keeping oneself silent; *śuciḥ*—being purified; *nārāyaṇa-param*—fully intent on Lord Nārāyaṇa; *varma*—armor; *sannahyet*—

put on oneself; *bhaye*—when fear; *āgate*—has come; *pādayoḥ*—on the two legs; *jānunoḥ*—on the two knees; *ūrvoḥ*—on the two thighs; *udare*—on the abdomen; *hṛdi*—on the heart; *atha*—thus; *urasi*—on the chest; *mukhe*—on the mouth; *śirasi*—on the head; *ānupūrvyāt*—one after another; *oṁkāra-ādīni*—beginning with *oṁkāra; vinyaset*—one should place; *oṁ*—the *praṇava; namaḥ*—obeisances; *nārāyaṇāya*—unto Nārāyaṇa, the Supreme Personality of Godhead; *iti*—thus; *viparyayam*—the reverse; *atha api*—moreover; *vā*—or.

TRANSLATION

Viśvarūpa said: If some form of fear arrives, one should first wash his hands and legs clean and then perform ācamana by chanting this mantra: oṁ apavitraḥ pavitro vā sarvāvasthāṁ gato 'pi vā/ yaḥ smaret puṇḍarīkākṣaṁ sa bahyābhyantaraḥ śuciḥ/ śrī-viṣṇu śrī-viṣṇu śrī-viṣṇu. Then one should touch kuśa grass and sit gravely and silently, facing north. When completely purified, one should touch the mantra composed of eight syllables to the eight parts of his body and touch the mantra composed of twelve syllables to his hands. Thus, in the following manner, he should bind himself with the Nārāyaṇa coat of armor. First, while chanting the mantra composed of eight syllables [oṁ namo nārāyaṇāya], beginning with the praṇava, the syllable oṁ, one should touch his hands to eight parts of his body, starting with the two feet and progressing systematically to the knees, thighs, abdomen, heart, chest, mouth and head. Then one should chant the mantra in reverse, beginning from the last syllable [ya], while touching the parts of his body in the reverse order. These two processes are known as utpatti-nyāsa and saṁhāra-nyāsa respectively.

TEXT 7

करन्यासं ततः कुर्याद् द्वादशाक्षरविद्यया ।
प्रणवादियकारान्तमङ्गुल्यङ्गुष्ठपर्वसु ॥ ७ ॥

kara-nyāsaṁ tataḥ kuryād
dvādaśākṣara-vidyayā
praṇavādi-ya-kārāntam
aṅguly-aṅguṣṭha-parvasu

kara-nyāsam—the ritual known as *kara-nyāsa,* which assigns the syllables of the *mantra* to the fingers; *tataḥ*—thereafter; *kuryāt*—should execute; *dvādaśa-akṣara*—composed of twelve syllables; *vidyayā*—with the *mantra; praṇava-ādi*—beginning with the *oṁkāra; ya-kāra-antam*—ending with the syllable *ya; aṅguli*—on the fingers, beginning with the index finger; *aṅguṣṭha-parvasu*—to the joints of the thumbs.

TRANSLATION

Then one should chant the mantra composed of twelve syllables [oṁ namo bhagavate vāsudevāya]. Preceding each syllable by the oṁkāra, one should place the syllables of the mantra on the tips of his fingers, beginning with the index finger of the right hand and concluding with the index finger of the left. The four remaining syllables should be placed on the joints of the thumbs.

TEXTS 8–10

न्यसेद्धृदय ओङ्कारं विकारमनु मूर्धनि ।
षकारं तु भ्रुवोर्मध्ये णकारं शिखया न्यसेत् ॥ ८ ॥
वेकारं नेत्रयोर्युञ्ज्यान्नकारं सर्वसन्धिषु ।
मकारमस्त्रमुद्दिश्य मन्त्रमूर्तिर्भवेद् बुधः ॥ ९ ॥
सविसर्गं फडन्तं तत् सर्वदिक्षु विनिर्दिशेत् ।
ॐ विष्णवे नम इति ॥१० ॥

nyased dhṛdaya oṁkāraṁ
vi-kāram anu mūrdhani
ṣa-kāraṁ tu bhruvor madhye
ṇa-kāraṁ śikhayā nyaset

ve-kāraṁ netrayor yuñjyān
na-kāraṁ sarva-sandhiṣu
ma-kāram astram uddiśya
mantra-mūrtir bhaved budhaḥ

savisargaṁ phaḍ-antaṁ tat
sarva-dikṣu vinirdiśet
oṁ viṣṇave nama iti

nyaset—should place; *hṛdaye*—on the heart; *oṁkāram*—the *praṇava, oṁkāra; vi-kāram*—the syllable *vi* of *viṣṇave; anu*—thereafter; *mūrdhani*—on the top of the head; *ṣa-kāram*—the syllable *ṣa; tu*—and; *bhruvoḥ madhye*—between the two eyebrows; *ṇa-kāram*—the syllable *ṇa; śikhayā*—on the *śikhā* on the head; *nyaset*—should place; *ve-kāram*—the syllable *ve; netrayoḥ*—between the two eyes; *yuñjyāt*—should be placed; *na-kāram*—the syllable *na* of the word *namaḥ; sarva-sandhiṣu*—on all the joints; *ma-kāram*—the syllable *ma* of the word *namaḥ; astram*—a weapon; *uddiśya*—thinking; *mantra-mūrtiḥ*—the form of the *mantra; bhavet*—should become; *budhaḥ*—an intelligent person; *sa-visargam*—with the *visarga* (*ḥ*); *phaṭ-antam*—ending with the sound *phaṭ; tat*—that; *sarva-dikṣu*—in all directions; *vinirdiśet*—should fix; *oṁ—praṇava; viṣṇave*—unto Lord Viṣṇu; *namaḥ*—obeisances; *iti*—thus.

TRANSLATION

One must then chant the mantra of six syllables [oṁ viṣṇave namaḥ]. One should place the syllable "oṁ" on his heart, the syllable "vi" on the top of his head, the syllable "ṣa" between his eyebrows, the syllable "ṇa" on his tuft of hair [śikhā], and the syllable "ve" between his eyes. The chanter of the mantra should then place the syllable "na" on all the joints of his body and meditate on the syllable "ma" as being a weapon. He should thus become the perfect personification of the mantra. Thereafter, adding visarga to the final syllable "ma," he should chant the mantra "maḥ astrāya phaṭ" in all directions, beginning from the east. In this way, all directions will be bound by the protective armor of the mantra.

TEXT 11

आत्मानं परमं ध्यायेद् ध्येयं षट्शक्तिभिर्युतम् ।
विद्यातेजस्तपोमूर्तिमिमं मन्त्रमुदाहरेत् ॥११॥

ātmānaṁ paramaṁ dhyāyed
dhyeyaṁ ṣaṭ-śaktibhir yutam
vidyā-tejas-tapo-mūrtim
imaṁ mantram udāharet

ātmānam—the self; *paramam*—the supreme; *dhyāyet*—one should meditate on; *dhyeyam*—worthy to be meditated on; *ṣaṭ-śaktibhiḥ*—the six opulences; *yutam*—possessed of; *vidyā*—learning; *tejaḥ*—influence; *tapaḥ*—austerity; *mūrtim*—personified; *imam*—this; *mantram*—mantra; *udāharet*—should chant.

TRANSLATION

After finishing this chanting, one should think himself qualitatively one with the Supreme Personality of Godhead, who is full in six opulences and is worthy to be meditated upon. Then one should chant the following protective prayer to Lord Nārāyaṇa, the Nārāyaṇa-kavaca.

TEXT 12

ॐ हरिर्विदध्यान्मम सर्वरक्षां
न्यस्ताङ्घ्रिपद्मः पतगेन्द्रपृष्ठे ।
दरारिचर्मासिगदेषुचाप-
पाशान् दधानोऽष्टगुणोऽष्टबाहुः ॥१२॥

oṁ harir vidadhyān mama sarva-rakṣāṁ
nyastāṅghri-padmaḥ patagendra-pṛṣṭhe
darāri-carmāsi-gadeṣu-cāpa-
pāśān dadhāno 'ṣṭa-guṇo 'ṣṭa-bāhuḥ

oṁ—O Lord; *hariḥ*—the Supreme Personality of Godhead; *vidadhyāt*—may He bestow; *mama*—my; *sarva-rakṣām*—protection from all sides; *nyasta*—placed; *aṅghri-padmaḥ*—whose lotus feet; *patagendra-pṛṣṭhe*—on the back of Garuḍa, the king of all birds; *dara*—conchshell; *ari*—disc; *carma*—shield; *asi*—sword; *gadā*—club; *iṣu*—arrows; *cāpa*—bow; *pāśān*—ropes; *dadhānaḥ*—holding; *aṣṭa*—possessing eight; *guṇaḥ*—perfections; *aṣṭa*—eight; *bāhuḥ*—arms.

TRANSLATION

The Supreme Lord, who sits on the back of the bird Garuḍa, touching him with His lotus feet, holds eight weapons—the conch-

shell, disc, shield, sword, club, arrows, bow and ropes. May that Supreme Personality of Godhead protect me at all times with His eight arms. He is all-powerful because He fully possesses the eight mystic powers [aṇimā, laghimā, etc.].

PURPORT

Thinking oneself one with the Supreme is called *ahaṅgrahopāsanā.* Through *ahaṅgrahopāsanā* one does not become God, but he thinks of himself as qualitatively one with the Supreme. Understanding that as a spirit soul he is equal in quality to the supreme soul the way the water of a river is of the same nature as the water of the sea, one should meditate upon the Supreme Lord, as described in this verse, and seek His protection. The living entities are always subordinate to the Supreme. Consequently their duty is to always seek the mercy of the Lord in order to be protected by Him in all circumstances.

TEXT 13

जलेषु मां रक्षतु मत्स्यमूर्ति-
यादोगणेभ्यो वरुणस्य पाशात् ।
स्थलेषु मायावटुवामनोऽव्यात्
त्रिविक्रमः खेऽवतु विश्वरूपः ॥१३॥

jaleṣu māṁ rakṣatu matsya-mūrtir
yādo-gaṇebhyo varuṇasya pāśāt
sthaleṣu māyāvaṭu-vāmano 'vyāt
trivikramaḥ khe 'vatu viśvarūpaḥ

jaleṣu—in the water; *mām*—me; *rakṣatu*—protect; *matsya-mūrtiḥ*—the Supreme Lord in the form of a great fish; *yādaḥ-gaṇebhyaḥ*—from fierce aquatic animals; *varuṇasya*—of the demigod known as Varuṇa; *pāśāt*—from the arresting rope; *sthaleṣu*—on the land; *māyā-vaṭu*—the merciful form of the Lord as a dwarf; *vāmanaḥ*—named Vāmanadeva; *avyāt*—may He protect; *trivikramaḥ*—Trivikrama, whose three gigantic steps took the three worlds from Bali; *khe*—in the sky; *avatu*—may the Lord protect; *viśvarūpaḥ*—the gigantic universal form.

TRANSLATION

May the Lord, who assumes the body of a great fish, protect me in the water from the fierce animals that are associates of the demigod Varuṇa. By expanding His illusory energy, the Lord assumed the form of the dwarf Vāmana. May Vāmana protect me on the land. Since the gigantic form of the Lord, Viśvarūpa, conquers the three worlds, may He protect me in the sky.

PURPORT

This *mantra* seeks the protection of the Supreme Personality of Godhead in the water, land and sky in His incarnations as the fish, Vāmanadeva and the Viśvarūpa.

TEXT 14

दुर्गेष्वटव्याजिमुखादिषु प्रभुः
पायान्नृसिंहोऽसुरयूथपारिः ।
विमुञ्चतो यस्य महाट्टहासं
दिशो विनेदुर्न्यपतंश्च गर्भाः ॥१४॥

durgeṣv aṭavy-āji-mukhādiṣu prabhuḥ
pāyān nṛsiṁho 'sura-yūthapāriḥ
vimuñcato yasya mahāṭṭa-hāsaṁ
diśo vinedur nyapataṁś ca garbhāḥ

durgeṣu—in places where travel is very difficult; *aṭavi*—in the dense forest; *āji-mukha-ādiṣu*—on the war front and so on; *prabhuḥ*—the Supreme Lord; *pāyāt*—may He protect; *nṛsiṁhaḥ*—Lord Nṛsiṁhadeva; *asura-yūthapa*—of Hiraṇyakaśipu, the leader of the demons; *ariḥ*—the enemy; *vimuñcataḥ*—releasing; *yasya*—of whom; *mahā-aṭṭa-hāsam*—great and fearful laughing; *diśaḥ*—all the directions; *vineduḥ*—resounded through; *nyapatan*—fell down; *ca*—and; *garbhāḥ*—the embryos of the wives of the demons.

TRANSLATION

May Lord Nṛsiṁhadeva, who appeared as the enemy of Hiraṇyakaśipu, protect me in all directions. His loud laughing

vibrated in all directions and caused the pregnant wives of the asuras to have miscarriages. May that Lord be kind enough to protect me in difficult places like the forest and battlefront.

TEXT 15

रक्षत्वसौ माध्वनि यज्ञकल्पः
स्वदंष्ट्रयोन्नीतधरो वराहः ।
रामोऽद्रिकूटेष्वथ विप्रवासे
सलक्ष्मणोऽव्याद् भरताग्रजोऽस्मान्॥ १५॥

rakṣatv asau mādhvani yajña-kalpaḥ
sva-daṁṣṭrayonnīta-dharo varāhaḥ
rāmo 'dri-kūṭeṣv atha vipravāse
salakṣmaṇo 'vyād bharatāgrajo 'smān

rakṣatu—may the Lord protect; *asau*—that; *mā*—me; *adhvani*—on the street; *yajña-kalpaḥ*—who is ascertained by performance of ritualistic ceremonies; *sva-daṁṣṭrayā*—by His own tusk; *unnīta*—raising; *dharaḥ*—the planet earth; *varāhaḥ*—Lord Boar; *rāmaḥ*—Lord Rāma; *adri-kūṭeṣu*—on the summits of the mountains; *atha*—then; *vipravāse*—in foreign countries; *sa-lakṣmaṇaḥ*—with His brother Lakṣmaṇa; *avyāt*—may He protect; *bharata-agrajaḥ*—the elder brother of Mahārāja Bharata; *asmān*—us.

TRANSLATION

The Supreme indestructible Lord is ascertained through the performance of ritualistic sacrifices and is therefore known as Yajñeśvara. In His incarnation as Lord Boar, He raised the planet earth from the water at the bottom of the universe and kept it on His pointed tusks. May that Lord protect me from rogues on the street. May Paraśurāma protect me on the tops of mountains, and may the elder brother of Bharata, Lord Rāmacandra, along with His brother Lakṣmaṇa, protect me in foreign countries.

PURPORT

There are three Rāmas. One Rāma is Paraśurāma (Jāmadāgnya), another Rāma is Lord Rāmacandra, and a third Rāma is Lord Balarāma.

In this verse the words *rāmo 'dri-kūṭeṣv atha* indicate Lord Paraśurāma. The brother of Bharata Mahārāja and Lakṣmaṇa is Lord Rāmacandra.

TEXT 16

मामुग्रधर्मादखिलात् प्रमादा-
न्नारायणः पातु नरश्च हासात् ।
दत्तस्त्वयोगादथ योगनाथः
पायाद् गुणेशः कपिलः कर्मबन्धात् ॥१६॥

mām ugra-dharmād akhilāt pramādān
nārāyaṇaḥ pātu naraś ca hāsāt
dattas tv ayogād atha yoga-nāthaḥ
pāyād guṇeśaḥ kapilaḥ karma-bandhāt

mām—me; *ugra-dharmāt*—from unnecessary religious principles; *akhilāt*—from all kinds of activities; *pramādāt*—which are enacted in madness; *nārāyaṇaḥ*—Lord Nārāyaṇa; *pātu*—may He protect; *naraḥ ca*—and Nara; *hāsāt*—from unnecessary pride; *dattaḥ*—Dattātreya; *tu*—of course; *ayogāt*—from the path of false *yoga; atha*—indeed; *yoga-nāthaḥ*—the master of all mystic powers; *pāyāt*—may He protect; *guṇa-īśaḥ*—the master of all spiritual qualities; *kapilaḥ*—Lord Kapila; *karma-bandhāt*—from the bondage of fruitive activities.

TRANSLATION

May Lord Nārāyaṇa protect me from unnecessarily following false religious systems and falling from my duties due to madness. May the Lord in His appearance as Nara protect me from unnecessary pride. May Lord Dattātreya, the master of all mystic power, protect me from falling while performing bhakti-yoga, and may Lord Kapila, the master of all good qualities, protect me from the material bondage of fruitive activities.

TEXT 17

सनत्कुमारोऽवतु कामदेवा-
द्धयशीर्षा मां पथि देवहेलनात् ।

देवर्षिवर्यः पुरुषार्चनान्तरात्
कूर्मो हरिर्मां निरयादशेषात् ॥१७॥

sanat-kumāro 'vatu kāmadevād
dhayaśīrṣā māṁ pathi deva-helanāt
devarṣi-varyaḥ puruṣārcanāntarāt
kūrmo harir māṁ nirayād aśeṣāt

sanat-kumāraḥ—the great *brahmacārī* named Sanat-kumāra; *avatu*—may he protect; *kāma-devāt*—from the hands of Cupid or lusty desire; *haya-śīrṣā*—Lord Hayagrīva, the incarnation of the Lord whose head is like that of a horse; *mām*—me; *pathi*—on the path; *deva-helanāt*—from neglecting to offer respectful obeisances to *brāhmaṇas*, Vaiṣṇavas and the Supreme Lord; *devarṣi-varyaḥ*—the best of the saintly sages, Nārada; *puruṣa-arcana-antarāt*—from the offenses in worshiping the Deity; *kūrmaḥ*—Lord Kūrma, the tortoise; *hariḥ*—the Supreme Personality of Godhead; *mām*—me; *nirayāt*—from hell; *aśeṣāt*—unlimited.

TRANSLATION

May Sanat-kumāra protect me from lusty desires. As I begin some auspicious activity, may Lord Hayagrīva protect me from being an offender by neglecting to offer respectful obeisances to the Supreme Lord. May Devarṣi Nārada protect me from committing offenses in worshiping the Deity, and may Lord Kūrma, the tortoise, protect me from falling to the unlimited hellish planets.

PURPORT

Lusty desires are very strong in everyone, and they are the greatest impediment to the discharge of devotional service. Therefore those who are very much influenced by lusty desires are advised to take shelter of Sanat-kumāra, the great *brahmacārī* devotee. Nārada Muni, who is the guide for *arcana*, is the author of the *Nārada-pañcarātra*, which prescribes the regulative principles for worshiping the Deity. Everyone engaged in Deity worship, whether at home or in the temple, should always seek the mercy of Devarṣi Nārada in order to avoid the thirty-two offenses while worshiping the Deity. These offenses in Deity worship are mentioned in *The Nectar of Devotion*.

TEXT 18

धन्वन्तरिर्भगवान् पात्वपथ्याद्
द्वन्द्वाद् भयादृषभो निर्जितात्मा ।
यज्ञश्च लोकादवताज्जनान्ताद्
बलो गणात् क्रोधवशादहीन्द्रः ॥१८॥

dhanvantarir bhagavān pātv apathyād
dvandvād bhayād ṛṣabho nirjitātmā
yajñaś ca lokād avatāj janāntād
balo gaṇāt krodha-vaśād ahīndraḥ

dhanvantariḥ—the incarnation Dhanvantari, the physician; *bhagavān*—the Supreme Personality of Godhead; *pātu*—may He protect me; *apathyāt*—from things injurious to the health, such as meat and intoxicants; *dvandvāt*—from duality; *bhayāt*—from fear; *ṛṣabhaḥ*—Lord Ṛṣabhadeva; *nirjita-ātmā*—who fully controlled his mind and self; *yajñaḥ*—Yajña; *ca*—and; *lokāt*—from the defamation of the populace; *avatāt*—may He protect; *jana-antāt*—from dangerous positions created by other people; *balaḥ*—Lord Balarāma; *gaṇāt*—from the hordes of; *krodha-vaśāt*—the angry serpents; *ahīndraḥ*—Lord Balarāma in the form of the serpent Śeṣa Nāga.

TRANSLATION

May the Supreme Personality of Godhead in His incarnation as Dhanvantari relieve me from undesirable eatables and protect me from physical illness. May Lord Ṛṣabhadeva, who conquered His inner and outer senses, protect me from fear produced by the duality of heat and cold. May Yajña protect me from defamation and harm from the populace, and may Lord Balarāma as Śeṣa protect me from envious serpents.

PURPORT

To live within this material world, one must face many dangers, as described herein. For example, undesirable food poses a danger to health, and therefore one must give up such food. The Dhanvantari incarnation can protect us in this regard. Since Lord Viṣṇu is the Supersoul of all living entities, if He likes He can save us from *adhibhautika* disturbances, disturbances from other living entities. Lord Balarāma is the Śeṣa incarnation, and therefore He can save us from angry serpents or envious persons, who are always ready to attack.

TEXT 19

द्वैपायनो भगवानप्रबोधाद्
बुद्धस्तु पाषण्डगणप्रमादात् ।
कल्किः कलेः कालमलात् प्रपातु
धर्मावनायोरुकृतावतारः ॥१९॥

dvaipāyano bhagavān aprabodhād
buddhas tu pāṣaṇḍa-gaṇa-pramādāt
kalkiḥ kaleḥ kāla-malāt prapātu
dharmāvanāyoru-kṛtāvatāraḥ

dvaipāyanaḥ—Śrīla Vyāsadeva, the giver of all Vedic knowledge; *bhagavān*—the most powerful incarnation of the Supreme Personality of Godhead; *aprabodhāt*—from ignorance of the *śāstra; buddhaḥ tu*—also Lord Buddha; *pāṣaṇḍa-gaṇa*—of atheists creating disillusionment for innocent persons; *pramādāt*—from the madness; *kalkiḥ*—Lord Kalki, the incarnation of Keśava; *kaleḥ*—of this Kali-yuga; *kāla-malāt*—from the darkness of the age; *prapātu*—may He protect; *dharma-avanāya*—for the protection of religious principles; *uru*—very great; *kṛta-avatāraḥ*—who took an incarnation.

TRANSLATION

May the Personality of Godhead in His incarnation as Vyāsadeva protect me from all kinds of ignorance resulting from the absence of Vedic knowledge. May Lord Buddhadeva protect me from activities opposed to Vedic principles and from laziness that causes one to madly forget the Vedic principles of knowledge and ritualistic action. May Kalkideva, the Supreme Personality of Godhead, who appeared as an incarnation to protect religious principles, protect me from the dirt of the age of Kali.

PURPORT

This verse mentions various incarnations of the Supreme Personality of Godhead who appear for various purposes. Śrīla Vyāsadeva, Mahāmuni, compiled the Vedic literature for the benefit of all human society. If one wants to be protected from the reactions of ignorance even in this age of Kali, one may consult the books left by Śrīla Vyāsadeva, namely the four *Vedas* (*Sāma*, *Yajur*, *Ṛg* and *Atharva*), the 108 *Upaniṣads*, *Vedānta-sūtra* (*Brahma-sūtra*), *Mahābhārata*, *Śrīmad-Bhāgavatam Mahā-purāṇa* (Vyāsadeva's commentary on the *Brahma-sūtra*) and the other seventeen *Purāṇas*. Only by the mercy of Śrīla Vyāsadeva do we have so many volumes of transcendental knowledge to save us from the clutches of ignorance.

As described by Śrīla Jayadeva Gosvāmī in his *Daśāvatāra-stotra*, Lord Buddha apparently decried the Vedic knowledge:

nindasi yajña-vidher ahaha śruti-jātaṁ
sadaya-hṛdaya-darśita-paśu-ghātam
keśava dhṛta-buddha-śarīra jaya jagad-īśa hare

The mission of Lord Buddha was to save people from the abominable activity of animal killing and to save the poor animals from being unnecessarily killed. When *pāṣaṇḍīs* were cheating by killing animals on the plea of sacrificing them in Vedic *yajñas*, the Lord said, "If the Vedic injunctions allow animal killing, I do not accept the Vedic principles." Thus he actually saved people who acted according to Vedic principles. One should therefore surrender to Lord Buddha so that he can help one avoid misusing the injunctions of the *Vedas*.

The Kalki *avatāra* is the fierce incarnation who vanquishes the class of the atheists born in this age of Kali. Now, in the beginning of Kali-yuga, many irreligious principles are in effect, and as Kali-yuga advances, many pseudo religious principles will certainly be introduced, and people will forget the real religious principles enunciated by Lord Kṛṣṇa before the beginning of Kali-yuga, namely principles of surrender unto the lotus feet of the Lord. Unfortunately, because of Kali-yuga, foolish people do not surrender to the lotus feet of Kṛṣṇa. Even most people who claim to belong to the Vedic system of religion are actually opposed to the Vedic principles. Every day they manufacture a new type of *dharma* on the plea that whatever one manufactures is also a path of liberation. Atheistic men generally say, *yata mata tata patha.* According to this view, there are hundreds and thousands of different opinions in human society, and each opinion is a valid religious principle. This philosophy of rascals has killed the religious principles mentioned in the *Vedas,* and such philosophies will become increasingly influential as Kali-yuga progresses. In the last stage of Kali-yuga, Kalkideva, the fierce incarnation of Keśava, will descend to kill all the atheists and will save only the devotees of the Lord.

TEXT 20

मां केशवो गदया प्रातरव्याद्
गोविन्द आसङ्गवमात्तवेणुः ।
नारायणः प्राह्ण उदात्तशक्ति-
र्मध्यन्दिने विष्णुररीन्द्रपाणिः ॥२०॥

māṁ keśavo gadayā prātar avyād
govinda āsaṅgavam ātta-veṇuḥ
nārāyaṇaḥ prāhṇa udātta-śaktir
madhyan-dine viṣṇur arīndra-pāṇiḥ

mām—me; *keśavaḥ*—Lord Keśava; *gadayā*—by His club; *prātaḥ*—in the morning hours; *avyāt*—may He protect; *govindaḥ*—Lord Govinda; *āsaṅgavam*—during the second part of the day; *ātta-veṇuḥ*—holding His flute; *nārāyaṇaḥ*—Lord Nārāyaṇa with four hands; *prāhṇaḥ*—during the third part of the day; *udātta-śaktiḥ*—controlling different types of potencies; *madhyam-dine*—during the fourth part of the day; *viṣṇuḥ*—Lord Viṣṇu; *arīndra-pāṇiḥ*—bearing the disc in His hand to kill the enemies.

TRANSLATION

May Lord Keśava protect me with His club in the first portion of the day, and may Govinda, who is always engaged in playing His flute, protect me in the second portion of the day. May Lord Nārāyaṇa, who is equipped with all potencies, protect me in the third part of the day, and may Lord Viṣṇu, who carries a disc to kill His enemies, protect me in the fourth part of the day.

PURPORT

According to Vedic astronomical calculations, day and night are each divided into thirty *ghaṭikās* (twenty-four minutes), instead of twelve hours. Generally, each day and each night is divided into six parts consisting of five *ghaṭikās*. In each of these six portions of the day and night, the Lord may be addressed for protection according to different names. Lord Keśava, the proprietor of the holy place of Mathurā, is the Lord of the first portion of the day, and Govinda, the Lord of Vṛndāvana, is the master of the second portion.

TEXT 21

देवोऽपराह्णे मधुहोग्रधन्वा
सायं त्रिधामावतु माधवो माम् ।
दोषे हृषीकेश उतार्धरात्रे
निशीथ एकोऽवतु पद्मनाभः ॥२१॥

devo 'parāhṇe madhu-hogradhanvā
sāyaṁ tri-dhāmāvatu mādhavo mām
doṣe hṛṣīkeśa utārdha-rātre
niśītha eko 'vatu padmanābhaḥ

devaḥ—the Lord; *aparāhṇe*—in the fifth part of the day; *madhu-hā*—named Madhusūdana; *ugra-dhanvā*—bearing the very fearful bow known as Śārṅga; *sāyam*—the sixth part of the day; *tri-dhāmā*—manifesting as the three deities Brahmā, Viṣṇu and Maheśvara; *avatu*—may He protect; *mādhavaḥ*—named Mādhava; *mām*—me; *doṣe*—during the first portion of the night; *hṛṣīkeśaḥ*—Lord Hṛṣīkeśa; *uta*—also; *ardha-rātre*—during the second part of the night; *niśīthe*—during the third part of the night; *ekaḥ*—alone; *avatu*—may He protect; *padmanābhaḥ*—Lord Padmanābha.

TRANSLATION

May Lord Madhusūdana, who carries a bow very fearful for the demons, protect me during the fifth part of the day. In the eve-

ning, may Lord Mādhava, appearing as Brahmā, Viṣṇu and Maheśvara, protect me, and in the beginning of night may Lord Hṛṣīkeśa protect me. At the dead of night [in the second and third parts of night] may Lord Padmanābha alone protect me.

TEXT 22

श्रीवत्सधामापररात्र ईशः
प्रत्यूष ईशोऽसिधरो जनार्दनः ।
दामोदरोऽव्यादनुसन्ध्यं प्रभाते
विश्वेश्वरो भगवान् कालमूर्तिः ॥२२॥

śrīvatsa-dhāmāpara-rātra īśaḥ
pratyūṣa īśo 'si-dharo janārdanaḥ
dāmodaro 'vyād anusandhyaṁ prabhāte
viśveśvaro bhagavān kāla-mūrtiḥ

śrīvatsa-dhāmā—the Lord, on whose chest the mark of Śrīvatsa is resting; *apara-rātre*—in the fourth part of the night; *īśaḥ*—the Supreme Lord; *pratyūṣe*—in the end of the night; *īśaḥ*—the Supreme Lord; *asi-dharaḥ*—carrying a sword in the hand; *janārdanaḥ*—Lord Janārdana; *dāmodaraḥ*—Lord Dāmodara; *avyāt*—may He protect; *anusandhyam*—during each junction or twilight; *prabhāte*—in the early morning (the sixth part of the night); *viśva-īśvaraḥ*—the Lord of the whole universe; *bhagavān*—the Supreme Personality of Godhead; *kāla-mūrtiḥ*—the personification of time.

TRANSLATION

May the Supreme Personality of Godhead, who bears the Śrīvatsa on His chest, protect me after midnight until the sky becomes pinkish. May Lord Janārdana, who carries a sword in His hand, protect me at the end of night [during the last four ghaṭikās of night]. May Lord Dāmodara protect me in the early morning, and may Lord Viśveśvara protect me during the junctions of day and night.

TEXT 23

चक्रं युगान्तानलतिग्मनेमि
भ्रमत् समन्ताद् भगवत्प्रयुक्तम् ।
दन्दग्धि दन्दग्ध्यरिसैन्यमाशु
कक्षं यथा वातसखो हुताशः ॥२३॥

cakraṁ yugāntānala-tigma-nemi
bhramat samantād bhagavat-prayuktam
dandagdhi dandagdhy ari-sainyam āśu
kakṣaṁ yathā vāta-sakho hutāśaḥ

cakram—the disc of the Lord; *yuga-anta*—at the end of the millennium; *anala*—like the fire of devastation; *tigma-nemi*—with a sharp rim; *bhramat*—wandering; *samantāt*—on all sides; *bhagavat-prayuktam*—being engaged by the Lord; *dandagdhi dandagdhi*—please burn completely, please burn completely; *ari-sainyam*—the army of our enemies; *āśu*—immediately; *kakṣam*—dry grass; *yathā*—like; *vāta-sakhaḥ*—the friend of the wind; *hutāśaḥ*—blazing fire.

TRANSLATION

Set into motion by the Supreme Personality of Godhead and wandering in all the four directions, the disc of the Supreme Lord has sharp edges as destructive as the fire of devastation at the end of the millennium. As a blazing fire burns dry grass to ashes with the assistance of the breeze, may that Sudarśana cakra burn our enemies to ashes.

TEXT 24

गदेऽशनिस्पर्शनविस्फुलिङ्गे
निष्पिण्ढि निष्पिण्ढ्यजितप्रियासि ।
कुष्माण्डवैनायकयक्षरक्षो-
भूतग्रहांश्चूर्णय चूर्णयारीन् ॥२४॥

gade 'śani-sparśana-visphuliṅge
niṣpiṇḍhi niṣpiṇḍhy ajita-priyāsi
kuṣmāṇḍa-vaināyaka-yakṣa-rakṣo-
bhūta-grahāṁś cūrṇaya cūrṇayārīn

gade—O club in the hands of the Supreme Personality of Godhead; *aśani*—like thunderbolts; *sparśana*—whose touch; *visphuliṅge*—giving off sparks of fire; *niṣpiṇḍhi niṣpiṇḍhi*—pound to pieces, pound to pieces; *ajita-priyā*—very dear to the Supreme Personality of Godhead; *asi*—you are; *kuṣmāṇḍa*—imps named Kuṣmāṇḍas; *vaināyaka*—ghosts named Vaināyakas; *yakṣa*—ghosts named Yakṣas; *rakṣaḥ*—ghosts named Rākṣasas; *bhūta*—ghosts named Bhūtas; *grahān*—and evil demons named Grahas; *cūrṇaya*—pulverize; *cūrṇaya*—pulverize; *arīn*—my enemies.

TRANSLATION

O club in the hand of the Supreme Personality of Godhead, you produce sparks of fire as powerful as thunderbolts, and you are extremely dear to the Lord. I am also His servant. Therefore kindly help me pound to pieces the evil living beings known as Kuṣmāṇḍas, Vaināyakas, Yakṣas, Rākṣasas, Bhūtas and Grahas. Please pulverize them.

TEXT 25

त्वं यातुधानप्रमथप्रेतमातृ-
पिशाचविप्रग्रहघोरदृष्टीन् ।
दरेन्द्र विद्रावय कृष्णपूरितो
भीमस्वनोऽरेर्हृदयानि कम्पयन् ॥२५॥

tvaṁ yātudhāna-pramatha-preta-mātṛ-
piśāca-vipragraha-ghora-dṛṣṭīn
darendra vidrāvaya kṛṣṇa-pūrito
bhīma-svano 'rer hṛdayāni kampayan

tvam—you; *yātudhāna*—Rākṣasas; *pramatha*—Pramathas; *preta*—Pretas; *mātṛ*—Mātās; *piśāca*—Piśācas; *vipra-graha*—*brāhmaṇa* ghosts;

ghora-dṛṣṭīn—who have very fearful eyes; *darendra*—O Pāñcajanya, the conchshell in the hands of the Lord; *vidrāvaya*—drive away; *kṛṣṇa-pūritaḥ*—being filled with air from the mouth of Kṛṣṇa; *bhīma-svanaḥ*—sounding extremely fearful; *areḥ*—of the enemy; *hṛdayāni*—the cores of the hearts; *kampayan*—causing to tremble.

TRANSLATION

O best of conchshells, O Pāñcajanya in the hands of the Lord, you are always filled with the breath of Lord Kṛṣṇa. Therefore you create a fearful sound vibration that causes trembling in the hearts of enemies like the Rākṣasas, Pramatha ghosts, Pretas, Mātās, Piśācas and brāhmaṇa ghosts with fearful eyes.

TEXT 26

त्वं तिग्मधारासिवरारिसैन्य-
मीशप्रयुक्तो मम छिन्धि छिन्धि ।
चक्षूंषि चर्मञ्छतचन्द्र छादय
द्विषामघोनां हर पापचक्षुषाम् ॥२६॥

tvaṁ tigma-dhārāsi-varāri-sainyam
īśa-prayukto mama chindhi chindhi
cakṣūṁṣi carmañ chata-candra chādaya
dviṣām aghonāṁ hara pāpa-cakṣuṣām

tvam—you; *tigma-dhāra-asi-vara*—O best of swords possessing very sharp blades; *ari-sainyam*—the soldiers of the enemy; *īśa-prayuktaḥ*—being engaged by the Supreme Personality of Godhead; *mama*—my; *chindhi chindhi*—chop to pieces, chop to pieces; *cakṣūṁṣi*—the eyes; *carman*—O shield; *śata-candra*—possessing brilliant circles like a hundred moons; *chādaya*—please cover; *dviṣām*—of those who are envious of me; *aghonām*—who are completely sinful; *hara*—please take away; *pāpa-cakṣuṣām*—of those whose eyes are very sinful.

TRANSLATION

O king of sharp-edged swords, you are engaged by the Supreme Personality of Godhead. Please cut the soldiers of my enemies to

pieces. Please cut them to pieces! O shield marked with a hundred brilliant moonlike circles, please cover the eyes of the sinful enemies. Pluck out their sinful eyes.

TEXTS 27–28

यन्नो भयं ग्रहेभ्योऽभूत् केतुभ्यो नृभ्य एव च ।
सरीसृपेभ्यो दंष्ट्रिभ्यो भूतेभ्योंऽहोभ्य एव च ॥२७॥
सर्वाण्येतानि भगवन्नामरूपानुकीर्तनात् ।
प्रयान्तु संक्षयं सद्यो ये नः श्रेयःप्रतीपकाः ॥२८॥

yan no bhayaṁ grahebhyo 'bhūt
ketubhyo nṛbhya eva ca
sarīsṛpebhyo daṁṣṭribhyo
bhūtebhyo 'ṁhobhya eva ca

sarvāṇy etāni bhagavan-
nāma-rūpānukīrtanāt
prayāntu saṅkṣayaṁ sadyo
ye naḥ śreyaḥ-pratīpakāḥ

yat—which; *naḥ*—our; *bhayam*—fear; *grahebhyaḥ*—from the Graha demons; *abhūt*—was; *ketubhyaḥ*—from meteors, or falling stars; *nṛbhyaḥ*—from envious human beings; *eva ca*—also; *sarīsṛpebhyaḥ*—from snakes or scorpions; *daṁṣṭribhyaḥ*—from animals with fierce teeth like tigers, wolves and boars; *bhūtebhyaḥ*—from ghosts or the material elements (earth, water, fire, etc.); *aṁhobhyaḥ*—from sinful activities; *eva ca*—as well as; *sarvāṇi etāni*—all these; *bhagavat-nāma-rūpa-anukīrtanāt*—by glorifying the transcendental form, name, attributes and paraphernalia of the Supreme Personality of Godhead; *prayāntu*—let them go; *saṅkṣayam*—to complete destruction; *sadyaḥ*—immediately; *ye*—which; *naḥ*—our; *śreyaḥ-pratīpakāḥ*—hindrances to well-being.

TRANSLATION

May the glorification of the transcendental name, form, qualities and paraphernalia of the Supreme Personality of Godhead protect

us from the influence of bad planets, meteors, envious human beings, serpents, scorpions, and animals like tigers and wolves. May it protect us from ghosts and the material elements like earth, water, fire and air, and may it also protect us from lightning and our past sins. We are always afraid of these hindrances to our auspicious life. Therefore, may they all be completely destroyed by the chanting of the Hare Kṛṣṇa mahā-mantra.

TEXT 29

गरुडो भगवान् स्तोत्रस्तोभश्छन्दोमयः प्रभुः ।
रक्षत्वशेषकृच्छ्रेभ्यो विष्वक्सेनः स्वनामभिः ॥२९॥

garuḍo bhagavān stotra-
stobhaś chandomayaḥ prabhuḥ
rakṣatv aśeṣa-kṛcchrebhyo
viṣvaksenaḥ sva-nāmabhiḥ

garuḍaḥ—His Holiness Garuḍa, the carrier of Lord Viṣṇu; *bhagavān*—as powerful as the Supreme Personality of Godhead; *stotra-stobhaḥ*—who is glorified by selected verses and songs; *chandaḥ-mayaḥ*—the personified *Vedas; prabhuḥ*—the lord; *rakṣatu*—may He protect; *aśeṣa-kṛcchrebhyaḥ*—from unlimited miseries; *viṣvaksenaḥ*—Lord Viṣvaksena; *sva-nāmabhiḥ*—by His holy names.

TRANSLATION

Lord Garuḍa, the carrier of Lord Viṣṇu, is the most worshipable lord, for he is as powerful as the Supreme Lord Himself. He is the personified Vedas and is worshiped by selected verses. May he protect us from all dangerous conditions, and may Lord Viṣvaksena, the Personality of Godhead, also protect us from all dangers by His holy names.

TEXT 30

सर्वापद्भ्यो हरेर्नामरूपयानायुधानि नः ।
बुद्धीन्द्रियमनःप्राणान् पान्तु पार्षदभूषणाः ॥३०॥

sarvāpadbhyo harer nāma-
rūpa-yānāyudhāni naḥ
buddhīndriya-manaḥ-prāṇān
pāntu pārṣada-bhūṣaṇāḥ

sarva-āpadbhyaḥ—from all kinds of danger; *hareḥ*—of the Supreme Personality of Godhead; *nāma*—the holy name; *rūpa*—the transcendental form; *yāna*—the carriers; *āyudhāni*—and all the weapons; *naḥ*—our; *buddhi*—intelligence; *indriya*—senses; *manaḥ*—mind; *prāṇān*—life air; *pāntu*—may they protect and maintain; *pārṣada-bhūṣaṇāḥ*—the decorations who are personal associates.

TRANSLATION

May the Supreme Personality of Godhead's holy names, His transcendental forms, His carriers and all the weapons decorating Him as personal associates protect our intelligence, senses, mind and life air from all dangers.

PURPORT

There are various associates of the transcendental Personality of Godhead, and His weapons and carrier are among them. In the spiritual world, nothing is material. The sword, bow, club, disc and everything decorating the personal body of the Lord are spiritual living force. Therefore the Lord is called *advaya-jñāna*, indicating that there is no difference between Him and His names, forms, qualities, weapons and so on. Anything pertaining to Him is in the same category of spiritual existence. They are all engaged in the service of the Lord in varieties of spiritual forms.

TEXT 31

यथा हि भगवानेव वस्तुतः सदसच्च यत् ।
सत्येनानेन नः सर्वे यान्तु नाशमुपद्रवाः ॥३१॥

yathā hi bhagavān eva
vastutaḥ sad asac ca yat
satyenānena naḥ sarve
yāntu nāśam upadravāḥ

yathā—just as; *hi*—indeed; *bhagavān*—the Supreme Personality of Godhead; *eva*—undoubtedly; *vastutaḥ*—at the ultimate issue; *sat*—manifested; *asat*—unmanifested; *ca*—and; *yat*—whatever; *satyena*—by the truth; *anena*—this; *naḥ*—our; *sarve*—all; *yāntu*—let them go; *nāśam*—to annihilation; *upadravāḥ*—disturbances.

TRANSLATION

The subtle and gross cosmic manifestation is material, but nevertheless it is nondifferent from the Supreme Personality of Godhead because He is ultimately the cause of all causes. Cause and effect are factually one because the cause is present in the effect. Therefore the Absolute Truth, the Supreme Personality of Godhead, can destroy all our dangers by any of His potent parts.

TEXTS 32–33

यथैकात्म्यानुभावानां विकल्परहितः स्वयम् ।
भूषणायुधलिङ्गाख्या धत्ते शक्तीः स्वमायया ॥३२॥
तेनैव सत्यमानेन सर्वज्ञो भगवान् हरिः ।
पातु सर्वैः स्वरूपैर्नः सदा सर्वत्र सर्वगः ॥३३॥

yathaikātmyānubhāvānāṁ
vikalpa-rahitaḥ svayam
bhūṣaṇāyudha-liṅgākhyā
dhatte śaktīḥ sva-māyayā

tenaiva satya-mānena
sarva-jño bhagavān hariḥ
pātu sarvaiḥ svarūpair naḥ
sadā sarvatra sarva-gaḥ

yathā—just as; *aikātmya*—in terms of oneness manifested in varieties; *anubhāvānām*—of those thinking; *vikalpa-rahitaḥ*—the absence of difference; *svayam*—Himself; *bhūṣaṇa*—decorations; *āyudha*—weapons; *liṅga-ākhyāḥ*—characteristics and different names; *dhatte*—possesses; *śaktīḥ*—potencies like wealth, influence, power, knowledge, beauty and renunciation; *sva-māyayā*—by expanding His spiritual energy; *tena eva*—by that; *satya-mānena*—true understanding; *sarva-jñaḥ*—omniscient; *bhagavān*—the Supreme Personality of Godhead; *hariḥ*—who can take away all the illusion of the living entities; *pātu*—may He protect; *sarvaiḥ*—with all; *sva-rūpaiḥ*—His forms; *naḥ*—us; *sadā*—always; *sarvatra*—everywhere; *sarva-gaḥ*—who is all-pervasive.

TRANSLATION

The Supreme Personality of Godhead, the living entities, the material energy, the spiritual energy and the entire creation are all individual substances. In the ultimate analysis, however, together they constitute the supreme one, the Personality of Godhead. Therefore those who are advanced in spiritual knowledge see unity in diversity. For such advanced persons, the Lord's bodily decorations, His name, His fame, His attributes and forms and the weapons in His hand are manifestations of the strength of His potency. According to their elevated spiritual understanding, the omniscient Lord, who manifests various forms, is present everywhere. May He always protect us everywhere from all calamities.

PURPORT

A person highly elevated in spiritual knowledge knows that nothing exists but the Supreme Personality of Godhead. This is also confirmed in *Bhagavad-gītā* (9.4) where Lord Kṛṣṇa says, *mayā tatam idaṁ sarvam,* indicating that everything we see is an expansion of His energy. This is confirmed in the *Viṣṇu Purāṇa* (1.22.52):

ekadeśa-sthitasyāgner
jyotsnā vistāriṇī yathā
parasya brahmaṇaḥ śaktis
tathedam akhilaṁ jagat

As a fire, although existing in one place, can expand its light and heat everywhere, so the omnipotent Lord, the Supreme Personality of Godhead, although situated in His spiritual abode, expands Himself everywhere, in both the material and spiritual worlds, by His various energies.

Since both cause and effect are the Supreme Lord, there is no difference between cause and effect. Consequently the ornaments and weapons of the Lord, being expansions of His spiritual energy, are not different from Him. There is no difference between the Lord and His variously presented energies. This is also confirmed in the *Padma Purāṇa:*

nāma cintāmaṇiḥ kṛṣṇaś
caitanya-rasa-vigrahaḥ
pūrṇaḥ śuddho nitya-mukto
'bhinnatvān nāma-nāminoḥ

The holy name of the Lord is fully identical with the Lord, not partially. The word *pūrṇa* means "complete." The Lord is omnipotent and omniscient, and similarly, His name, form, qualities, paraphernalia and everything pertaining to Him are complete, pure, eternal and free from material contamination. The prayer to the ornaments and carriers of the Lord is not false, for they are as good as the Lord. Since the Lord is all-pervasive, He exists in everything, and everything exists in Him. Therefore even worship of the Lord's weapons or ornaments has the same potency as worship of the Lord. Māyāvādīs refuse to accept the form of the Lord, or they say that the form of the Lord is *māyā,* or false, but one should note very carefully that this is not acceptable. Although the Lord's original form and His impersonal expansion are one, the Lord maintains His form, qualities and abode eternally. Therefore this prayer says, *pātu sarvaiḥ svarūpair naḥ sadā sarvatra sarva-gaḥ:* "May the Lord, who is all-pervasive in His various forms, protect us everywhere." The Lord is always present everywhere by His name, form, qualities, attributes and paraphernalia, and they all have equal power to protect the devotees. Śrīla Madhvācārya explains this as follows:

eka eva paro viṣṇur
bhūṣāheti dhvajeṣv ajaḥ
tat-tac-chakti-pradatvena
svayam eva vyavasthitaḥ
satyenānena māṁ devaḥ
pātu sarveśvaro hariḥ

TEXT 34

विदिक्षु दिक्षूर्ध्वमधः समन्ता-
दन्तर्बहिर्भगवान् नारसिंहः ।
प्रहापयँल्लोकभयं स्वनेन
स्वतेजसा ग्रस्तसमस्ततेजाः ॥३४॥

vidikṣu dikṣūrdhvam adhaḥ samantād
antar bahir bhagavān nārasiṁhaḥ
prahāpayal loka-bhayaṁ svanena
sva-tejasā grasta-samasta-tejāḥ

vidikṣu—in all corners; *dikṣu*—in all directions (east, west, north and south); *ūrdhvam*—above; *adhaḥ*—below; *samantāt*—on all sides; *antaḥ*—internally; *bahiḥ*—externally; *bhagavān*—the Supreme Personality of Godhead; *nārasiṁhaḥ*—in the form of Nṛsiṁhadeva (half-lion and half-man); *prahāpayan*—completely destroying; *loka-bhayam*—fear created by animals, poison, weapons, water, air, fire and so on; *svanena*—by His roar or the vibration of His name by His devotee Prahlāda Mahārāja; *sva-tejasā*—by His personal effulgence; *grasta*—covered; *samasta*—all other; *tejāḥ*—influences.

TRANSLATION

Prahlāda Mahārāja loudly chanted the holy name of Lord Nṛsiṁhadeva. May Lord Nṛsiṁhadeva, roaring for His devotee Prahlāda Mahārāja, protect us from all fear of dangers created by stalwart leaders in all directions through poison, weapons, water, fire, air and so on. May the Lord cover their influence by His own transcendental influence. May Nṛsiṁhadeva protect us in all directions and in all corners, above, below, within and without.

TEXT 35

मघवन्निदमाख्यातं वर्म नारायणात्मकम् ।
विजेष्यसेऽञ्जसा येन दंशितोऽसुरयूथपान् ॥३५॥

maghavann idam ākhyātaṁ
varma nārāyaṇātmakam
vijeṣyase 'ñjasā yena
daṁśito 'sura-yūthapān

maghavan—O King Indra; *idam*—this; *ākhyātam*—described; *varma*—mystic armor; *nārāyaṇa-ātmakam*—related to Nārāyaṇa; *vijeṣyase*—you will conquer; *añjasā*—very easily; *yena*—by which; *daṁśitaḥ*—being protected; *asura-yūthapān*—the chief leaders of the demons.

TRANSLATION

Viśvarūpa continued: O Indra, this mystic armor related to Lord Nārāyaṇa has been described by me to you. By putting on this protective covering, you will certainly be able to conquer the leaders of the demons.

TEXT 36

एतद् धारयमाणस्तु यं यं पश्यति चक्षुषा ।
पदा वा संस्पृशेत् सद्यः साध्वसात् स विमुच्यते॥३६॥

etad dhārayamāṇas tu
yaṁ yaṁ paśyati cakṣuṣā
padā vā saṁspṛśet sadyaḥ
sādhvasāt sa vimucyate

etat—this; *dhārayamāṇaḥ*—a person employing; *tu*—but; *yam yam*—whomever; *paśyati*—he sees; *cakṣuṣā*—by his eyes; *padā*—by his feet; *vā*—or; *saṁspṛśet*—may touch; *sadyaḥ*—immediately; *sādhvasāt*—from all fear; *saḥ*—he; *vimucyate*—is freed.

TRANSLATION

If one employs this armor, whomever he sees with his eyes or touches with his feet is immediately freed from all the abovementioned dangers.

TEXT 37

न कुतश्चिद् भयं तस्य विद्यां धारयतो भवेत् ।
राजदस्युग्रहादिभ्यो व्याध्यादिभ्यश्च कर्हिचित् ॥३७॥

na kutaścid bhayaṁ tasya
vidyāṁ dhārayato bhavet
rāja-dasyu-grahādibhyo
vyādhy-ādibhyaś ca karhicit

na—not; *kutaścit*—from anywhere; *bhayam*—fear; *tasya*—of him; *vidyām*—this mystical prayer; *dhārayataḥ*—employing; *bhavet*—may appear; *rāja*—from the government; *dasyu*—from rogues and thieves; *graha-ādibhyaḥ*—from demons and so on; *vyādhi-ādibhyaḥ*—from diseases and so on; *ca*—also; *karhicit*—at any time.

TRANSLATION

This prayer, Nārāyaṇa-kavaca, constitutes subtle knowledge transcendentally connected with Nārāyaṇa. One who employs this prayer is never disturbed or put in danger by the government, by plunderers, by evil demons or by any type of disease.

TEXT 38

इमां विद्यां पुरा कश्चित् कौशिको धारयन् द्विजः ।
योगधारणया स्वाङ्गं जहौ स मरुधन्वनि ॥३८॥

imāṁ vidyāṁ purā kaścit
kauśiko dhārayan dvijaḥ
yoga-dhāraṇayā svāṅgaṁ
jahau sa maru-dhanvani

imām—this; *vidyām*—prayer; *purā*—formerly; *kaścit*—someone; *kauśikaḥ*—Kauśika; *dhārayan*—using; *dvijaḥ*—a *brāhmaṇa; yoga-dhāraṇayā*—by mystic power; *sva-aṅgam*—his own body; *jahau*—gave up; *saḥ*—he; *maru-dhanvani*—in the desert.

TRANSLATION

O King of heaven, a brāhmaṇa named Kauśika formerly used this armor when he purposely gave up his body in the desert by mystic power.

TEXT 39

तस्योपरि विमानेन गन्धर्वपतिरेकदा ।
ययौ चित्ररथः स्त्रीभिर्वृतो यत्र द्विजक्षयः ॥३९॥

tasyopari vimānena
gandharva-patir ekadā
yayau citrarathaḥ strībhir
vṛto yatra dvija-kṣayaḥ

tasya—his dead body; *upari*—above; *vimānena*—by airplane; *gandharva-patiḥ*—the King of Gandharvaloka, Citraratha; *ekadā*—once upon a time; *yayau*—went; *citrarathaḥ*—Citraratha; *strībhiḥ*—by many beautiful women; *vṛtaḥ*—surrounded; *yatra*—where; *dvija-kṣayaḥ*—the *brāhmaṇa* Kauśika had died.

TRANSLATION

Surrounded by many beautiful women, Citraratha, the King of Gandharvaloka, was once passing in his airplane over the brāhmaṇa's body at the spot where the brāhmaṇa had died.

TEXT 40

गगनान्न्यपतत् सद्यः सविमानो ह्यवाक्शिराः ।
स वालिखिल्यवचनादस्थीन्यादाय विस्मितः ।
प्रास्य प्राचीसरस्वत्यां स्नात्वा धाम स्वमन्वगात् ॥४०॥

gaganān nyapatat sadyaḥ
savimāno hy avāk-śirāḥ
sa vālikhilya-vacanād
asthīny ādāya vismitaḥ
prāsya prācī-sarasvatyāṁ
snātvā dhāma svam anvagāt

gaganāt—from the sky; *nyapatat*—fell; *sadyaḥ*—suddenly; *sa-vimānaḥ*—with his airplane; *hi*—certainly; *avāk-śirāḥ*—with his head downward; *saḥ*—he; *vālikhilya*—of the great sages named the Vālikhilyas; *vacanāt*—by the instructions; *asthīni*—all the bones; *ādāya*—taking; *vismitaḥ*—struck with wonder; *prāsya*—throwing; *prācī-sarasvatyām*—in the River Sarasvatī, which flows to the east; *snātvā*—bathing in that river; *dhāma*—to the abode; *svam*—his own; *anvagāt*—returned.

TRANSLATION

Suddenly Citraratha was forced to fall from the sky headfirst with his airplane. Struck with wonder, he was ordered by the great sages named the Vālikhilyas to throw the brāhmaṇa's bones in the nearby River Sarasvatī. He had to do this and bathe in the river before returning to his own abode.

TEXT 41

श्रीशुक उवाच
य इदं शृणुयात् काले यो धारयति चादृतः ।
तं नमस्यन्ति भूतानि मुच्यते सर्वतो भयात् ॥४१॥

śrī-śuka uvāca
ya idaṁ śṛṇuyāt kāle
yo dhārayati cādṛtaḥ
taṁ namasyanti bhūtāni
mucyate sarvato bhayāt

śrī-śukaḥ uvāca—Śrī Śukadeva Gosvāmī said; *yaḥ*—anyone who; *idam*—this; *śṛṇuyāt*—may hear; *kāle*—at a time of fear; *yaḥ*—anyone who; *dhārayati*—employs this prayer; *ca*—also; *ādṛtaḥ*—with faith and adoration; *tam*—unto him; *namasyanti*—offer respectful obeisances; *bhūtāni*—all living beings; *mucyate*—is released; *sarvataḥ*—from all; *bhayāt*—fearful conditions.

TRANSLATION

Śrī Śukadeva Gosvāmī said: My dear Mahārāja Parīkṣit, one who employs this armor or hears about it with faith and veneration

when afraid because of any conditions in the material world is immediately freed from all dangers and is worshiped by all living entities.

TEXT 42

एतां विद्यामधिगतो विश्वरूपाच्छतक्रतुः ।
त्रैलोक्यलक्ष्मीं बुभुजे विनिर्जित्य मृधेऽसुरान् ॥४२॥

etāṁ vidyām adhigato
viśvarūpāc chatakratuḥ
trailokya-lakṣmīṁ bubhuje
vinirjitya mṛdhe 'surān

etām—this; *vidyām*—prayer; *adhigataḥ*—received; *viśvarūpāt*—from the *brāhmaṇa* Viśvarūpa; *śata-kratuḥ*—Indra, the King of heaven; *trailokya-lakṣmīm*—all the opulence of the three worlds; *bubhuje*—enjoyed; *vinirjitya*—conquering; *mṛdhe*—in battle; *asurān*—all the demons.

TRANSLATION

King Indra, who performed one hundred sacrifices, received this prayer of protection from Viśvarūpa. After conquering the demons, he enjoyed all the opulences of the three worlds.

PURPORT

This mystical mantric armor given by Viśvarūpa to Indra, the King of heaven, acted powerfully, with the effect that Indra was able to conquer the *asuras* and enjoy the opulence of the three worlds without impediments. In this regard, Madhvācārya points out:

vidyāḥ karmāṇi ca sadā
guroḥ prāptāḥ phala-pradāḥ
anyathā naiva phaladāḥ
prasannoktāḥ phala-pradāḥ

One must receive all kinds of *mantras* from a bona fide spiritual master; otherwise the *mantras* will not be fruitful. This is also indicated in *Bhagavad-gītā* (4.34):

tad viddhi praṇipātena
paripraśnena sevayā
upadekṣyanti te jñānaṁ
jñāninas tattva-darśinaḥ

"Just try to learn the truth by approaching a spiritual master. Inquire from him submissively and render service unto him. The self-realized soul can impart knowledge unto you because he has seen the truth." All *mantras* should be received through the authorized *guru*, and the disciple must satisfy the *guru* in all respects, after surrendering at his lotus feet. In the *Padma Purāṇa* it is also said, *sampradāya-vihīnā ye mantrās te niṣphalā matāḥ*. There are four *sampradāyas*, or disciplic successions, namely the Brahma-sampradāya, the Rudra-sampradāya, the Śrī-sampradāya and the Kumāra-sampradāya. If one wants to advance in spiritual power, one must receive his *mantras* from one of these bona fide *sampradāyas;* otherwise he will never successfully advance in spiritual life.

Thus end the Bhaktivedanta purports of the Sixth Canto, Eighth Chapter, of the Śrīmad-Bhāgavatam, *entitled "The Nārāyaṇa-kavaca Shield."*

CHAPTER NINE

Appearance of the Demon Vṛtrāsura

As described in this chapter, Indra, the King of heaven, killed Viśvarūpa, and therefore Viśvarūpa's father performed a *yajña* to kill Indra. When Vṛtrāsura appeared from that *yajña*, the demigods, in fear, sought shelter of the Supreme Personality of Godhead and glorified Him.

Because of affection for the demons, Viśvarūpa secretly supplied them the remnants of *yajña*. When Indra learned about this, he beheaded Viśvarūpa, but he later regretted killing Viśvarūpa because Viśvarūpa was a *brāhmaṇa*. Although competent to neutralize the sinful reactions for killing a *brāhmaṇa*, Indra did not do so. Instead he accepted the reactions. Later, he distributed these reactions among the land, water, trees and women in general. Since the land accepted one fourth of the sinful reactions, a portion of the land turned into desert. The trees were also given one fourth of the sinful reactions, and therefore they drip sap, which is prohibited for drinking. Because women accepted one fourth of the sinful reactions, they are untouchable during their menstrual period. Since water was also infested with sinful reactions, when bubbles appear in water it cannot be used for any purpose.

After Viśvarūpa was killed, his father, Tvaṣṭā, performed a sacrifice to kill King Indra. Unfortunately, if *mantras* are chanted irregularly, they yield an opposite result. This happened when Tvaṣṭā performed this *yajña*. While performing the sacrifice to kill Indra, Tvaṣṭā chanted a *mantra* to increase Indra's enemies, but because he chanted the *mantra* wrong, the sacrifice produced an *asura* named Vṛtrāsura, of whom Indra was the enemy. When Vṛtrāsura was generated from the sacrifice, his fierce features made the whole world afraid, and his personal effulgence diminished even the power of the demigods. Finding no other means of protection, the demigods began to worship the Supreme Personality of Godhead, the enjoyer of all the results of sacrifice, who is supreme throughout the entire universe. The demigods all worshiped Him because ultimately no one but Him can protect a living entity from fear and danger. Seeking shelter of a demigod instead of worshiping the Supreme

Personality of Godhead is compared to trying to cross the ocean by grasping the tail of a dog. A dog can swim, but that does not mean that one can cross the ocean by grasping a dog's tail.

Being pleased with the demigods, the Supreme Personality of Godhead advised them to approach Dadhīci to beg him for the bones of his own body. Dadhīci would comply with the request of the demigods, and with the help of his bones Vṛtrāsura could be killed.

TEXT 1

श्रीशुक उवाच
तस्यासन् विश्वरूपस्य शिरांसि त्रीणि भारत ।
सोमपीथं सुरापीथमन्नादमिति शुश्रुम ॥ १ ॥

śrī-śuka uvāca
tasyāsan viśvarūpasya
śirāṁsi trīṇi bhārata
soma-pīthaṁ surā-pītham
annādam iti śuśruma

śrī-śukaḥ uvāca—Śrī Śukadeva Gosvāmī said; *tasya*—of him; *āsan*—there were; *viśvarūpasya*—of Viśvarūpa, the priest of the demigods; *śirāṁsi*—heads; *trīṇi*—three; *bhārata*—O Mahārāja Parīkṣit; *soma-pītham*—used for drinking the beverage *soma; surā-pītham*—used for drinking wine; *anna-adam*—used for eating; *iti*—thus; *śuśruma*—I have heard by the *paramparā* system.

TRANSLATION

Śrī Śukadeva Gosvāmī continued: Viśvarūpa, who was engaged as the priest of the demigods, had three heads. He used one to drink the beverage soma-rasa, another to drink wine and the third to eat food. O King Parīkṣit, thus I have heard from authorities.

PURPORT

One cannot directly perceive the kingdom of heaven, its king and other inhabitants, or how they perform their various engagements, for no one can go to the heavenly planets. Although modern scientists have invented many powerful space vehicles, they cannot even go to the moon, not to speak of other planets. By direct experience one cannot learn anything beyond the range of human perception. One must hear from authorities. Therefore Śukadeva Gosvāmī, a great personality, says, "What I am describing to you, O King, is what I have heard from authoritative sources." This is the Vedic system. The Vedic knowledge is called *śruti* because it must be received by being heard from authorities. It is beyond the realm of our false experimental knowledge.

TEXT 2

स वै बर्हिषि देवेभ्यो भागं प्रत्यक्षमुच्चकैः ।
अददद् यस्य पितरो देवाः सप्रश्रयं नृप ॥ २ ॥

sa vai barhiṣi devebhyo
bhāgaṁ pratyakṣam uccakaiḥ
adadad yasya pitaro
devāḥ sapraśrayaṁ nṛpa

saḥ—he (Viśvarūpa); *vai*—indeed; *barhiṣi*—in the sacrificial fire; *devebhyaḥ*—unto the particular demigods; *bhāgam*—the proper share; *pratyakṣam*—visibly; *uccakaiḥ*—by loud chanting of the *mantras; adadat*—offered; *yasya*—of whom; *pitaraḥ*—the fathers; *devāḥ*—demigods; *sa-praśrayam*—very humbly in a gentle voice; *nṛpa*—O King Parīkṣit.

TRANSLATION

O Mahārāja Parīkṣit, the demigods were related to Viśvarūpa from his father's side, and therefore he visibly offered clarified butter in the fire while chanting mantras such as "indrāya idaṁ svāhā" ["this is meant for King Indra"] and "idam agnaye" ["this is for the demigod of fire"]. He loudly chanted these mantras and offered each of the demigods his proper share.

TEXT 3

स एव हि ददौ भागं परोक्षमसुरान् प्रति ।
यजमानोऽवहद् भागं मातृस्नेहवशानुगः ॥ ३ ॥

sa eva hi dadau bhāgaṁ
parokṣam asurān prati
yajamāno 'vahad bhāgaṁ
mātṛ-sneha-vaśānugaḥ

saḥ—he (Viśvarūpa); *eva*—indeed; *hi*—certainly; *dadau*—offered; *bhāgam*—share; *parokṣam*—without the knowledge of the demigods; *asurān*—the demons; *prati*—unto; *yajamānaḥ*—performing sacrifice; *avahat*—offered; *bhāgam*—share; *mātṛ-sneha*—by affection for his mother; *vaśa-anugaḥ*—being compelled.

TRANSLATION

Although offering clarified butter in the sacrificial fire in the name of the demigods, without the knowledge of the demigods he also offered oblations to the demons because they were his relatives through his mother.

PURPORT

Because of Viśvarūpa's affection for the families of both the demigods and the demons, he appeased the Supreme Lord on behalf of both dynasties. When he offered oblations in the fire on behalf of the *asuras*, he did so secretly, without the knowledge of the demigods.

TEXT 4

तद्‌ देवहेलनं तस्य धर्मालीकं सुरेश्वरः ।
आलक्ष्य तरसा भीतस्तच्छीर्षाण्यच्छिनद्‌ रुषा ॥४ ॥

tad deva-helanaṁ tasya
dharmālīkaṁ sureśvaraḥ
ālakṣya tarasā bhītas
tac-chīrṣāṇy acchinad ruṣā

tat—that; *deva-helanam*—offense to the demigods; *tasya*—of him (Viśvarūpa); *dharma-alīkam*—cheating in religious principles (pretending to be the priest of the demigods, but secretly acting as the priest of the demons also); *sura-īśvaraḥ*—the king of the demigods; *ālakṣya*—observing; *tarasā*—quickly; *bhītaḥ*—being afraid (that the demons would gain strength by being blessed by Viśvarūpa); *tat*—his (Viśvarūpa's); *śīrṣāṇi*—heads; *acchinat*—cut off; *ruṣā*—with great anger.

TRANSLATION

Once upon a time, however, the King of heaven, Indra, understood that Viśvarūpa was secretly cheating the demigods by offering oblations on behalf of the demons. He became extremely afraid of being defeated by the demons, and in great anger at Viśvarūpa he cut Viśvarūpa's three heads from his shoulders.

TEXT 5

सोमपीथं तु यत् तस्य शिर आसीत् कपिञ्जलः ।
कलविङ्कः सुरापीथमन्नादं यत् स तित्तिरिः ॥ ५ ॥

soma-pītham tu yat tasya
śira āsīt kapiñjalaḥ
kalaviṅkaḥ surā-pītham
annādaṁ yat sa tittiriḥ

soma-pītham—used for drinking *soma-rasa; tu*—however; *yat*—which; *tasya*—of him (Viśvarūpa); *śiraḥ*—the head; *āsīt*—became; *kapiñjalaḥ*—a francolin partridge; *kalaviṅkaḥ*—a sparrow; *surā-pītham*—meant for drinking wine; *anna-adam*—used for eating food; *yat*—which; *saḥ*—that; *tittiriḥ*—a common partridge.

TRANSLATION

Thereafter, the head meant for drinking soma-rasa was transformed into a kapiñjala [francolin partridge]. Similarly, the head meant for drinking wine was transformed into a kalaviṅka [sparrow], and the head meant for eating food became a tittiri [common partridge].

TEXT 6

ब्रह्महत्यामञ्जलिना जग्राह यदपीश्वरः ।
संवत्सरान्ते तदघं भूतानां स विशुद्धये ।
भूम्यम्बुद्रुमयोषिद्भ्यश्चतुर्धा व्यभजद्धरिः ॥ ६ ॥

brahma-hatyām añjalinā
jagrāha yad apīśvaraḥ
saṁvatsarānte tad aghaṁ
bhūtānāṁ sa viśuddhaye
bhūmy-ambu-druma-yoṣidbhyaś
caturdhā vyabhajad dhariḥ

brahma-hatyām—the sinful reaction for killing a *brāhmaṇa; añjalinā*—with folded hands; *jagrāha*—assumed the responsibility for; *yat api*—although; *īśvaraḥ*—very powerful; *saṁvatsara-ante*—after one year; *tat agham*—that sinful reaction; *bhūtānām*—of the material elements; *saḥ*—he; *viśuddhaye*—for purification; *bhūmi*—unto the earth; *ambu*—water; *druma*—trees; *yoṣidbhyaḥ*—and unto women; *caturdhā*—in four divisions; *vyabhajat*—divided; *hariḥ*—King Indra.

TRANSLATION

Although Indra was so powerful that he could neutralize the sinful reactions for killing a brāhmaṇa, he repentantly accepted the burden of these reactions with folded hands. He suffered for one year, and then to purify himself he distributed the reactions for this sinful killing among the earth, water, trees and women.

TEXT 7

भूमिस्तुरीयं जग्राह खातपूरवरेण वै ।
ईरिणं ब्रह्महत्याया रूपं भूमौ प्रदृश्यते ॥ ७ ॥

bhūmis turīyaṁ jagrāha
khāta-pūra-vareṇa vai
īriṇaṁ brahma-hatyāyā
rūpaṁ bhūmau pradṛśyate

bhūmiḥ—the earth; *turīyam*—one fourth; *jagrāha*—accepted; *khāta-pūra*—of the filling of holes; *vareṇa*—because of the benediction; *vai*—indeed; *īriṇam*—the deserts; *brahma-hatyāyāḥ*—of the reaction for killing a *brāhmaṇa; rūpam*—form; *bhūmau*—on the earth; *pradṛśyate*—is visible.

TRANSLATION

In return for King Indra's benediction that ditches in the earth would be filled automatically, the land accepted one fourth of the sinful reactions for killing a brāhmaṇa. Because of those sinful reactions, we find many deserts on the surface of the earth.

PURPORT

Because deserts are manifestations of the earth's diseased condition, no auspicious ritualistic ceremony can be performed in a desert. Persons destined to live in deserts are understood to be sharing the reactions for the sin of *brahma-hatyā*, the killing of a *brāhmaṇa.*

TEXT 8

तुर्यं छेदविरोहेण वरेण जगृहुर्द्रुमाः ।
तेषां निर्यासरूपेण ब्रह्महत्या प्रदृश्यते ॥ ८ ॥

turyaṁ cheda-viroheṇa
vareṇa jagṛhur drumāḥ
teṣāṁ niryāsa-rūpeṇa
brahma-hatyā pradṛśyate

turyam—one fourth; *cheda*—although being cut; *viroheṇa*—of growing again; *vareṇa*—because of the benediction; *jagṛhuḥ*—accepted; *drumāḥ*—the trees; *teṣām*—of them; *niryāsa-rūpeṇa*—by the liquid oozing from the trees; *brahma-hatyā*—the reaction for killing a *brāhmaṇa; pradṛśyate*—is visible.

TRANSLATION

In return for Indra's benediction that their branches and twigs would grow back when trimmed, the trees accepted one fourth of

the reactions for killing a brāhmaṇa. These reactions are visible in the flowing of sap from trees. [Therefore one is forbidden to drink this sap.]

TEXT 9

शश्वत्कामवरेणांहस्तुरीयं जगृहुः स्त्रियः ।
रजोरूपेण तास्वंहो मासि मासि प्रदृश्यते ॥ ९ ॥

śaśvat-kāma-vareṇāṁhas
turīyaṁ jagṛhuḥ striyaḥ
rajo-rūpeṇa tāsv aṁho
māsi māsi pradṛśyate

śaśvat—perpetual; *kāma*—of sexual desire; *vareṇa*—because of the benediction; *aṁhaḥ*—the sinful reaction for killing a *brāhmaṇa; turīyam*—one fourth; *jagṛhuḥ*—accepted; *striyaḥ*—women; *rajaḥ-rūpeṇa*—in the form of the menstrual period; *tāsu*—in them; *aṁhaḥ*—the sinful reaction; *māsi māsi*—every month; *pradṛśyate*—is visible.

TRANSLATION

In return for Lord Indra's benediction that they would be able to enjoy lusty desires continuously, even during pregnancy for as long as sex is not injurious to the embryo, women accepted one fourth of the sinful reactions. As a result of those reactions, women manifest the signs of menstruation every month.

PURPORT

Women as a class are very lusty, and apparently their continuous lusty desires are never satisfied. In return for Lord Indra's benediction that there would be no cessation to their lusty desires, women accepted one fourth of the sinful reactions for killing a *brāhmaṇa.*

TEXT 10

द्रव्यभूयोवरेणापस्तुरीयं जगृहुर्मलम् ।
तासु बुद्बुदफेनाभ्यां दृष्टं तद्धरति क्षिपन् ॥१०॥

dravya-bhūyo-vareṇāpas
turīyaṁ jagṛhur malam
tāsu budbuda-phenābhyāṁ
dṛṣṭaṁ tad dharati kṣipan

dravya—other things; *bhūyaḥ*—of increasing; *vareṇa*—by the benediction; *āpaḥ*—water; *turīyam*—one fourth; *jagṛhuḥ*—accepted; *malam*—the sinful reaction; *tāsu*—in the water; *budbuda-phenābhyām*—by bubbles and foam; *dṛṣṭam*—visible; *tat*—that; *harati*—one collects; *kṣipan*—throwing away.

TRANSLATION

And in return for King Indra's benediction that water would increase the volume of other substances with which it was mixed, water accepted one fourth of the sinful reactions. Therefore there are bubbles and foam in water. When one collects water, these should be avoided.

PURPORT

If water is mixed with milk, fruit juice or other similar substances, it increases their volume, and no one can understand which has increased. In return for this benediction, water accepted one fourth of Indra's sinful reactions. These sinful reactions are visible in foam and bubbles. Therefore one should avoid foam and bubbles while collecting drinking water.

TEXT 11

हतपुत्रस्ततस्त्वष्टा जुहावेन्द्राय शत्रवे ।
इन्द्रशत्रो विवर्धस्व माचिरं जहि विद्विषम् ॥११॥

hata-putras tatas tvaṣṭā
juhāvendrāya śatrave
indra-śatro vivardhasva
mā ciraṁ jahi vidviṣam

hata-putraḥ—who lost his son; *tataḥ*—thereafter; *tvaṣṭā*—Tvaṣṭā; *juhāva*—performed a sacrifice; *indrāya*—of Indra; *śatrave*—for creating an enemy; *indra-śatro*—O enemy of Indra; *vivardhasva*—increase; *mā*—not; *ciram*—after a long time; *jahi*—kill; *vidviṣam*—your enemy.

TRANSLATION

After Viśvarūpa was killed, his father, Tvaṣṭā, performed ritualistic ceremonies to kill Indra. He offered oblations in the sacrificial fire, saying, "O enemy of Indra, flourish to kill your enemy without delay."

PURPORT

There was some defect in Tvaṣṭā's chanting of the *mantra* because he chanted it long instead of short, and therefore the meaning changed. Tvaṣṭā intended to chant the word *indra-śatro,* meaning, "O enemy of Indra." In this *mantra,* the word *indra* is in the possessive case (*ṣaṣṭhī*), and the word *indra-śatro* is called a *tat-puruṣa* compound (*tatpuruṣa-samāsa*). Unfortunately, instead of chanting the *mantra* short, Tvaṣṭā chanted it long, and its meaning changed from "the enemy of Indra" to "Indra, who is an enemy." Consequently instead of an enemy of Indra's, there emerged the body of Vṛtrāsura, of whom Indra was the enemy.

TEXT 12

अथान्वाहार्यपचनादुत्थितो घोरदर्शनः ।
कृतान्त इव लोकानां युगान्तसमये यथा ॥१२॥

athānvāhārya-pacanād
utthito ghora-darśanaḥ
kṛtānta iva lokānāṁ
yugānta-samaye yathā

atha—thereafter; *anvāhārya-pacanāt*—from the fire known as Anvāhārya; *utthitaḥ*—arisen; *ghora-darśanaḥ*—appearing very fearful; *kṛtāntaḥ*—personified annihilation; *iva*—like; *lokānām*—of all the planets; *yuga-anta*—of the end of the millennium; *samaye*—at the time; *yathā*—just as.

TRANSLATION

Thereafter, from the southern side of the sacrificial fire known as Anvāhārya came a fearful personality who looked like the destroyer of the entire creation at the end of the millennium.

TEXTS 13–17

विष्वग्विवर्धमानं तमिषुमात्रं दिने दिने ।
दग्धशैलप्रतीकाशं सन्ध्याभ्रानीकवर्चसम् ॥१३॥
तप्तताम्रशिखाश्मश्रुं मध्याह्नार्कोग्रलोचनम् ॥१४॥
देदीप्यमाने त्रिशिखे शूल आरोप्य रोदसी ।
नृत्यन्तमुन्नदन्तं च चालयन्तं पदा महीम् ॥१५॥
दरीगम्भीरवक्त्रेण पिबता च नभस्तलम् ।
लिहता जिह्वयर्क्षाणि ग्रसता भुवनत्रयम् ॥१६॥
महता रौद्रदंष्ट्रेण जृम्भमाणं मुहुर्मुहुः ।
वित्रस्ता दुद्रुवुर्लोका वीक्ष्य सर्वे दिशो दश ॥१७॥

viṣvag vivardhamānaṁ tam
iṣu-mātraṁ dine dine
dagdha-śaila-pratīkāśaṁ
sandhyābhrānīka-varcasam

tapta-tāmra-śikhā-śmaśruṁ
madhyāhnārkogra-locanam

dedīpyamāne tri-śikhe
śūla āropya rodasī
nṛtyantam unnadantaṁ ca
cālayantaṁ padā mahīm

darī-gambhīra-vaktreṇa
pibatā ca nabhastalam
lihatā jihvayarkṣāṇi
grasatā bhuvana-trayam

mahatā raudra-daṁṣṭreṇa
jṛmbhamāṇaṁ muhur muhuḥ
vitrastā dudruvur lokā
vīkṣya sarve diśo daśa

viṣvak—all around; *vivardhamānam*—increasing; *tam*—him; *iṣu-mātram*—an arrow's flight; *dine dine*—day after day; *dagdha*—burnt; *śaila*—mountain; *pratīkāśam*—resembling; *sandhyā*—in the evening; *abhra-anīka*—like an array of clouds; *varcasam*—having an effulgence; *tapta*—melted; *tāmra*—like copper; *śikhā*—hair; *śmaśrum*—moustache and beard; *madhyāhna*—at midday; *arka*—like the sun; *ugra-locanam*—having powerful eyes; *dedīpyamāne*—blazing; *tri-śikhe*—three-pointed; *śūle*—on his spear; *āropya*—keeping; *rodasī*—heaven and earth; *nṛtyantam*—dancing; *unnadantam*—shouting loudly; *ca*—and; *cālayantam*—moving; *padā*—by his foot; *mahīm*—the earth; *darī-gambhīra*—as deep as a cave; *vaktreṇa*—by the mouth; *pibatā*—drinking; *ca*—also; *nabhastalam*—the sky; *lihatā*—licking up; *jihvayā*—by the tongue; *ṛkṣāṇi*—the stars; *grasatā*—swallowing; *bhuvana-trayam*—the three worlds; *mahatā*—very great; *raudra-daṁṣṭreṇa*—with fearful teeth; *jṛmbhamāṇam*—yawning; *muhuḥ muhuḥ*—again and again; *vitrastāḥ*—fearful; *dudruvuḥ*—ran; *lokāḥ*—people; *vīkṣya*—seeing; *sarve*—all; *diśaḥ daśa*—ten directions.

TRANSLATION

Like arrows released in the four directions, the demon's body grew, day after day. Tall and blackish, he appeared like a burnt hill and was as lustrous as a bright array of clouds in the evening. The hair on the demon's body and his beard and moustache were the color of melted copper, and his eyes were piercing like the midday sun. He appeared unconquerable, as if holding the three worlds on the points of his blazing trident. Dancing and shouting with a loud voice, he made the entire surface of the earth tremble as if from an earthquake. As he yawned again and again, he seemed to be trying to swallow the whole sky with his mouth, which was as deep as a cave. He seemed to be licking up all the stars in the sky with his tongue and eating the entire universe with his long, sharp teeth. Seeing this gigantic demon, everyone, in great fear, ran here and there in all directions.

TEXT 18

येनावृता इमे लोकास्तपसा त्वाष्ट्रमूर्तिना ।
स वै वृत्र इति प्रोक्तः पापः परमदारुणः ॥१८॥

yenāvṛtā ime lokās
tapasā tvāṣṭra-mūrtinā
sa vai vṛtra iti proktaḥ
pāpaḥ parama-dāruṇaḥ

yena—by whom; *āvṛtāḥ*—covered; *ime*—all these; *lokāḥ*—planets; *tapasā*—by the austerity; *tvāṣṭra-mūrtinā*—in the form of the son of Tvaṣṭā; *saḥ*—he; *vai*—indeed; *vṛtraḥ*—Vṛtra; *iti*—thus; *proktaḥ*—called; *pāpaḥ*—personified sin; *parama-dāruṇaḥ*—very fearful.

TRANSLATION

That very fearful demon, who was actually the son of Tvaṣṭā, covered all the planetary systems by dint of austerity. Therefore he was named Vṛtra, or one who covers everything.

PURPORT

In the *Vedas* it is said, *sa imāl̐ lokān āvṛṇot tad vṛtrasya vṛtratvam:* because the demon covered all the planetary systems, his name was Vṛtrāsura.

TEXT 19

तं निजघ्नुरभिद्रुत्य सगणा विबुधर्षभाः ।
स्वैः स्वैर्दिव्यास्त्रशस्त्रौघैः सोऽग्रसत् तानि कृत्स्नशः ॥१९॥

taṁ nijaghnur abhidrutya
sagaṇā vibudharṣabhāḥ
svaiḥ svair divyāstra-śastraughaiḥ
so 'grasat tāni kṛtsnaśaḥ

tam—him; *nijaghnuḥ*—struck; *abhidrutya*—running to; *sa-gaṇāḥ*—with soldiers; *vibudha-ṛṣabhāḥ*—all the great demigods; *svaiḥ svaiḥ*—with their own respective; *divya*—transcendental; *astra*—bows and arrows; *śastra-oghaiḥ*—different weapons; *saḥ*—he (Vṛtra); *agrasat*—swallowed; *tāni*—them (the weapons); *kṛtsnaśaḥ*—all together.

TRANSLATION

The demigods, headed by Indra, charged the demon with their soldiers, striking him with their own transcendental bows and

arrows and other weapons, but Vṛtrāsura swallowed all their weapons.

TEXT 20

ततस्ते विस्मिताः सर्वे विषण्णा ग्रस्ततेजसः ।
प्रत्यञ्चमादिपुरुषमुपतस्थुः समाहिताः ॥२०॥

tatas te vismitāḥ sarve
viṣaṇṇā grasta-tejasaḥ
pratyañcam ādi-puruṣam
upatasthuḥ samāhitāḥ

tataḥ—thereafter; *te*—they (the demigods); *vismitāḥ*—being struck with wonder; *sarve*—all; *viṣaṇṇāḥ*—being very morose; *grasta-tejasaḥ*—having lost all their personal strength; *pratyañcam*—to the Supersoul; *ādi-puruṣam*—the original person; *upatasthuḥ*—prayed; *samāhitāḥ*—all gathered together.

TRANSLATION

Struck with wonder and disappointment upon seeing the strength of the demon, the demigods lost their own strength. Therefore they all met together to try to please the Supersoul, the Supreme Personality of Godhead, Nārāyaṇa, by worshiping Him.

TEXT 21

श्रीदेवा ऊचुः
वाय्वम्बराग्न्यप्क्षितयस्त्रिलोका
ब्रह्मादयो ये वयमुद्विजन्तः ।
हराम यस्मै बलिमन्तकोऽसौ
बिभेति यस्मादरणं ततो नः ॥२१॥

śrī-devā ūcuḥ
vāyv-ambarāgny-ap-kṣitayas tri-lokā
brahmādayo ye vayam udvijantaḥ
harāma yasmai balim antako 'sau
bibheti yasmād araṇaṁ tato naḥ

śrī-devāḥ ūcuḥ—the demigods said; *vāyu*—composed of air; *ambara*—sky; *agni*—fire; *ap*—water; *kṣitayaḥ*—and land; *tri-lokāḥ*—the three worlds; *brahma-ādayaḥ*—beginning from Lord Brahmā; *ye*—who; *vayam*—we; *udvijantaḥ*—being very much afraid; *harāma*—offer; *yasmai*—unto whom; *balim*—presentation; *antakaḥ*—the destroyer, death; *asau*—that; *bibheti*—fears; *yasmāt*—from whom; *araṇam*—shelter; *tataḥ*—therefore; *naḥ*—our.

TRANSLATION

The demigods said: The three worlds are created by the five elements—namely ether, air, fire, water and earth—which are controlled by various demigods, beginning from Lord Brahmā. Being very much afraid that the time factor will end our existence, we offer presentations unto time by performing our work as time dictates. The time factor himself, however, is afraid of the Supreme Personality of Godhead. Therefore let us now worship that Supreme Lord, who alone can give us full protection.

PURPORT

When one is afraid of being killed, one must take shelter of the Supreme Personality of Godhead. He is worshiped by all the demigods, beginning from Brahmā, although they are in charge of the various elements of this material world. The words *bibheti yasmāt* indicate that all the demons, regardless of how great and powerful, fear the Supreme Personality of Godhead. The demigods, being afraid of death, took shelter of the Lord and offered Him these prayers. Although the time factor is fearful to everyone, fear personified is afraid of the Supreme Lord, who is therefore known as *abhaya*, fearless. Taking shelter of the Supreme Lord brings actual fearlessness, and therefore the demigods decided to take shelter of the Lord.

TEXT 22

अविस्मितं तं परिपूर्णकामं
स्वेनैव लाभेन समं प्रशान्तम् ।

विनोपसर्पत्यपरं हि बालिशः
श्वलाङ्गुलेनातितितर्ति सिन्धुम् ॥२२॥

avismitaṁ taṁ paripūrṇa-kāmaṁ
svenaiva lābhena samaṁ praśāntam
vinopasarpaty aparaṁ hi bāliśaḥ
śva-lāṅgulenātititarti sindhum

avismitam—who is never struck with wonder; *tam*—Him; *paripūrṇa-kāmam*—who is fully satisfied; *svena*—by His own; *eva*—indeed; *lābhena*—achievements; *samam*—equipoised; *praśāntam*—very steady; *vinā*—without; *upasarpati*—approaches; *aparam*—another; *hi*—indeed; *bāliśaḥ*—a fool; *śva*—of a dog; *lāṅgulena*—by the tail; *atititarti*—wants to cross; *sindhum*—the sea.

TRANSLATION

Free from all material conceptions of existence and never wonderstruck by anything, the Lord is always jubilant and fully satisfied by His own spiritual perfection. He has no material designations, and therefore He is steady and unattached. That Supreme Personality of Godhead is the only shelter of everyone. Anyone desiring to be protected by others is certainly a great fool who desires to cross the sea by holding the tail of a dog.

PURPORT

A dog can swim in the water, but if a dog dives in the ocean and someone wants to cross the ocean by holding the dog's tail, he is certainly fool number one. A dog cannot cross the ocean, nor can a person cross the ocean by catching a dog's tail. Similarly, one who desires to cross the ocean of nescience should not seek the shelter of any demigod or anyone else but the fearless shelter of the Supreme Personality of Godhead. *Śrīmad-Bhāgavatam* (10.14.58) therefore says:

samāśritā ye pada-pallava-plavaṁ
mahat-padaṁ puṇya-yaśo-murāreḥ

bhavāmbudhir vatsa-padaṁ paraṁ padaṁ
padaṁ padaṁ yad vipadāṁ na teṣām

The Lord's lotus feet are an indestructible boat, and if one takes shelter of that boat he can easily cross the ocean of nescience. Consequently there are no dangers for a devotee although he lives within this material world, which is full of dangers at every step. One should seek the shelter of the all-powerful instead of trying to be protected by one's own concocted ideas.

TEXT 23

यस्योरुशृङ्गे जगतीं स्वनावं
मनुर्यथाबध्य ततार दुर्गम् ।
स एव नस्त्वाष्ट्रभयाद् दुरन्तात्
त्राताश्रितान् वारिचरोऽपि नूनम् ॥२३॥

yasyoru-śṛṅge jagatīṁ sva-nāvaṁ
manur yathābadhya tatāra durgam
sa eva nas tvāṣṭra-bhayād durantāt
trātāśritān vāricaro 'pi nūnam

yasya—of whom; *uru*—very strong and high; *śṛṅge*—on the horn; *jagatīm*—in the form of the world; *sva-nāvam*—his own boat; *manuḥ*—Manu, King Satyavrata; *yathā*—just as; *ābadhya*—binding; *tatāra*—crossed; *durgam*—the very difficult to cross (inundation); *saḥ*—He (the Supreme Personality of Godhead); *eva*—certainly; *naḥ*—us; *tvāṣṭra-bhayāt*—from fear of the son of Tvaṣṭā; *durantāt*—endless; *trātā*—deliverer; *āśritān*—dependents (like us); *vāri-caraḥ api*—although taking the form of a fish; *nūnam*—indeed.

TRANSLATION

The Manu named King Satyavrata formerly saved himself by tying the small boat of the entire world to the horn of the Matsya avatāra, the fish incarnation. By the grace of the Matsya avatāra,

Manu saved himself from the great danger of the flood. May that same fish incarnation save us from the great and fearful danger caused by the son of Tvaṣṭā.

TEXT 24

पुरा स्वयम्भूरपि संयमाम्भ-
स्युदीर्णवातोर्मिरवैः कराले ।
एकोऽरविन्दात् पतितस्ततार
तस्माद् भयाद् येन स नोऽस्तु पारः॥२४॥

purā svayambhūr api saṁyamāmbhasy
udīrṇa-vātormi-ravaiḥ karāle
eko 'ravindāt patitas tatāra
tasmād bhayād yena sa no 'stu pāraḥ

purā—formerly (during the time of creation); *svayambhūḥ*—Lord Brahmā; *api*—also; *saṁyama-ambhasi*—in the water of inundation; *udīrṇa*—very high; *vāta*—of wind; *ūrmi*—and of waves; *ravaiḥ*—by the sounds; *karāle*—very fearful; *ekaḥ*—alone; *aravindāt*—from the lotus seat; *patitaḥ*—almost fallen; *tatāra*—escaped; *tasmāt*—from that; *bhayāt*—fearful situation; *yena*—by whom (the Lord); *saḥ*—He; *naḥ*—of us; *astu*—let there be; *pāraḥ*—deliverance.

TRANSLATION

In the beginning of creation, a tremendous wind caused fierce waves of inundating water. The great waves made such a horrible sound that Lord Brahmā almost fell from his seat on the lotus into the water of devastation, but he was saved with the help of the Lord. Thus we also expect the Lord to protect us from this dangerous condition.

TEXT 25

य एक ईशो निजमायया नः
ससर्ज येनानुसृजाम विश्वम् ।

वयं न यस्यापि पुरः समीहतः
पश्याम लिङ्गं पृथगीशमानिनः ॥२५॥

ya eka īśo nija-māyayā naḥ
sasarja yenānusṛjāma viśvam
vayaṁ na yasyāpi puraḥ samīhataḥ
paśyāma liṅgaṁ pṛthag īśa-māninaḥ

yaḥ—He who; *ekaḥ*—one; *īśaḥ*—controller; *nija-māyayā*—by His transcendental potency; *naḥ*—us; *sasarja*—created; *yena*—by whom (through whose mercy); *anusṛjāma*—we also create; *viśvam*—the universe; *vayam*—we; *na*—not; *yasya*—of whom; *api*—although; *puraḥ*—in front of us; *samīhataḥ*—of Him who is acting; *paśyāma*—see; *liṅgam*—the form; *pṛthak*—separate; *īśa*—as controllers; *māninaḥ*—thinking of ourselves.

TRANSLATION

The Supreme Personality of Godhead, who created us by His external potency and by whose mercy we expand the creation of the universe, is always situated before us as the Supersoul, but we cannot see His form. We are unable to see Him because all of us think that we are separate and independent gods.

PURPORT

Here is an explanation of why the conditioned soul cannot see the Supreme Personality of Godhead face to face. Even though the Lord appears before us as Lord Kṛṣṇa or Lord Rāmacandra and lives in human society as a leader or king, the conditioned soul cannot understand Him. *Avajānanti māṁ mūḍhā mānuṣīṁ tanum āśritam:* rascals (*mūḍhas*) deride the Supreme Personality of Godhead, thinking Him an ordinary human being. However insignificant we are, we think that we are also God, that we can create a universe or that we can create another God. This is why we cannot see or understand the Supreme Personality of Godhead. In this regard, Śrīla Madhvācārya says:

liṅgam eva paśyāmaḥ
kadācid abhimānas tu

devānām api sann iva
prāyaḥ kāleṣu nāsty eva
tāratamyena so 'pi tu

We are all conditioned to various degrees, but we think that we are God. This is why we cannot understand who God is or see Him face to face.

TEXTS 26-27

यो नः सपत्नैर्भृशमर्द्यमानान्
देवर्षितिर्यङ्नृषु नित्य एव ।
कृतावतारस्तनुभिः स्वमायया
कृत्वात्मसात् पाति युगे युगे च ॥२६॥
तमेव देवं वयमात्मदैवतं
परं प्रधानं पुरुषं विश्वमन्यम् ।
व्रजाम सर्वे शरणं शरण्यं
स्वानां स नो धास्यति शं महात्मा॥२७॥

yo naḥ sapatnair bhṛśam ardyamānān
devarṣi-tiryaṅ-nṛṣu nitya eva
kṛtāvatāras tanubhiḥ sva-māyayā
kṛtvātmasāt pāti yuge yuge ca

tam eva devaṁ vayam ātma-daivataṁ
paraṁ pradhānaṁ puruṣaṁ viśvam anyam
vrajāma sarve śaraṇaṁ śaraṇyaṁ
svānāṁ sa no dhāsyati śaṁ mahātmā

yaḥ—He who; *naḥ*—us; *sapatnaiḥ*—by our enemies, the demons; *bhṛśam*—almost always; *ardyamānān*—being persecuted; *deva*—among the demigods; *ṛṣi*—the saintly persons; *tiryak*—the animals; *nṛṣu*—and men; *nityaḥ*—always; *eva*—certainly; *kṛta-avatāraḥ*—appearing as an incarnation; *tanubhiḥ*—with different forms; *sva-māyayā*—by His internal potency; *kṛtvā ātmasāt*—considering very near and dear to Him; *pāti*—protects; *yuge yuge*—in every millennium;

ca—and; *tam*—Him; *eva*—indeed; *devam*—the Supreme Lord; *vayam*—all of us; *ātma-daivatam*—the Lord of all living entities; *param*—transcendental; *pradhānam*—the original cause of the total material energy; *puruṣam*—the supreme enjoyer; *viśvam*—whose energy constitutes this universe; *anyam*—separately situated; *vrajāma*—we approach; *sarve*—all; *śaraṇam*—shelter; *śaraṇyam*—suitable as shelter; *svānām*—unto His own devotees; *saḥ*—He; *naḥ*—unto us; *dhāsyati*—shall give; *śam*—good fortune; *mahātmā*—the Supersoul.

TRANSLATION

By His inconceivable internal potency, the Supreme Personality of Godhead expands into various transcendental bodies as Vāmanadeva, the incarnation of strength among the demigods; Paraśurāma, the incarnation among saints; Nṛsiṁhadeva and Varāha, incarnations among animals; and Matsya and Kūrma, incarnations among aquatics. He accepts various transcendental bodies among all types of living entities, and among human beings He especially appears as Lord Kṛṣṇa and Lord Rāma. By His causeless mercy, He protects the demigods, who are always harassed by the demons. He is the supreme worshipable Deity of all living entities. He is the supreme cause, represented as the male and female creative energies. Although different from this universe, He exists in His universal form [virāṭa-rūpa]. In our fearful condition, let us take shelter of Him, for we are sure that the Supreme Lord, the Supreme Soul, will give us His protection.

PURPORT

In this verse, the Supreme Personality of Godhead, Viṣṇu, is ascertained to be the original cause of creation. Śrīdhara Svāmī, in his commentary *Bhāvārtha-dīpikā*, replies to the idea that *prakṛti* and *puruṣa* are the causes of the cosmic manifestation. As stated herein, *paraṁ pradhānaṁ puruṣaṁ viśvam anyam:* "He is the supreme cause, represented as the male and female creative energies. Although different from this universe, He exists in His universal form [*virāṭa-rūpa*]." The word *prakṛti*, which is used to indicate the source of generation, refers to the material energy of the Supreme Lord, and the word *puruṣa* refers to the living entities, who are the superior energy of the Lord. Both the *prakṛti* and *puruṣa* ultimately enter the Supreme Lord, as stated in *Bhagavad-gītā* (*prakṛtiṁ yānti māmikām*).

Although *prakṛti* and *puruṣa* superficially appear to be the causes of the material manifestation, both are emanations of different energies of the Supreme Lord. Therefore the Supreme Lord is the cause of *prakṛti* and *puruṣa*. He is the original cause (*sarva-kāraṇa-kāraṇam*). The *Nāradīya Purāṇa* says:

avikāro 'pi paramaḥ
prakṛtis tu vikāriṇī
anupraviśya govindaḥ
prakṛtiś cābhidhīyate

Both the *prakṛti* and *puruṣa*, which are inferior and superior energies, are emanations from the Supreme Personality of Godhead. As explained in *Bhagavad-gītā* (*gām āviśya*), the Lord enters the *prakṛti*, and then the *prakṛti* creates different manifestations. The *prakṛti* is not independent or beyond His energies. Vāsudeva, Lord Śrī Kṛṣṇa, is the original cause of everything. Therefore the Lord says in *Bhagavad-gītā* (10.8):

ahaṁ sarvasya prabhavo
mattaḥ sarvaṁ pravartate
iti matvā bhajante māṁ
budhā bhāva-samanvitāḥ

"I am the source of all spiritual and material worlds. Everything emanates from Me. The wise who perfectly know this engage in My devotional service and worship Me with all their hearts." In *Śrīmad-Bhāgavatam* (2.9.33) the Lord also says, *aham evāsam evāgre:* "Only I existed before the creation." This is confirmed in the *Brahmāṇḍa Purāṇa* as follows:

smṛtir avyavadhānena
prakṛtitvam iti sthitiḥ
ubhayātmaka-sūtitvād
vāsudevaḥ paraḥ pumān
prakṛtiḥ puruṣaś ceti
śabdair eko 'bhidhīyate

To generate the universe, the Lord acts indirectly as the *puruṣa* and directly as the *prakṛti.* Because both energies emanate from Lord Vāsudeva, the all-pervasive Supreme Personality of Godhead, He is known as both *prakṛti* and *puruṣa.* Therefore Vāsudeva is the cause of everything (*sarva-kāraṇa-kāraṇam*).

TEXT 28

श्रीशुक उवाच
इति तेषां महाराज सुराणामुपतिष्ठताम् ।
प्रतीच्यां दिश्यभूदाविः शङ्खचक्रगदाधरः ॥२८॥

śrī-śuka uvāca
iti teṣāṁ mahārāja
surāṇām upatiṣṭhatām
pratīcyāṁ diśy abhūd āviḥ
śaṅkha-cakra-gadā-dharaḥ

śrī-śukaḥ uvāca—Śrī Śukadeva Gosvāmī said; *iti*—thus; *teṣām*—of them; *mahārāja*—O King; *surāṇām*—of the demigods; *upatiṣṭhatām*—praying; *pratīcyām*—inside; *diśi*—in the direction; *abhūt*—became; *āviḥ*—visible; *śaṅkha-cakra-gadā-dharaḥ*—bearing the transcendental weapons: the conchshell, disc and club.

TRANSLATION

Śrī Śukadeva Gosvāmī said: My dear King, when all the demigods offered Him their prayers, the Supreme Personality of Godhead, Lord Hari, carrying His weapons, the conchshell, disc and club, appeared first within their hearts and then before them.

TEXTS 29–30

आत्मतुल्यैः षोडशभिर्विना श्रीवत्सकौस्तुभौ ।
पर्युपासितमुन्निद्रशरदम्बुरुहेक्षणम् ॥२९॥
दृष्ट्वा तमवनौ सर्व ईक्षणाह्लादविक्लवाः ।
दण्डवत् पतिता राजञ्छनैरुत्थाय तुष्टुवुः ॥३०॥

ātma-tulyaiḥ ṣoḍaśabhir
vinā śrīvatsa-kaustubhau
paryupāsitam unnidra-
śarad-amburuhekṣaṇam

dṛṣṭvā tam avanau sarva
īkṣaṇāhlāda-viklavāḥ
daṇḍavat patitā rājañ
chanair utthāya tuṣṭuvuḥ

ātma-tulyaiḥ—almost equal to Himself; *ṣoḍaśabhiḥ*—by sixteen (servants); *vinā*—without; *śrīvatsa-kaustubhau*—the Śrīvatsa mark and Kaustubha jewel; *paryupāsitam*—being attended on all sides; *unnidra*—blooming; *śarat*—of the autumn; *amburuha*—like lotus flowers; *īkṣaṇam*—having eyes; *dṛṣṭvā*—seeing; *tam*—Him (the Supreme Personality of Godhead, Nārāyaṇa); *avanau*—on the ground; *sarve*—all of them; *īkṣaṇa*—from directly seeing; *āhlāda*—with happiness; *viklavāḥ*—being overwhelmed; *daṇḍa-vat*—like a stick; *patitāḥ*—fell; *rājan*—O King; *śanaiḥ*—slowly; *utthāya*—standing up; *tuṣṭuvuḥ*—offered prayers.

TRANSLATION

Surrounding and serving the Supreme Personality of Godhead, Nārāyaṇa, were sixteen personal attendants, decorated with ornaments and appearing exactly like Him but without the mark of Śrīvatsa and the Kaustubha jewel. O King, when all the demigods saw the Supreme Lord in that posture, smiling with eyes like the petals of lotuses grown in autumn, they were overwhelmed with happiness and immediately fell down like rods, offering daṇḍavats. Then they slowly rose and pleased the Lord by offering Him prayers.

PURPORT

In Vaikuṇṭhaloka the Supreme Personality of Godhead has four hands and decorations like the Śrīvatsa mark on His chest and the gem known as Kaustubha. These are special indications of the Supreme Personality of Godhead. The Lord's personal attendants and other devotees in Vaikuṇṭha have the same features, except for the Śrīvatsa mark and the Kaustubha gem.

TEXT 31

श्रीदेवा ऊचुः
नमस्ते यज्ञवीर्याय वयसे उत ते नमः ।
नमस्ते ह्यस्तचक्राय नमः सुपुरुहूतये ॥३१॥

śrī-devā ūcuḥ
namas te yajña-vīryāya
vayase uta te namaḥ
namas te hy asta-cakrāya
namaḥ supuru-hūtaye

śrī-devāḥ ūcuḥ—the demigods said; *namaḥ*—obeisances; *te*—unto You; *yajña-vīryāya*—unto the Supreme Personality of Godhead, who is able to give the results of sacrifice; *vayase*—who is the time factor, which ends the results of *yajña; uta*—although; *te*—unto You; *namaḥ*—obeisances; *namaḥ*—obeisances; *te*—unto You; *hi*—indeed; *asta-cakrāya*—who throws the disc; *namaḥ*—respectful obeisances; *supuru-hūtaye*—having varieties of transcendental names.

TRANSLATION

The demigods said: O Supreme Personality of Godhead, You are competent to give the results of sacrifice, and You are also the time factor that destroys all such results in due course. You are the one who releases the cakra to kill the demons. O Lord, who possesses many varieties of names, we offer our respectful obeisances unto You.

TEXT 32

यत् ते गतीनां तिसृणामीशितुः परमं पदम् ।
नार्वाचीनो विसर्गस्य धातर्वेदितुमर्हति ॥३२॥

yat te gatīnāṁ tisṛṇām
īśituḥ paramaṁ padam
nārvācīno visargasya
dhātar veditum arhati

yat—which; *te*—of You; *gatīnām tisṛṇām*—of the three destinations (the heavenly planets, the earthly planets and hell); *īśituḥ*—who are the controller; *paramam padam*—the supreme abode, Vaikuṇṭhaloka; *na*—not; *arvācīnaḥ*—a person appearing after; *visargasya*—the creation; *dhātaḥ*—O supreme controller; *veditum*—to understand; *arhati*—is able.

TRANSLATION

O supreme controller, You control the three destinations [promotion to the heavenly planets, birth as a human being, and condemnation in hell], yet Your supreme abode is Vaikuṇṭhadhāma. Since we appeared after You created this cosmic manifestation, Your activities are impossible for us to understand. We therefore have nothing to offer You but our humble obeisances.

PURPORT

An inexperienced man generally does not know what to beg from the Supreme Personality of Godhead. Everyone is under the jurisdiction of the created material world, and no one knows what benediction to ask when praying to the Supreme Lord. People generally pray to be promoted to the heavenly planets because they have no information of Vaikuṇṭhaloka. Śrīla Madhvācārya quotes the following verse:

deva-lokāt pitṛ-lokāt
nirayāc cāpi yat param
tisṛbhyaḥ paramaṁ sthānaṁ
vaiṣṇavaṁ viduṣāṁ gatiḥ

There are different planetary systems, known as Devaloka (the planets of the demigods), Pitṛloka (the planet of the Pitās) and Niraya (the hellish planets). When one transcends these various planetary systems and enters Vaikuṇṭhaloka, he achieves the ultimate resort of the Vaiṣṇavas. Vaiṣṇavas have nothing to do with the other planetary systems.

TEXT 33

ॐ नमस्तेऽस्तु भगवन् नारायण वासुदेवादिपुरुष महापुरुष महानुभाव परममङ्गल परमकल्याण परमकारुणिक केवल जगदाधार लोकैकनाथ सर्वेश्वर लक्ष्मीनाथ परमहंसपरिव्राजकैः परमेणात्मयोगसमाधिना परिभावितपरिस्फुटपारमहंस्यधर्मेणोद्घाटिततमःकपाटद्वारे चित्तेऽपावृत आत्मलोके स्वयमुपलब्धनिजसुखानुभवो भवान् ॥ ३३ ॥

oṁ namas te 'stu bhagavan nārāyaṇa vāsudevādi-puruṣa mahā-puruṣa mahānubhāva parama-maṅgala parama-kalyāṇa parama-kāruṇika kevala jagad-ādhāra lokaika-nātha sarveśvara lakṣmī-nātha paramahaṁsa-parivrājakaiḥ parameṇātma-yoga-samādhinā paribhāvita-parisphuṭa-pāramahaṁsya-dharmeṇodghāṭita-tamaḥ-kapāṭa-dvāre citte 'pāvṛta ātma-loke svayam upalabdha-nija-sukhānubhavo bhavān.

oṁ—O Lord; *namaḥ*—respectful obeisances; *te*—unto You; *astu*—let there be; *bhagavan*—O Supreme Personality of Godhead; *nārāyaṇa*—the resort of all living entities, Nārāyaṇa; *vāsudeva*—Lord Vāsudeva, Śrī Kṛṣṇa; *ādi-puruṣa*—the original person; *mahā-puruṣa*—the most exalted personality; *mahā-anubhāva*—the supremely opulent; *parama-maṅgala*—the most auspicious; *parama-kalyāṇa*—the supreme benediction; *parama-kāruṇika*—the supremely merciful; *kevala*—changeless; *jagat-ādhāra*—the support of the cosmic manifestation; *loka-eka-nātha*—the only proprietor of all the planetary systems; *sarva-īśvara*—the supreme controller; *lakṣmī-nātha*—the husband of the goddess of fortune; *paramahaṁsa-parivrājakaiḥ*—by the topmost *sannyāsīs* wandering all over the world; *parameṇa*—by supreme; *ātma-yoga-samādhinā*—absorption in *bhakti-yoga; paribhāvita*—fully purified; *parisphuṭa*—and fully manifested; *pāramahaṁsya-dharmeṇa*—by executing the transcendental process of devotional service; *udghāṭita*—pushed open; *tamaḥ*—of illusory existence; *kapāṭa*—in which the door; *dvāre*—existing as the entrance; *citte*—in the mind; *apāvṛte*—without contamination; *ātma-loke*—in the spiritual world; *svayam*—personally; *upalabdha*—experiencing; *nija*—personal; *sukha-anubhavaḥ*—perception of happiness; *bhavān*—Your Lordship.

TRANSLATION

O Supreme Personality of Godhead, O Nārāyaṇa, O Vāsudeva, original person! O most exalted person, supreme experience, welfare personified! O supreme benediction, supremely merciful and changeless! O support of the cosmic manifestation, sole proprietor of all planetary systems, master of everything and husband of the goddess of fortune! Your Lordship is realized by the topmost sannyāsīs, who wander about the world to preach Kṛṣṇa consciousness, fully absorbed in samādhi through bhakti-yoga. Because their minds are concentrated upon You, they can receive the conception of Your personality in their fully purified hearts. When the darkness in their hearts is completely eradicated and You are revealed to them, the transcendental bliss they enjoy is the transcendental form of Your Lordship. No one but such persons can realize You. Therefore we simply offer You our respectful obeisances.

PURPORT

The Supreme Personality of Godhead has numerous transcendental names pertaining to different grades of revelation to various grades of devotees and transcendentalists. When He is realized in His impersonal form He is called the Supreme Brahman, when realized as the Paramātmā He is called *antaryāmī*, and when He expands Himself in different forms for material creation He is called Kṣīrodakaśāyī Viṣṇu, Garbhodakaśāyī Viṣṇu and Kāraṇodakaśāyī Viṣṇu. When He is realized as Vāsudeva, Saṅkarṣaṇa, Pradyumna and Aniruddha—the Caturvyūha, who are beyond the three forms of Viṣṇu—He is the Vaikuṇṭha Nārāyaṇa. Above realization of Nārāyaṇa is realization of Baladeva, and above that is realization of Kṛṣṇa. All these realizations are possible when one engages fully in devotional service. The covered core of one's heart is then completely open to receiving an understanding of the Supreme Personality of Godhead in His various forms.

TEXT 34

दुरवबोध इव तवायं विहारयोगो यदशरणोऽशरीर इदमनवेक्षितास्मत्समवाय
आत्मनैवाविक्रियमाणेन सगुणमगुणः सृजसि पासि हरसि ॥ ३४ ॥

duravabodha iva tavāyaṁ vihāra-yogo yad aśaraṇo 'śarīra idam
anavekṣitāsmat-samavāya ātmanaivāvikriyamāṇena saguṇam aguṇaḥ
sṛjasi pāsi harasi.

duravabodhaḥ—difficult to understand; *iva*—quite; *tava*—Your; *ayam*—this; *vihāra-yogaḥ*—engagement in the pastimes of material creation, maintenance and annihilation; *yat*—which; *aśaraṇaḥ*—not dependent on any other support; *aśarīraḥ*—without having a material body; *idam*—this; *anavekṣita*—without waiting for; *asmat*—of us; *samavāyaḥ*—the cooperation; *ātmanā*—by Your own self; *eva*—indeed; *avikriyamāṇena*—without being transformed; *sa-guṇam*—the material modes of nature; *aguṇaḥ*—although transcendental to such material qualities; *sṛjasi*—You create; *pāsi*—maintain; *harasi*—annihilate.

TRANSLATION

O Lord, You need no support, and although You have no material body, You do not need cooperation from us. Since You are the cause of the cosmic manifestation and You supply its material ingredients without being transformed, You create, maintain and annihilate this cosmic manifestation by Yourself. Nevertheless, although You appear engaged in material activity, You are transcendental to all material qualities. Consequently these transcendental activities of Yours are extremely difficult to understand.

PURPORT

The *Brahma-saṁhitā* (5.37) says, *goloka eva nivasaty akhilātma-bhūtaḥ:* the Supreme Personality of Godhead, Kṛṣṇa, is always situated in Goloka Vṛndāvana. It is also said, *vṛndāvanaṁ parityajya padam ekaṁ na gacchati:* Kṛṣṇa never goes even a step from Vṛndāvana. Nevertheless, although Kṛṣṇa is situated in His own abode, Goloka Vṛndāvana, He is simultaneously all-pervading and is therefore present everywhere. This is very difficult for a conditioned soul to understand, but devotees can understand how Kṛṣṇa, without undergoing any changes, can simultaneously be in His abode and be all-pervasive. The demigods are understood to be various limbs of the Supreme Lord's body, although the Supreme Lord has no material body and does not need anyone's help. He is spread everywhere (*mayā tatam idaṁ sarvaṁ jagad avyakta-mūrtinā*). Nevertheless, He is not present everywhere in His spiritual form. According to the Māyāvāda philosophy, the Supreme Truth, being all-pervasive, does not need a transcendental form. The Māyāvādīs suppose that since His form is distributed everywhere, He has no form. This is untrue. The Lord keeps His transcendental form, and at the same time He extends everywhere, in every nook and corner of the material creation.

TEXT 35

**अथ तत्र भवान् किं देवदत्तवदिह गुणविसर्गपतितः पारतन्त्र्येण स्वकृतकुशला-
कुशलं फलमुपाददात्याहोस्विदात्माराम उपशमशीलः समञ्जसदर्शन उदास्त इति
ह वाव न विदामः ॥ ३५ ॥**

atha tatra bhavān kiṁ devadattavad iha guṇa-visarga-patitaḥ pāratantryeṇa sva-kṛta-kuśalākuśalaṁ phalam upādadāty āhosvid ātmārāma upaśama-śīlaḥ samañjasa-darśana udāsta iti ha vāva na vidāmaḥ.

atha—therefore; *tatra*—in that; *bhavān*—Your Lordship; *kim*—whether; *deva-datta-vat*—like an ordinary human being, forced by the fruits of his activities; *iha*—in this material world; *guṇa-visarga-patitaḥ*—fallen in a material body impelled by the modes of material nature; *pāratantryeṇa*—by dependence on the conditions of time, space, activity and nature; *sva-kṛta*—executed by oneself; *kuśala*—auspicious; *akuśalam*—inauspicious; *phalam*—results of action; *upādadāti*—accepts; *āhosvit*—or; *ātmārāmaḥ*—completely self-satisfied; *upaśama-śīlaḥ*—self-controlled in nature; *samañjasa-darśanaḥ*—not deprived of full spiritual potencies; *udāste*—remains neutral as the witness; *iti*—thus; *ha vāva*—certainly; *na vidāmaḥ*—we do not understand.

TRANSLATION

These are our inquiries. The ordinary conditioned soul is subject to the material laws, and he thus receives the fruits of his actions. Does Your Lordship, like an ordinary human being, exist

within this material world in a body produced by the material modes? Do You enjoy or suffer the good or bad results of actions under the influence of time, past work and so forth? Or, on the contrary, are You present here only as a neutral witness who is self-sufficient, free from all material desires, and always full of spiritual potency? We certainly cannot understand Your actual position.

PURPORT

In *Bhagavad-gītā* Kṛṣṇa says that He descends to this material world for two purposes, namely *paritrāṇāya sādhūnāṁ vināśāya ca duṣkṛtām*—to relieve the devotees and kill demons or nondevotees. These two kinds of action are the same for the Absolute Truth. When the Lord comes to punish the demons, He bestows His favor upon them, and similarly when He delivers His devotees and gives them relief, He also bestows His favor. Thus the Lord bestows His favor equally upon the conditioned souls. When a conditioned soul gives relief to others he acts piously, and when he gives trouble to others he acts impiously, but the Lord is neither pious nor impious; He is always full in His spiritual potency, by which He shows equal mercy to the punishable and the protectable. The Lord is *apāpa-viddham;* He is never contaminated by the reactions of so-called sinful activities. When Kṛṣṇa was present on this earth, He killed many inimical nondevotees, but they all received *sārūpya;* in other words, they returned to their original spiritual bodies. One who does not know the Lord's position says that God is unkind to him but merciful to others. Actually the Lord says in *Bhagavad-gītā* (9.29), *samo 'haṁ sarva-bhūteṣu na me dveṣyo 'sti na priyaḥ:* "I am equal to everyone. No one is My enemy, and no one is My friend." But He also says, *ye bhajanti tu māṁ bhaktyā mayi te teṣu cāpy aham:* "If one becomes My devotee and fully surrenders unto Me, I give him special attention."

TEXT 36

न हि विरोध उभयं भगवत्यपरिमितगुणगण ईश्वरेऽनवगाह्यमाहात्म्येऽर्वाची-
नविकल्पवितर्कविचारप्रमाणाभासकुतर्कशास्त्रकलिलान्तःकरणाश्रयदुरवग्रहवादि-

नां विवादानवसर उपरतसमस्तमायामये केवल एवात्ममायामन्तर्धाय को न्वर्थो दुर्घट इव भवति स्वरूपद्वयाभावात् ॥ ३६ ॥

na hi virodha ubhayaṁ bhagavaty aparimita-guṇa-gaṇa īśvare
'navagāhya-māhātmye 'rvācīna-vikalpa-vitarka-vicāra-pramāṇābhāsa-
kutarka-śāstra-kalilāntaḥkaraṇāśraya-duravagraha-vādināṁ
vivādānavasara uparata-samasta-māyāmaye kevala evātma-māyām
antardhāya ko nv artho durghaṭa iva bhavati svarūpa-dvayābhāvāt.

na—not; *hi*—certainly; *virodhaḥ*—contradiction; *ubhayam*—both; *bhagavati*—in the Supreme Personality of Godhead; *aparimita*—unlimited; *guṇa-gaṇe*—whose transcendental attributes; *īśvare*—in the supreme controller; *anavagāhya*—possessing; *māhātmye*—unfathomable ability and glories; *arvācīna*—recent; *vikalpa*—full of equivocal calculations; *vitarka*—opposing arguments; *vicāra*—judgments; *pramāṇa-ābhāsa*—imperfect evidence; *kutarka*—useless arguments; *śāstra*—by unauthorized scriptures; *kalila*—agitated; *antaḥkaraṇa*—minds; *āśraya*—whose shelter; *duravagraha*—with wicked obstinacies; *vādinām*—of theorists; *vivāda*—of the controversies; *anavasare*—not within the range; *uparata*—withdrawn; *samasta*—from whom all; *māyā-maye*—illusory energy; *kevale*—without a second; *eva*—indeed; *ātma-māyām*—the illusory energy, which can do and undo the inconceivable; *antardhāya*—placing between; *kaḥ*—what; *nu*—indeed; *arthaḥ*—meaning; *durghaṭaḥ*—impossible; *iva*—as it were; *bhavati*—is; *sva-rūpa*—natures; *dvaya*—of two; *abhāvāt*—due to the absence.

TRANSLATION

O Supreme Personality of Godhead, all contradictions can be reconciled in You. O Lord, since You are the Supreme Person, the reservoir of unlimited spiritual qualities, the supreme controller, Your unlimited glories are inconceivable to the conditioned souls. Many modern theologians argue about right and wrong without knowing what is actually right. Their arguments are always false and their judgments inconclusive because they have no authorized evidence with which to gain knowledge of You. Because their minds are agitated by scriptures containing false conclusions, they

are unable to understand the truth concerning You. Furthermore, because of polluted eagerness to arrive at the right conclusion, their theories are incapable of revealing You, who are transcendental to their material conceptions. You are one without a second, and therefore in You contradictions like doing and not doing, happiness and distress, are not contradictory. Your potency is so great that it can do and undo anything as You like. With the help of that potency, what is impossible for You? Since there is no duality in Your constitutional position, You can do everything by the influence of Your energy.

PURPORT

The Supreme Personality of Godhead, being self-sufficient, is full of transcendental bliss (*ātmārāma*). He enjoys bliss in two ways—when He appears happy and when He appears distressed. Distinctions and contradictions are impossible in Him because only from Him have they emanated. The Supreme Personality of Godhead is the reservoir of all knowledge, all potency, all strength, opulence and influence. There is no limit to His powers. Since He is full in all transcendental attributes, nothing abominable from the material world can exist in Him. He is transcendental and spiritual, and therefore conceptions of material happiness and distress do not apply to Him.

We should not be astonished to find contradictions in the Supreme Personality of Godhead. Actually there are no contradictions. That is the meaning of His being supreme. Because He is all-powerful, He is not subject to the conditioned soul's arguments regarding His existence or nonexistence. He is pleased to protect His devotees by killing their enemies. He enjoys both the killing and the protecting.

Such freedom from duality applies not only to the Lord but also to His devotees. In Vṛndāvana, the damsels of Vrajabhūmi enjoy transcendental bliss in the company of the Supreme Personality of Godhead, Kṛṣṇa, and they feel the same transcendental bliss in separation when Kṛṣṇa and Balarāma leave Vṛndāvana for Mathurā. There is no question of material pains or pleasures for either the Supreme Personality of Godhead or His pure devotees, although they are sometimes superficially said to be distressed or happy. One who is *ātmārāma* is blissful in both ways.

Nondevotees cannot understand the contradictions present in the Supreme Lord or His devotees. Therefore in *Bhagavad-gītā* the Lord says, *bhaktyā mām abhijānāti:* the transcendental pastimes can be understood through devotional service; to nondevotees they are inconceivable. *Acintyāḥ khalu ye bhāvā na tāṁs tarkeṇa yojayet:* the Supreme Lord and His form, name, pastimes and paraphernalia are inconceivable to nondevotees, and one should not try to understand such realities simply by logical arguments. They will not bring one to the right conclusion about the Absolute Truth.

TEXT 37

समविषममतीनां मतमनुसरसि यथा रज्जुखण्डः सर्पादिधियाम् ॥ ३७॥

sama-viṣama-matīnāṁ matam anusarasi yathā rajju-khaṇḍaḥ sarpādi-dhiyām.

sama—equal or proper; *viṣama*—and unequal or mistaken; *matīnām*—of those having intelligence; *matam*—conclusion; *anusarasi*—You follow; *yathā*—just as; *rajju-khaṇḍaḥ*—a piece of rope; *sarpa-ādi*—a snake, etc.; *dhiyām*—of those who perceive.

TRANSLATION

A rope causes fear for a bewildered person who considers it a snake, but not for a person with proper intelligence who knows it to be only a rope. Similarly, You, as the Supersoul in everyone's heart, inspire fear or fearlessness according to one's intelligence, but in You there is no duality.

PURPORT

In *Bhagavad-gītā* (4.11) the Lord says, *ye yathā māṁ prapadyante tāṁs tathaiva bhajāmy aham:* "As one surrenders unto Me, I reward him accordingly." The Supreme Personality of Godhead is the reservoir of everything, including all knowledge, all truth and all contradictions. The example cited herein is very appropriate. A rope is one truth, but some mistake it for a snake, whereas others know it to be a rope. Similarly, devotees who know the Supreme Personality of Godhead do not see contradictions in Him, but nondevotees regard Him as the snakelike source of all fear. For example, when Nṛsiṁhadeva appeared, Prahlāda Mahārāja saw the Lord as the supreme solace, whereas his father, a demon, saw Him as the ultimate death. As stated in *Śrīmad-Bhāgavatam* (11.2.37), *bhayaṁ dvitīyābhiniveśataḥ syāt:* fear results from being absorbed in duality. When one is in knowledge of duality, one knows both fear and bliss. The same Supreme Lord is a source of bliss to devotees and fear to nondevotees who have a poor fund of knowledge. God is one, but people understand the Absolute Truth from different angles of vision. The unintelligent see contradictions in Him, but sober devotees find no contradictions.

TEXT 38

स एव हि पुनः सर्ववस्तुनि वस्तुस्वरूपः सर्वेश्वरः सकलजगत्कारणकारणभूतः सर्वप्रत्यगात्मत्वात् सर्वगुणाभासोपलक्षित एक एव पर्यवशेषितः ॥ ३८ ॥

sa eva hi punaḥ sarva-vastuni vastu-svarūpaḥ sarveśvaraḥ sakala-jagat-kāraṇa-kāraṇa-bhūtaḥ sarva-pratyag-ātmatvāt sarva-guṇābhāsopalakṣita eka eva paryavaśeṣitaḥ.

saḥ—He (the Supreme Personality of Godhead); *eva*—indeed; *hi*—certainly; *punaḥ*—again; *sarva-vastuni*—in everything, material and spiritual; *vastu-svarūpaḥ*—the substance; *sarva-īśvaraḥ*—the controller of everything; *sakala-jagat*—of the whole universe; *kāraṇa*—of the causes; *kāraṇa-bhūtaḥ*—existing as the cause; *sarva-pratyak-ātmat-vāt*—because of being the Supersoul of every living being, or being present in everything, even the atom; *sarva-guṇa*—of all the effects of the material modes of nature (such as intelligence and the senses); *ābhāsa*—by the manifestations; *upalakṣitaḥ*—perceived; *ekaḥ*—alone; *eva*—indeed; *paryavaśeṣitaḥ*—left remaining.

TRANSLATION

With deliberation, one will see that the Supreme Soul, although manifested in different ways, is actually the basic principle of everything. The total material energy is the cause of the material manifestation, but the material energy is caused by Him.

Therefore He is the cause of all causes, the manifester of intelligence and the senses. He is perceived as the Supersoul of everything. Without Him, everything would be dead. You, as that Supersoul, the supreme controller, are the only one remaining.

PURPORT

The words *sarva-vastuni vastu-svarūpaḥ* indicate that the Supreme Lord is the active principle of everything. As described in the *Brahma-saṁhitā* (5.35):

eko 'py asau racayituṁ jagad-aṇḍa-koṭiṁ
yac-chaktir asti jagad-aṇḍa-cayā yad-antaḥ
aṇḍāntara-stha-paramāṇu-cayāntara-sthaṁ
govindam ādi-puruṣaṁ tam ahaṁ bhajāmi

"I worship the Personality of Godhead, Govinda, who enters the existence of every universe and every atom by one of His plenary portions and thus manifests His infinite energy throughout the material creation." By His one plenary portion as Paramātmā, *antaryāmī*, the Lord is all-pervading throughout the unlimited universes. He is the *pratyak*, or *antaryāmī*, of all living entities. The Lord says in *Bhagavad-gītā* (13.3), *kṣetrajñaṁ cāpi māṁ viddhi sarva-kṣetreṣu bhārata:* "O scion of Bharata, you should understand that I am also the knower in all bodies." Because the Lord is the Supersoul, He is the active principle of every living entity and even the atom (*aṇḍāntara-stha-paramāṇu-cayāntara-stham*). He is the actual reality. According to various stages of intelligence, one realizes the presence of the Supreme in everything through the manifestations of His energy. The entire world is permeated by the three *guṇas*, and one can understand His presence according to one's modes of material nature.

TEXT 39

अथ ह वाव तव महिमामृतरससमुद्रविप्रुषा सकृदवलीढया स्वमनसि निष्यन्द-
मानानवरतसुखेन विस्मारितदृष्टश्रुतविषयसुखलेशाभासाः परमभागवता
एकान्तिनो भगवति सर्वभूतप्रियसुहृदि सर्वात्मनि नितरां निरन्तरं निर्वृत-

मनसः कथमु ह वा एते मधुमथन पुनः स्वार्थकुशला ह्यात्मप्रियसुहृदः साधवस्त्वच्चरणाम्बुजानुसेवां विसृजन्ति न यत्र पुनरयं संसारपर्यावर्तः ॥ ३९ ॥

atha ha vāva tava mahimāmṛta-rasa-samudra-vipruṣā sakṛd avalīḍhayā sva-manasi niṣyandamānānavarata-sukhena vismārita-dṛṣṭa-śruta-viṣaya-sukha-leśābhāsāḥ parama-bhāgavatā ekāntino bhagavati sarva-bhūta-priya-suhṛdi sarvātmani nitarāṁ nirantaraṁ nirvṛta-manasaḥ katham u ha vā ete madhumathana punaḥ svārtha-kuśalā hy ātma-priya-suhṛdaḥ sādhavas tvac-caraṇāmbujānusevāṁ visṛjanti na yatra punar ayaṁ saṁsāra-paryāvartaḥ.

atha ha—therefore; *vāva*—indeed; *tava*—Your; *mahima*—of glories; *amṛta*—of the nectar; *rasa*—of the mellow; *samudra*—of the ocean; *vipruṣā*—by a drop; *sakṛt*—only once; *avalīḍhayā*—tasted; *sva-manasi*—in his mind; *niṣyandamāna*—flowing; *anavarata*—continuously; *sukhena*—by the transcendental bliss; *vismārita*—forgotten; *dṛṣṭa*—from material sight; *śruta*—and sound; *viṣaya-sukha*—of the material happiness; *leśa-ābhāsāḥ*—the dim reflection of a tiny portion; *parama-bhāgavatāḥ*—great, exalted devotees; *ekāntinaḥ*—who have faith only in the Supreme Lord and nothing else; *bhagavati*—in the Supreme Personality of Godhead; *sarva-bhūta*—to all living entities; *priya*—who is dearmost; *suhṛdi*—the friend; *sarva-ātmani*—the Supersoul of all; *nitarām*—completely; *nirantaram*—continuously; *nirvṛta*—with happiness; *manasaḥ*—those whose minds; *katham*—how; *u ha*—then; *vā*—or; *ete*—these; *madhu-mathana*—O killer of the Madhu demon; *punaḥ*—again; *sva-artha-kuśalāḥ*—who are expert in the interest of life; *hi*—indeed; *ātma-priya-suhṛdaḥ*—who have accepted You as the Supersoul, dearmost lover and friend; *sādhavaḥ*—the devotees; *tvat-caraṇa-ambuja-anusevām*—service to the lotus feet of Your Lordship; *visṛjanti*—can give up; *na*—not; *yatra*—wherein; *punaḥ*—again; *ayam*—this; *saṁsāra-paryāvartaḥ*—repetition of birth and death within the material world.

TRANSLATION

Therefore, O killer of the Madhu demon, incessant transcendental bliss flows in the minds of those who have even once tasted

but a drop of the nectar from the ocean of Your glories. Such exalted devotees forget the tiny reflection of so-called material happiness produced from the material senses of sight and sound. Free from all desires, such devotees are the real friends of all living entities. Offering their minds unto You and enjoying transcendental bliss, they are expert in achieving the real goal of life. O Lord, You are the soul and dear friend of such devotees, who never need return to this material world. How could they give up engagement in Your devotional service?

PURPORT

Although nondevotees, because of their meager knowledge and speculative habits, cannot understand the real nature of the Lord, a devotee who has once tasted the nectar from the Lord's lotus feet can realize what transcendental pleasure there is in the Lord's devotional service. A devotee knows that simply by rendering service to the Lord, he serves everyone. Therefore devotees are real friends to all living entities. Only a pure devotee can preach the glories of the Lord for the benefit of all conditioned souls.

TEXT 40

त्रिभुवनात्मभवन त्रिविक्रम त्रिनयन त्रिलोकमनोहरानुभाव तवैव विभूतयो दितिजदनुजादयश्चापि तेषामुपक्रमसमयोऽयमिति स्वात्ममायया सुरनरमृगमिश्रितजलचराकृतिभिर्यथापराधं दण्डं दण्डधर दधर्थ एवमेनमपि भगवञ्जहि त्वाष्ट्रमुत यदि मन्यसे ॥४०॥

tri-bhuvanātma-bhavana trivikrama tri-nayana tri-loka-manoharānubhāva tavaiva vibhūtayo ditija-danujādayaś cāpi teṣām upakrama-samayo 'yam iti svātma-māyayā sura-nara-mṛga-miśrita-jalacarākṛtibhir yathāparādhaṁ daṇḍaṁ daṇḍa-dhara dadhartha evam enam api bhagavañ jahi tvāṣṭram uta yadi manyase.

tri-bhuvana-ātma-bhavana—O Lord, You are the shelter of the three worlds because You are the Supersoul of the three worlds; *tri-vikrama*—O Lord, who assumes the form of Vāmana, Your power and opulence are distributed throughout the three worlds; *tri-nayana*—O maintainer and seer of the three worlds; *tri-loka-manohara-anubhāva*—O You who are perceived as the most beautiful within the three worlds; *tava*—of You; *eva*—certainly; *vibhūtayaḥ*—the expansions of energy; *diti-ja-danu-ja-ādayaḥ*—the demoniac sons of Diti, and the Dānavas, another type of demon; *ca*—and; *api*—also (the human beings); *teṣām*—of all of them; *upakrama-samayaḥ*—the time of enterprise; *ayam*—this; *iti*—thus; *sva-ātma-māyayā*—by Your own energy; *sura-nara-mṛga-miśrita-jalacara-ākṛtibhiḥ*—with different forms like those of the demigods, human beings, animals, mixtures and aquatics (the incarnations Vāmana, Lord Rāmacandra, Kṛṣṇa, Varāha, Hayagrīva, Nṛsiṁha, Matsya and Kūrma); *yathā-aparādham*—according to their offenses; *daṇḍam*—punishment; *daṇḍa-dhara*—O supreme chastiser; *dadhartha*—You awarded; *evam*—thus; *enam*—this one (Vṛtrāsura); *api*—also; *bhagavan*—O Supreme Personality of Godhead; *jahi*—kill; *tvāṣṭram*—the son of Tvaṣṭā; *uta*—indeed; *yadi manyase*—if You think it proper.

TRANSLATION

O Lord, O personified three worlds, father of the three worlds! O strength of the three worlds, in the form of the Vāmana incarnation! O three-eyed form of Nṛsiṁhadeva! O most beautiful person within the three worlds! Everything and everyone, including human beings and even the Daitya demons and the Dānavas, is but an expansion of Your energy. O supremely powerful one, You have always appeared in Your forms as the various incarnations to punish the demons as soon as they become very powerful. You appear as Lord Vāmanadeva, Lord Rāma and Lord Kṛṣṇa. You appear sometimes as an animal like Lord Boar, sometimes a mixed incarnation like Lord Nṛsiṁhadeva and Lord Hayagrīva, and sometimes an aquatic like Lord Fish and Lord Tortoise. Assuming such various forms, You have always punished the demons and Dānavas. We therefore pray that Your Lordship appear today as another incarnation, if You so desire, to kill the great demon Vṛtrāsura.

PURPORT

There are two kinds of devotees, known as *sakāma* and *akāma*. Pure devotees are *akāma*, whereas devotees in the upper planetary systems, such as the demigods, are called *sakāma* because they still want to enjoy material opulence. Because of their pious activities, the *sakāma* devotees are promoted to the higher planetary systems, but at heart they still desire to lord it over the material resources. The *sakāma* devotees are sometimes disturbed by the demons and Rākṣasas, but the Lord is so kind that He always saves them by appearing as an incarnation. The Lord's incarnations are so powerful that Lord Vāmanadeva covered the entire universe with two steps and therefore had no place for His third step. The Lord is called Trivikrama because He showed His strength by delivering the entire universe with merely three steps.

The difference between *sakāma* and *akāma* devotees is that when *sakāma* devotees, like the demigods, fall into difficulty, they approach the Supreme Personality of Godhead for relief, whereas *akāma* devotees, even in the greatest danger, never disturb the Lord for material benefits. Even if an *akāma* devotee is suffering, he thinks this is due to his past impious activities and agrees to suffer the consequences. He never disturbs the Lord. *Sakāma* devotees immediately pray to the Lord as soon as they are in difficulty, but they are regarded as pious because they consider themselves fully dependent on the mercy of the Lord. As stated in *Śrīmad-Bhāgavatam* (10.14.8):

tat te 'nukampāṁ susamīkṣamāṇo
bhuñjāna evātma-kṛtaṁ vipākam
hṛd-vāg-vapurbhir vidadhan namas te
jīveta yo mukti-pade sa dāya-bhāk

Even while suffering in the midst of difficulties, devotees simply offer their prayers and service more enthusiastically. In this way they become firmly fixed in devotional service and eligible to return home, back to Godhead, without a doubt. *Sakāma* devotees, of course, achieve from the Lord the results they desire from their prayers, but they do not immediately become fit to return to Godhead. It is to be noted herein that Lord Viṣṇu, in His various incarnations, is always the protector of His devotees. Śrīla Madhvācārya says: *vividhaṁ bhāva-pātratvāt sarve viṣṇor vibhūtayaḥ.* Kṛṣṇa is the original Personality of Godhead (*kṛṣṇas tu bhagavān svayam*). All the other incarnations proceed from Lord Viṣṇu.

TEXT 41

अस्माकं तावकानां ततत नतानां हरे तव चरणनलिनयुगलध्यानानु-
बद्धहृदयनिगडानां स्वलिङ्गविवरणेनात्मसात्कृतानामनुकम्पानुरञ्जितविशदरुचिर-
शिशिरस्मितावलोकेन विगलितमधुरमुखरसामृतकलया चान्तस्तापमनघार्हसि
शमयितुम् ॥४१॥

*asmākaṁ tāvakānāṁ tatatata natānāṁ hare tava caraṇa-nalina-
yugala-dhyānānubaddha-hṛdaya-nigaḍānāṁ sva-liṅga-
vivaraṇenātmasāt-kṛtānām anukampānurañjita-viśada-rucira-śiśira-
smitāvalokena vigalita-madhura-mukha-rasāmṛta-kalayā cāntas tāpam
anaghārhasi śamayitum.*

asmākam—of us; *tāvakānām*—who are wholly and solely dependent upon You; *tata-tata*—O grandfather, father of the father; *natānām*—who are fully surrendered unto You; *hare*—O Lord Hari; *tava*—Your; *caraṇa*—on the feet; *nalina-yugala*—like two blue lotus flowers; *dhyāna*—by meditation; *anubaddha*—bound; *hṛdaya*—in the heart; *nigaḍānām*—whose chains; *sva-liṅga-vivaraṇena*—by manifesting Your own form; *ātmasāt-kṛtānām*—of those You have accepted as Your own; *anukampā*—by compassion; *anurañjita*—being colored; *viśada*—bright; *rucira*—very pleasing; *śiśira*—cool; *smita*—with a smile; *avalokena*—by Your glance; *vigalita*—melted with compassion; *madhura-mukha-rasa*—of the very sweet words from Your mouth; *amṛta-kalayā*—by the drops of nectar; *ca*—and; *antaḥ*—within the cores of our hearts; *tāpam*—the great pain; *anagha*—O supreme pure; *arhasi*—You deserve; *śamayitum*—to curb.

TRANSLATION

O supreme protector, O grandfather, O supreme pure, O Lord! We are all surrendered souls at Your lotus feet. Indeed, our minds are bound to Your lotus feet in meditation by chains of love. Now please manifest Your incarnation. Accepting us as Your own eternal servants and devotees, be pleased with us and sympathetic toward us. By Your love-filled glance, with its cool and pleasing

smile of sympathy, and by the sweet, nectarean words emanating from Your beautiful face, free us from the anxiety caused by this Vṛtrāsura, who always pains the cores of our hearts.

PURPORT

Lord Brahmā is considered the father of the demigods, but Kṛṣṇa, or Lord Viṣṇu, is the father of Brahmā because Brahmā took birth from the lotus flower growing from the Lord's abdomen.

TEXT 42

अथ भगवंस्तवास्माभिरखिलजगदुत्पत्तिस्थितिलयनिमित्तायमानदिव्यमाया-
विनोदस्यसकलजीवनिकायानामन्तर्हृदयेषु बहिरपि च ब्रह्मप्रत्यगात्मस्वरूपेण
प्रधानरूपेण च यथादेशकालदेहावस्थानविशेषं तदुपादानोपलम्भकतयानुभवतः
सर्वप्रत्ययसाक्षिण आकाशशरीरस्य साक्षात्परब्रह्मणः परमात्मनः कियानिह
वार्थविशेषो विज्ञापनीयः स्याद् विस्फुलिङ्गादिभिरिव हिरण्यरेतसः ॥ ४२ ॥

atha bhagavaṁs tavāsmābhir akhila-jagad-utpatti-sthiti-laya-nimittāyamāna-divya-māyā-vinodasya sakala-jīva-nikāyānām antar-hṛdayeṣu bahir api ca brahma-pratyag-ātma-svarūpeṇa pradhāna-rūpeṇa ca yathā-deśa-kāla-dehāvasthāna-viśeṣaṁ tad-upādānopalambhakatayānubhavataḥ sarva-pratyaya-sākṣiṇa ākāśa-śarīrasya sākṣāt para-brahmaṇaḥ paramātmanaḥ kiyān iha vārtha-viśeṣo vijñāpanīyaḥ syād visphuliṅgādibhir iva hiraṇya-retasaḥ.

atha—therefore; *bhagavan*—O Lord; *tava*—of You; *asmābhiḥ*—by us; *akhila*—all; *jagat*—of the material world; *utpatti*—of the creation; *sthiti*—maintenance; *laya*—and annihilation; *nimittāyamāna*—being the cause; *divya-māyā*—with the spiritual energy; *vinodasya*—of You, who amuse Yourself; *sakala*—all; *jīva-nikāyānām*—of the hordes of living entities; *antaḥ-hṛdayeṣu*—in the cores of the hearts; *bahiḥ api*—externally also; *ca*—and; *brahma*—of impersonal Brahman, or the Absolute Truth; *pratyak-ātma*—of the Supersoul; *sva-rūpeṇa*—by Your forms; *pradhāna-rūpeṇa*—by Your form as the external ingredients; *ca*—also; *yathā*—according to; *deśa-kāla-deha-avasthāna*—of country, time, body and position; *viśeṣam*—the particulars; *tat*—of them;

upādāna—of the material causes; *upalambhakatayā*—by being the exhibitor; *anubhavataḥ*—witnessing; *sarva-pratyaya-sākṣiṇaḥ*—the witness of all different activities; *ākāśa-śarīrasya*—the Supersoul of the whole universe; *sākṣāt*—directly; *para-brahmaṇaḥ*—the Supreme Absolute Truth; *paramātmanaḥ*—the Supersoul; *kiyān*—of what extent; *iha*—herein; *vā*—or; *artha-viśeṣaḥ*—special necessity; *vijñāpanīyaḥ*—to be informed; *syāt*—may be; *visphuliṅga-ādibhiḥ*—by the sparks of the fire; *iva*—like; *hiraṇya-retasaḥ*—to the original fire.

TRANSLATION

O Lord, as the small sparks of a fire cannot possibly perform the actions of the whole fire, we sparks of Your Lordship cannot inform You of the necessities of our lives. You are the complete whole. Therefore, of what do we need to inform You? You know everything because You are the original cause of the cosmic manifestation, the maintainer and the annihilator of the entire universal creation. You always engage in Your pastimes with Your spiritual and material energies, for You are the controller of all these varied energies. You exist within all living entities, within the cosmic manifestation, and also beyond them. You exist internally as Parabrahman and externally as the ingredients of the material creation. Therefore, although manifested in various stages, at different times and places, and in various bodies, You, the Personality of Godhead, are the original cause of all causes. Indeed, You are the original element. You are the witness of all activities, but because You are as great as the sky, You are never touched by any of them. You are the witness of everything as Parabrahman and Paramātmā. O Supreme Personality of Godhead, nothing is unknown to You.

PURPORT

The Absolute Truth exists in three phases of spiritual understanding—Brahman, Paramātmā and Bhagavān (*brahmeti paramātmeti bhagavān iti śabdyate*). Bhagavān, the Supreme Personality of Godhead, is the cause of Brahman and Paramātmā. Brahman, the impersonal Absolute Truth, is all-pervading, and Paramātmā is locally situated in everyone's heart, but Bhagavān, who is worshipable by the devotees, is the original cause of all causes. A pure devotee is aware that since nothing is unknown to the Supreme Personality of Godhead, He need not be informed of a devotee's conveniences and inconveniences. A pure devotee knows that there is no need to ask the Absolute Truth for any material necessities. Therefore, while informing the Supreme Lord about their distress in being attacked by Vṛtrāsura, the demigods apologized for offering prayers for their safety. A neophyte devotee, of course, approaches the Supreme Lord for relief from distress or poverty, or for speculative knowledge of the Lord. *Bhagavad-gītā* (7.16) mentions four kinds of pious men who begin devotional service to the Lord—one who is distressed (*ārta*), one in need of money (*arthārthī*), one who is inquisitive (*jijñāsu*) and one who is searching for the Absolute Truth (*jñānī*). A pure devotee, however, knows that since the Lord is omnipresent and omniscient, there is no need to offer prayers or worship Him for one's personal benefit. A pure devotee always engages in the service of the Lord without demanding anything. The Lord is present everywhere and knows the necessities of His devotees; consequently there is no need to disturb Him by asking Him for material benefits.

TEXT 43

अत एव स्वयं तदुपकल्पयास्माकं भगवतः परमगुरोस्तव चरणशतपलाशच्छायां विविधवृजिनसंसारपरिश्रमोपशमनीमुपसृतानां वयं यत्कामेनोपसादिताः ॥४३॥

ata eva svayaṁ tad upakalpayāsmākaṁ bhagavataḥ parama-guros tava
caraṇa-śata-palāśac-chāyāṁ vividha-vṛjina-saṁsāra-
pariśramopaśamanīṁ upasṛtānāṁ vayaṁ yat-kāmenopasāditāḥ.

ata eva—therefore; *svayam*—Yourself; *tat*—that; *upakalpaya*—please arrange; *asmākam*—of us; *bhagavataḥ*—of the Supreme Personality of Godhead; *parama-guroḥ*—the supreme spiritual master; *tava*—of You; *caraṇa*—of the feet; *śata-palāśat*—like lotus flowers with hundreds of petals; *chāyām*—the shade; *vividha*—various; *vṛjina*—with dangerous positions; *saṁsāra*—of this conditioned life; *pariśrama*—the pain; *upaśamanīm*—relieving; *upasṛtānām*—the devotees who have taken shelter at Your lotus feet; *vayam*—we; *yat*—for which; *kāmena*—by the desires; *upasāditāḥ*—caused to come near (the shelter of Your lotus feet).

TRANSLATION

Dear Lord, You are omniscient, and therefore You know very well why we have taken shelter at Your lotus feet, which provide shade that gives relief from all material disturbances. Since You are the supreme spiritual master and You know everything, we have sought shelter of Your lotus feet for instruction. Please give us relief by counteracting our present distress. Your lotus feet are the only shelter for a fully surrendered devotee and are the only means for subduing all the tribulations of this material world.

PURPORT

One need only seek shelter of the shade of the Lord's lotus feet. Then all the material tribulations that disturb him will be subdued, just as when one comes under the shadow of a big tree, the disturbances caused by the heat of the scorching sun are immediately mitigated, without one's asking for relief. Therefore the whole concern of the conditioned soul should be the lotus feet of the Lord. The conditioned soul suffering from various tribulations because of existing in this material world can be relieved only when he seeks shelter at the Lord's lotus feet.

TEXT 44

अथो ईश जहि त्वाष्ट्रं ग्रसन्तं भुवनत्रयम् ।
ग्रस्तानि येन नः कृष्ण तेजांस्यस्त्रायुधानि च ॥४४॥

atho īśa jahi tvāṣṭraṁ
grasantaṁ bhuvana-trayam
grastāni yena naḥ kṛṣṇa
tejāṁsy astrāyudhāni ca

atho—therefore; *īśa*—O supreme controller; *jahi*—kill; *tvāṣṭram*—the demon Vṛtrāsura, son of Tvaṣṭā; *grasantam*—who is devouring; *bhuvana-trayam*—the three worlds; *grastāni*—devoured; *yena*—by whom; *naḥ*—our; *kṛṣṇa*—O Lord Kṛṣṇa; *tejāṁsi*—all strength and prowess; *astra*—arrows; *āyudhāni*—and other weapons; *ca*—also.

TRANSLATION

Therefore, O Lord, O supreme controller, O Lord Kṛṣṇa, please annihilate this dangerous demon Vṛtrāsura, Tvaṣṭā's son, who has already swallowed all our weapons, our paraphernalia for fighting, and our strength and influence.

PURPORT

The Lord says in *Bhagavad-gītā* (7.15–16):

na māṁ duṣkṛtino mūḍhāḥ
prapadyante narādhamāḥ
māyayāpahṛta-jñānā
āsuraṁ bhāvam āśritāḥ

catur-vidhā bhajante māṁ
janāḥ sukṛtino 'rjuna
ārto jijñāsur arthārthī
jñānī ca bharatarṣabha

"Those miscreants who are grossly foolish, lowest among mankind, whose knowledge is stolen by illusion, and who partake of the atheistic nature of demons, do not surrender unto Me. O best among the Bhāratas [Arjuna], four kinds of pious men render devotional service unto Me—the distressed, the desirer of wealth, the inquisitive, and he who is searching for knowledge of the Absolute."

The four classes of neophyte devotees who approach the Supreme Personality of Godhead to offer devotional service because of material motives are not pure devotees, but the advantage for such materialistic devotees is that they sometimes give up their material desires and become pure. When the demigods are utterly helpless, they approach the Supreme Personality of Godhead in grief and with tears in their eyes, praying to the Lord, and thus they become almost pure devotees, free from material desires. Admitting that they have forgotten pure devotional service because of extensive material opportunities, they fully surrender to the Lord, leaving to His consideration whether to maintain them or annihilate them. Such surrender is necessary. Bhaktivinoda

Ṭhākura sings, *mārabi rākhabi—yo icchā tohārā:* "O Lord, I fully surrender unto Your lotus feet. Now, as You desire, You may protect me or annihilate me. You have the full right to do either."

TEXT 45

हंसाय दहृनिलयाय निरीक्षकाय
कृष्णाय मृष्टयशसे निरुपक्रमाय ।
सत्संग्रहाय भवपान्थनिजाश्रमाप्ता-
वन्ते परीष्टगतये हरये नमस्ते ॥४५॥

haṁsāya dahra-nilayāya nirīkṣakāya
kṛṣṇāya mṛṣṭa-yaśase nirupakramāya
sat-saṁgrahāya bhava-pāntha-nijāśramāptāv
ante parīṣṭa-gataye haraye namas te

haṁsāya—unto the most exalted and pure (*pavitraṁ paramam*, the supreme pure); *dahra*—in the core of the heart; *nilayāya*—whose abode; *nirīkṣakāya*—supervising the activities of the individual soul; *kṛṣṇāya*—unto the Supersoul, who is a partial manifestation of Kṛṣṇa; *mṛṣṭa-yaśase*—whose reputation is very bright; *nirupakramāya*—who has no beginning; *sat-saṁgrahāya*—understood only by pure devotees; *bhava-pāntha-nija-āśrama-āptau*—being obtainment of the shelter of Kṛṣṇa for persons within this material world; *ante*—at the ultimate end; *parīṣṭa-gataye*—unto Him who is the ultimate goal, the highest success of life; *haraye*—unto the Supreme Personality of Godhead; *namaḥ*—respectful obeisances; *te*—unto You.

TRANSLATION

O Lord, O supreme pure, You live within the core of everyone's heart and observe all the desires and activities of the conditioned souls. O Supreme Personality of Godhead known as Lord Kṛṣṇa, Your reputation is bright and illuminating. You have no beginning, for You are the beginning of everything. This is understood by pure devotees because You are easily accessible to the pure and

truthful. When the conditioned souls are liberated and sheltered at Your lotus feet after roving throughout the material world for many millions of years, they attain the highest success of life. Therefore, O Lord, O Supreme Personality of Godhead, we offer our respectful obeisances at Your lotus feet.

PURPORT

The demigods certainly wanted Lord Viṣṇu to relieve their anxiety, but now they directly approach Lord Kṛṣṇa, for although there is no difference between Lord Kṛṣṇa and Lord Viṣṇu, Kṛṣṇa descends to this planet in His Vāsudeva feature for the purpose of *paritrāṇāya sādhūnāṁ vināśāya ca duṣkṛtām*—protecting His devotees and annihilating the miscreants. Demons, or atheists, always disturb the demigods, or devotees, and therefore Kṛṣṇa descends to punish the atheists and demons and fulfill the desire of His devotees. Kṛṣṇa, being the original cause of everything, is the Supreme Person, above even Viṣṇu and Nārāyaṇa, although there is no difference between these different forms of the Lord. As explained in *Brahma-saṁhitā* (5.46):

dīpārcir eva hi daśāntaram abhyupetya
dīpāyate vivṛta-hetu-samāna-dharmā
yas tādṛg eva hi ca viṣṇutayā vibhāti
govindam ādi-puruṣaṁ tam ahaṁ bhajāmi

Kṛṣṇa expands Himself as Viṣṇu the way a bright candle kindles another. Although there is no difference between the power of one candle and another, Kṛṣṇa is compared to the original candle.

The word *mṛṣṭa-yaśase* is significant herein because Kṛṣṇa is always famous for relieving His devotee from danger. A devotee who has sacrificed everything for the service of Kṛṣṇa and whose only source of relief is the Lord is known as *akiñcana.*

As expressed in the prayers offered by Queen Kuntī, the Lord is *akiñcana-vitta,* the property of such a devotee. Those who are liberated from the bondage of conditioned life are elevated to the spiritual world, where they achieve five kinds of liberation—*sāyujya, sālokya, sārūpya, sārṣṭi* and *sāmīpya.* They personally associate with the Lord in five mellows—*śānta, dāsya, sakhya, vātsalya* and *mādhurya.* These *rasas* are all emanations from Kṛṣṇa. As described by Viśvanātha Cakravartī Ṭhākura, the original mellow, *ādi-rasa,* is conjugal love. Kṛṣṇa is the origin of pure and spiritual conjugal love.

TEXT 46

श्रीशुक उवाच
अथैवमीडितो राजन् सादरं त्रिदशैर्हरिः ।
स्वमुपस्थानमाकर्ण्य प्राह तानभिनन्दितः ॥४६॥

śrī-śuka uvāca
athaivam īḍito rājan
sādaraṁ tri-daśair hariḥ
svam upasthānam ākarṇya
prāha tān abhinanditaḥ

śrī-śukaḥ uvāca—Śrī Śukadeva Gosvāmī said; *atha*—thereafter; *evam*—in this way; *īḍitaḥ*—being worshiped and offered obeisances; *rājan*—O King; *sa-ādaram*—with proper respect; *tri-daśaiḥ*—by all the demigods from the higher planetary systems; *hariḥ*—the Supreme Personality of Godhead; *svam upasthānam*—their prayer glorifying Him; *ākarṇya*—hearing; *prāha*—replied; *tān*—unto them (the demigods); *abhinanditaḥ*—being pleased.

TRANSLATION

Śrī Śukadeva Gosvāmī continued: O King Parīkṣit, when the demigods offered the Lord their sincere prayers in this way, the Lord listened by His causeless mercy. Being pleased, He then replied to the demigods.

TEXT 47

श्रीभगवानुवाच
प्रीतोऽहं वः सुरश्रेष्ठा मदुपस्थानविद्यया ।
आत्मैश्वर्यस्मृतिः पुंसां भक्तिश्चैव यया मयि ॥४७॥

śrī-bhagavān uvāca
prīto 'haṁ vaḥ sura-śreṣṭhā
mad-upasthāna-vidyayā
ātmaiśvarya-smṛtiḥ puṁsāṁ
bhaktiś caiva yayā mayi

śrī-bhagavān uvāca—the Supreme Personality of Godhead said; *prītaḥ*—pleased; *aham*—I; *vaḥ*—of you; *sura-śreṣṭhāḥ*—O best of the demigods; *mat-upasthāna-vidyayā*—by the highly advanced knowledge and prayers offered unto Me; *ātma-aiśvarya-smṛtiḥ*—remembrance of the exalted transcendental position of Me, the Supreme Personality of Godhead; *puṁsām*—of men; *bhaktiḥ*—devotional service; *ca*—and; *eva*—certainly; *yayā*—by which; *mayi*—unto Me.

TRANSLATION

The Supreme Personality of Godhead said: O beloved demigods, you have offered your prayers to Me with great knowledge, and I am certainly most pleased with you. A person is liberated by such knowledge, and thus he remembers My exalted position, which is above the conditions of material life. Such a devotee is fully purified by offering prayers in full knowledge. This is the source of devotional service to Me.

PURPORT

Another name of the Supreme Personality of Godhead is Uttamaśloka, which means that He is offered prayers with selected verses. *Bhakti* means *śravaṇaṁ kīrtanaṁ viṣṇoḥ*, chanting and hearing about Lord Viṣṇu. Impersonalists cannot be purified, for they do not offer personal prayers to the Supreme Personality of Godhead. Even though they sometimes offer prayers, the prayers are not directed toward the Supreme Person. Impersonalists sometimes show their incomplete knowledge by addressing the Lord as being nameless. They always offer prayers indirectly, saying, "You are this, You are that," but they do not know to whom they are praying. A devotee, however, always offers personal prayers. A devotee says, *govindam ādi-puruṣaṁ tam ahaṁ bhajāmi:* "I offer my respectful obeisances unto Govinda, unto Kṛṣṇa." That is the way to offer prayers. If one continues to offer such personal prayers to the Supreme Personality of Godhead, he is eligible to become a pure devotee and return home, back to Godhead.

TEXT 48

किं दुरापं मयि प्रीते तथापि विबुधर्षभाः ।
मय्येकान्तमतिर्नान्यन्मत्तो वाञ्छति तत्त्ववित् ॥४८॥

kiṁ durāpaṁ mayi prīte
tathāpi vibudharṣabhāḥ
mayy ekānta-matir nānyan
matto vāñchati tattva-vit

kim—what; *durāpam*—difficult to obtain; *mayi*—when I; *prīte*—satisfied; *tathāpi*—still; *vibudha-ṛṣabhāḥ*—O best of the intelligent demigods; *mayi*—in Me; *ekānta*—exclusively fixed; *matiḥ*—whose attention; *na anyat*—not anything other; *mattaḥ*—than Me; *vāñchati*—desires; *tattva-vit*—one who knows the truth.

TRANSLATION

O best of the intelligent demigods, although it is true that nothing is difficult for one to obtain when I am pleased with him, a pure devotee, whose mind is exclusively fixed upon Me, does not ask Me for anything but the opportunity to engage in devotional service.

PURPORT

When the demigods finished offering their prayers, they anxiously waited for their enemy Vṛtrāsura to be killed. This means that the demigods are not pure devotees. Although without difficulty one can get anything he desires if the Lord is pleased, the demigods aspire for material profit by pleasing the Lord. The Lord wanted the demigods to pray for unalloyed devotional service, but instead they prayed for an opportunity to kill their enemy. This is the difference between a pure devotee and a devotee on the material platform. Indirectly, the Lord regretted that the demigods did not ask for pure devotional service.

TEXT 49

न वेद कृपणः श्रेय आत्मनो गुणवस्तुदृक् ।
तस्य तानिच्छतो यच्छेद् यदि सोऽपि तथाविधः ।।४९।।

na veda kṛpaṇaḥ śreya
ātmano guṇa-vastu-dṛk
tasya tān icchato yacched
yadi so 'pi tathā-vidhaḥ

na—not; *veda*—knows; *kṛpaṇaḥ*—a miserly living entity; *śreyaḥ*—the ultimate necessity; *ātmanaḥ*—of the soul; *guṇa-vastu-dṛk*—who is attracted by the creation of the modes of material nature; *tasya*—of him; *tān*—things created by the material energy; *icchataḥ*—desiring; *yacchet*—one bestows; *yadi*—if; *saḥ api*—he also; *tathā-vidhaḥ*—of the kind (a foolish *kṛpaṇa* who does not know his real self-interest).

TRANSLATION

Those who think material assets to be everything or to be the ultimate goal of life are called misers [kṛpaṇas]. They do not know the ultimate necessity of the soul. Moreover, if one awards that which is desired by such fools, he must also be considered foolish.

PURPORT

There are two classes of men—namely the *kṛpaṇa* and the *brāhmaṇa.* A *brāhmaṇa* is one who knows Brahman, the Absolute Truth, and who thus knows his real interest. A *kṛpaṇa,* however, is one who has a material, bodily concept of life. Not knowing how to utilize his human or demigod life, a *kṛpaṇa* is attracted by things created by the material modes of nature. The *kṛpaṇas,* who always desire material benefits, are foolish, whereas *brāhmaṇas,* who always desire spiritual benefits, are intelligent. If a *kṛpaṇa,* not knowing his self-interest, foolishly asks for something material, one who awards it to him is also foolish. Kṛṣṇa, however, is not a foolish person; He is supremely intelligent. If someone comes to Kṛṣṇa asking for material benefits, Kṛṣṇa does not award him the material things he desires. Instead, the Lord gives him intelligence so that he will forget his material desires and become attached to the Lord's lotus feet. In such cases, although the *kṛpaṇa* offers prayers to Lord Kṛṣṇa for material things, the Lord takes away whatever material possessions the *kṛpaṇa* has and gives him the sense to become a devotee. As stated by the Lord in the *Caitanya-caritāmṛta* (*Madhya* 22.39):

āmi—vijña, ei mūrkhe 'viṣaya' kene diba?
sva-caraṇāmṛta diyā 'viṣaya' bhulāiba

"Since I am very intelligent, why should I give this fool material prosperity? Instead I shall induce him to take the nectar of the shelter of My lotus feet and make him forget illusory material enjoyment." If one sincerely prays to God for material possessions in exchange for devotional service, the Lord, who is not foolish like such an unintelligent devotee, shows him special favor by taking away whatever material possessions he has and gradually giving him the intelligence to be satisfied only by rendering service to His lotus feet. Śrīla Viśvanātha Cakravartī Ṭhākura comments in this regard that if a foolish child requests his mother to give him poison, the mother, being intelligent, will certainly not give him poison, even though he requests it. A materialist does not know that to accept material possessions means to accept poison, or the repetition of birth and death. An intelligent person, a *brāhmaṇa*, aspires for liberation from material bondage. That is the real self-interest of a human being.

TEXT 50

स्वयं निःश्रेयसं विद्वान् न वक्त्यज्ञाय कर्म हि ।
न राति रोगिणोऽपथ्यं वाञ्छतोऽपि भिषक्तमः ॥५०॥

svayaṁ niḥśreyasaṁ vidvān
na vakty ajñāya karma hi
na rāti rogiṇo 'pathyaṁ
vāñchato 'pi bhiṣaktamaḥ

svayam—personally; *niḥśreyasam*—the supreme goal of life, namely the means of obtaining ecstatic love for the Supreme Personality of Godhead; *vit-vān*—one who is accomplished in devotional service; *na*—not;

vakti—teaches; *ajñāya*—unto a foolish person not conversant with the ultimate goal of life; *karma*—fruitive activities; *hi*—indeed; *na*—not; *rāti*—administers; *rogiṇaḥ*—unto the patient; *apathyam*—something unconsumable; *vāñchataḥ*—desiring; *api*—although; *bhiṣak-tamaḥ*—an experienced physician.

TRANSLATION

A pure devotee who is fully accomplished in the science of devotional service will never instruct a foolish person to engage in fruitive activities for material enjoyment, not to speak of helping him in such activities. Such a devotee is like an experienced physician, who never encourages a patient to eat food injurious to his health, even if the patient desires it.

PURPORT

Here is the difference between the benedictions awarded by the demigods and those awarded by the Supreme Personality of Godhead, Viṣṇu. Devotees of the demigods ask for benedictions simply for sense gratification, and therefore they have been described in *Bhagavad-gītā* (7.20) as bereft of intelligence.

kāmais tais tair hṛta-jñānāḥ
prapadyante 'nya-devatāḥ
taṁ taṁ niyamam āsthāya
prakṛtyā niyatāḥ svayā

"Those whose minds are distorted by material desires surrender unto demigods and follow the particular rules and regulations of worship according to their own natures."

Conditioned souls are generally bereft of intelligence because of profound desires for sense gratification. They do not know what benedictions to ask. Therefore nondevotees are advised in the *śāstras* to worship various demigods to achieve material benefits. For example, if one wants a beautiful wife, he is advised to worship Umā, or goddess Durgā. If one wants to be cured of a disease, he is advised to worship the sun-god. All requests for benedictions from the demigods, however, are due to material lust. The benedictions will be finished at the end of the cosmic manifestation, along with those who bestow them. If one approaches Lord Viṣṇu for benedictions, the Lord will give him a benediction that will help him return home, back to Godhead. This is also confirmed by the Lord Himself in *Bhagavad-gītā* (10.10):

teṣāṁ satata-yuktānāṁ
bhajatāṁ prīti-pūrvakam
dadāmi buddhi-yogaṁ taṁ
yena mām upayānti te

Lord Viṣṇu, or Lord Kṛṣṇa, instructs a devotee who constantly engages in His service how to approach Him at the end of his material body. The Lord says in *Bhagavad-gītā* (4.9):

janma karma ca me divyam
evaṁ yo vetti tattvataḥ
tyaktvā dehaṁ punar janma
naiti mām eti so 'rjuna

"One who knows the transcendental nature of My appearance and activities, does not, upon leaving the body, take his birth again in this material world, but attains My eternal abode, O Arjuna." This is the benediction of Lord Viṣṇu, Kṛṣṇa. After giving up his body, a devotee returns home, back to Godhead.

A devotee may foolishly ask for material benedictions, but Lord Kṛṣṇa does not give him such benedictions, despite the devotee's prayers. Therefore people who are very attached to material life do not generally become devotees of Kṛṣṇa or Viṣṇu. Instead they become devotees of the demigods (*kāmais tais tair hṛta-jñānāḥ prapadyante 'nya-devatāḥ*). The benedictions of the demigods, however, are condemned in *Bhagavad-gītā. Antavat tu phalaṁ teṣāṁ tad bhavaty alpa-medhasām:* "Men of small intelligence worship the demigods, and their fruits are limited and temporary." A non-Vaiṣṇava, one who is not engaged in the service of the Supreme Personality of Godhead, is considered a fool with a small quantity of brain substance.

TEXT 51

मघवन् यात भद्रं वो दध्यञ्चमृषिसत्तमम् ।
विद्याव्रततपःसारं गात्रं याचत मा चिरम् ॥५१॥

maghavan yāta bhadraṁ vo
dadhyañcam ṛṣi-sattamam
vidyā-vrata-tapaḥ-sāraṁ
gātraṁ yācata mā ciram

maghavan—O Indra; *yāta*—go; *bhadram*—good fortune; *vaḥ*—to all of you; *dadhyañcam*—to Dadhyañca; *ṛṣi-sat-tamam*—the most exalted saintly person; *vidyā*—of education; *vrata*—vow; *tapaḥ*—and austerities; *sāram*—the essence; *gātram*—his body; *yācata*—ask for; *mā ciram*—without delay.

TRANSLATION

O Maghavan [Indra], all good fortune unto you. I advise you to approach the exalted saint Dadhyañca [Dadhīci]. He has become very accomplished in knowledge, vows and austerities, and his body is very strong. Go ask him for his body without delay.

PURPORT

Everyone in this material world, from Lord Brahmā down to the ant, is eager to keep his body comfortable. A pure devotee may also be comfortable, but he is not eager for such a benediction. Since Maghavan, the King of heaven, still aspired for a comfortable bodily situation, Lord Viṣṇu advised him to ask Dadhyañca for his body, which was very strong due to his knowledge, vows and austerity.

TEXT 52

स वा अधिगतो दध्यङ्ङश्विभ्यां ब्रह्म निष्कलम् ।
यद् वा अश्वशिरो नाम तयोरमरतां व्यधात् ॥५२॥

sa vā adhigato dadhyaṅṅ
aśvibhyāṁ brahma niṣkalam

yad vā aśvaśiro nāma
tayor amaratāṁ vyadhāt

saḥ—he; *vā*—certainly; *adhigataḥ*—having obtained; *dadhyaṅ*—Dadhyañca; *aśvibhyām*—to the two Aśvinī-kumāras; *brahma*—spiritual knowledge; *niṣkalam*—pure; *yat vā*—by which; *aśvaśiraḥ*—Aśvaśira; *nāma*—named; *tayoḥ*—of the two; *amaratām*—liberation in one's life; *vyadhāt*—awarded.

TRANSLATION

That saintly Dadhyañca, who is also known as Dadhīci, personally assimilated the spiritual science and then delivered it to the Aśvinī-kumāras. It is said that Dadhyañca gave them mantras through the head of a horse. Therefore the mantras are called Aśvaśira. After obtaining the mantras of spiritual science from Dadhīci, the Aśvinī-kumāras became jīvan-mukta, liberated even in this life.

PURPORT

The following story is narrated by many *ācāryas* in their commentaries:

niśamyātharvaṇaṁ dakṣaṁ pravargya-brahmavidyayoḥ. dadhyañcaṁ samupāgamya tam ūcatur athāśvinau. bhagavan dehi nau vidyām iti śrutvā sa cābravīt. karmaṇy avasthito 'dyāhaṁ paścād vakṣyāmi gacchatam. tayor nirgatayor eva śakra āgatya taṁ munim. uvāca bhiṣajor vidyāṁ mā vādīr aśvinor mune. yadi mad-vākyam ullaṅghya bravīṣi sahasaiva te. śiraś-chindyāṁ na sandeha ity uktvā sa yayau hariḥ. indre gate tathābhyetya nāsatyāv ūcatur dvijam. tan-mukhād indra-gaditaṁ śrutvā tāv ūcatuḥ punaḥ. āvāṁ tava śiraś chittvā pūrvam aśvasya mastakam. sandhāsyāvas tato brūhi tena vidyāṁ ca nau dvija. tasminn indreṇa sañchinne punaḥ sandhāya mastakam. nijaṁ te dakṣiṇāṁ dattvā gamiṣyāvo yathāgatam. etac chrutvā tadovāca dadhyaṅṅ ātharvaṇas tayoḥ pravargyaṁ brahma-vidyāṁ ca sat-kṛto 'satya-śaṅkitaḥ.

The great saint Dadhīci had perfect knowledge of how to perform fruitive activities, and he had advanced spiritual knowledge as well. Knowing this, the Aśvinī-kumāras once approached him and begged him to instruct them in spiritual science (*brahma-vidyā*). Dadhīci Muni replied, "I am now engaged in arranging sacrifices for fruitive activities. Come back some time later." When the Aśvinī-kumāras left, Indra, the

King of heaven, approached Dadhīci and said, "My dear Muni, the Aśvinī-kumāras are only physicians. Please do not instruct them in spiritual science. If you impart the spiritual science to them despite my warning, I shall punish you by cutting off your head." After warning Dadhīci in this way, Indra returned to heaven. The Aśvinī-kumāras, who understood Indra's desires, returned and begged Dadhīci for *brahma-vidyā.* When the great saint Dadhīci informed them of Indra's threat, the Aśvinī-kumāras replied, "Let us first cut off your head and replace it with the head of a horse. You can instruct *brahma-vidyā* through the horse's head, and when Indra returns and cuts off that head, we shall reward you and restore your original head." Since Dadhīci had promised to impart *brahma-vidyā* to the Aśvinī-kumāras, he agreed to their proposal. Therefore, because Dadhīci imparted *brahma-vidyā* through the mouth of a horse, this *brahma-vidyā* is also known as Aśvaśira.

TEXT 53

दध्यङ्ङाथर्वणस्त्वष्ट्रे वर्माभेद्यं मदात्मकम् ।
विश्वरूपाय यत् प्रादात् त्वष्टा यत् त्वमधास्ततः ॥५३॥

dadhyaṅṅ ātharvaṇas tvaṣṭre
varmābhedyaṁ mad-ātmakam
viśvarūpāya yat prādāt
tvaṣṭā yat tvam adhās tataḥ

dadhyaṅ—Dadhyañca; *ātharvaṇaḥ*—the son of Atharvā; *tvaṣṭre*—unto Tvaṣṭā; *varma*—the protective covering known as Nārāyaṇa-kavaca; *abhedyam*—invincible; *mat-ātmakam*—consisting of Myself; *viśvarūpāya*—unto Viśvarūpa; *yat*—which; *prādāt*—delivered; *tvaṣṭā*—Tvaṣṭā; *yat*—which; *tvam*—you; *adhāḥ*—received; *tataḥ*—from him.

TRANSLATION

Dadhyañca's invincible protective covering known as the Nārāyaṇa-kavaca was given to Tvaṣṭā, who delivered it to his son Viśvarūpa, from whom you have received it. Because of this Nārāyaṇa-kavaca, Dadhīci's body is now very strong. You should therefore beg him for his body.

TEXT 54

युष्मभ्यं याचितोऽश्विभ्यां धर्मज्ञोऽङ्गानि दास्यति ।
ततस्तैरायुधश्रेष्ठो विश्वकर्मविनिर्मितः ।
येन वृत्रशिरो हर्ता मत्तेजउपबृंहितः ॥५४॥

yuṣmabhyaṁ yācito 'śvibhyāṁ
dharma-jño 'ṅgāni dāsyati
tatas tair āyudha-śreṣṭho
viśvakarma-vinirmitaḥ
yena vṛtra-śiro hartā
mat-teja-upabṛṁhitaḥ

yuṣmabhyam—for all of you; *yācitaḥ*—being asked; *aśvibhyām*—by the Aśvinī-kumāras; *dharma-jñaḥ*—Dadhīci, who knows the principles of religion; *aṅgāni*—his limbs; *dāsyati*—will give; *tataḥ*—after that; *taiḥ*—by those bones; *āyudha*—of weapons; *śreṣṭhaḥ*—the most powerful (the thunderbolt); *viśvakarma-vinirmitaḥ*—manufactured by Viśvakarmā; *yena*—by which; *vṛtra-śiraḥ*—the head of Vṛtrāsura; *hartā*—will be taken away; *mat-tejaḥ*—by My strength; *upabṛṁhitaḥ*—increased.

TRANSLATION

When the Aśvinī-kumāras beg for Dadhyañca's body on your behalf, he will surely give it because of affection. Do not doubt this, for Dadhyañca is very experienced in religious understanding. When Dadhyañca awards you his body, Viśvakarmā will prepare a thunderbolt from his bones. This thunderbolt will certainly kill Vṛtrāsura because it will be invested with My power.

TEXT 55

तस्मिन् विनिहते यूयं तेजोऽस्त्रायुधसम्पदः ।
भूयः प्राप्स्यथ भद्रं वो न हिंसन्ति च मत्परान् ॥५५॥

tasmin vinihate yūyaṁ
tejo-'strāyudha-sampadaḥ

bhūyaḥ prāpsyatha bhadraṁ vo
na hiṁsanti ca mat-parān

tasmin—when he (Vṛtrāsura); *vinihate*—is killed; *yūyam*—all of you; *tejaḥ*—power; *astra*—arrows; *āyudha*—other weapons; *sampadaḥ*—and opulence; *bhūyaḥ*—again; *prāpsyatha*—will obtain; *bhadram*—all good fortune; *vaḥ*—unto you; *na*—not; *hiṁsanti*—hurt; *ca*—also; *mat-parān*—My devotees.

TRANSLATION

When Vṛtrāsura is killed because of My spiritual strength, you will regain your strength, weapons and wealth. Thus there will be all good fortune for all of you. Although Vṛtrāsura can destroy all the three worlds, do not fear that he will harm you. He is also a devotee and will never be envious of you.

PURPORT

A devotee of the Lord is never envious of anyone, what to speak of other devotees. As revealed later, Vṛtrāsura was also a devotee. Therefore he was not expected to be envious of the demigods. Indeed, of his own accord, he would try to benefit the demigods. A devotee does not hesitate to give up his own body for a better cause. Cāṇakya Paṇḍita said, *san-nimitte varaṁ tyāgo vināśe niyate sati.* After all, all one's material possessions, including his body, will be destroyed in due course of time. Therefore if the body and other possessions can be utilized for a better cause, a devotee never hesitates to give up even his own body. Because Lord Viṣṇu wanted to save the demigods, Vṛtrāsura, even though able to swallow the three worlds, would agree to be killed by the demigods. For a devotee there is no difference between living and dying because in this life a devotee engages in devotional service, and after giving up his body, he engages in the same service in the spiritual world. His devotional service is never hindered.

Thus end the Bhaktivedanta purports to the Ninth Chapter, Sixth Canto, of the Śrīmad-Bhāgavatam, *entitled "Appearance of the Demon Vṛtrāsura."*

CHAPTER TEN

The Battle Between the Demigods and Vṛtrāsura

As described in this chapter, after Indra obtained the body of Dadhīci, a thunderbolt was prepared from Dadhīci's bones, and a fight took place between Vṛtrāsura and the demigods.

Following the order of the Supreme Personality of Godhead, the demigods approached Dadhīci Muni and begged for his body. Dadhīci Muni, just to hear from the demigods about the principles of religion, jokingly refused to relinquish his body, but for higher purposes he thereafter agreed to give it up, for after death the body is usually eaten by low animals like dogs and jackals. Dadhīci Muni first merged his gross body made of five elements into the original stock of five elements and then engaged his soul at the lotus feet of the Supreme Personality of Godhead. Thus he gave up his gross body. With the help of Viśvakarmā, the demigods then prepared a thunderbolt from Dadhīci's bones. Armed with the thunderbolt weapon, they prepared themselves to fight and got up on the backs of elephants.

At the end of Satya-yuga and the beginning of Tretā-yuga, a great fight took place between the demigods and the *asuras*. Unable to tolerate the effulgence of the demigods, the *asuras* fled the battle, leaving Vṛtrāsura, their commander in chief, to fight for himself. Vṛtrāsura, however, seeing the demons fleeing, instructed them in the importance of fighting and dying in the battlefield. One who is victorious in battle gains material possessions, and one who dies in the battlefield attains a residence at once in the celestial heavens. In either way, the fighter benefits.

TEXT 1

श्रीबादरायणिरुवाच

इन्द्रमेवं समादिश्य भगवान् विश्वभावनः ।
पश्यतामनिमेषाणां तत्रैवान्तर्दधे हरिः ॥ १ ॥

śrī-bādarāyaṇir uvāca
indram evaṁ samādiśya
bhagavān viśva-bhāvanaḥ
paśyatām animeṣāṇāṁ
tatraivāntardadhe hariḥ

śrī-bādarāyaṇiḥ uvāca—Śrī Śukadeva Gosvāmī said; *indram*—Indra, the heavenly King; *evam*—thus; *samādiśya*—after instructing; *bhagavān*—the Supreme Personality of Godhead; *viśva-bhāvanaḥ*—the original cause of all cosmic manifestations; *paśyatām animeṣāṇām*—while the demigods were looking on; *tatra*—then and there; *eva*—indeed; *antardadhe*—disappeared; *hariḥ*—the Lord.

TRANSLATION

Śrī Śukadeva Gosvāmī said: After instructing Indra in this way, the Supreme Personality of Godhead, Hari, the cause of the cosmic manifestation, then and there disappeared from the presence of the onlooking demigods.

TEXT 2

तथाभियाचितो देवैर्ऋषिराथर्वणो महान् ।
मोदमान उवाचेदं प्रहसन्निव भारत ॥ २ ॥

tathābhiyācito devair
ṛṣir ātharvaṇo mahān
modamāna uvācedaṁ
prahasann iva bhārata

tathā—in that manner; *abhiyācitaḥ*—being begged; *devaiḥ*—by the demigods; *ṛṣiḥ*—the great saintly person; *ātharvaṇaḥ*—Dadhīci, the son of Atharvā; *mahān*—the great personality; *modamānaḥ*—being merry; *uvāca*—said; *idam*—this; *prahasan*—smiling; *iva*—somewhat; *bhārata*—O Mahārāja Parīkṣit.

TRANSLATION

O King Parīkṣit, following the Lord's instructions, the demigods approached Dadhīci, the son of Atharvā. He was very

liberal, and when they begged him to give them his body, he at once partially agreed. However, just to hear religious instructions from them, he smiled and jokingly spoke as follows.

TEXT 3

अपि वृन्दारका यूयं न जानीथ शरीरिणाम् ।
संस्थायां यस्त्वभिद्रोहो दुःसहश्चेतनापहः ॥ ३ ॥

api vṛndārakā yūyaṁ
na jānītha śarīriṇām
saṁsthāyāṁ yas tv abhidroho
duḥsahaś cetanāpahaḥ

api—although; *vṛndārakāḥ*—O demigods; *yūyam*—all of you; *na jānītha*—do not know; *śarīriṇām*—of those who have material bodies; *saṁsthāyām*—at the time of death, or while quitting this body; *yaḥ*—which; *tu*—then; *abhidrohaḥ*—severe pain; *duḥsahaḥ*—unbearable; *cetana*—the consciousness; *apahaḥ*—which takes away.

TRANSLATION

O elevated demigods, at the time of death, severe, unbearable pain takes away the consciousness of all living entities who have accepted material bodies. Don't you know about this pain?

TEXT 4

जिजीविषूणां जीवानामात्मा प्रेष्ठ इहेप्सितः ।
क उत्सहेत तं दातुं भिक्षमाणाय विष्णवे ॥ ४ ॥

jijīviṣūṇāṁ jīvānām
ātmā preṣṭha ihepsitaḥ
ka utsaheta taṁ dātuṁ
bhikṣamāṇāya viṣṇave

jijīviṣūṇām—aspiring to remain alive; *jīvānām*—of all living entities; *ātmā*—the body; *preṣṭhaḥ*—very dear; *iha*—here; *īpsitaḥ*—desired;

kaḥ—who; *utsaheta*—can bear; *tam*—that body; *dātum*—to deliver; *bhikṣamāṇāya*—begging; *viṣṇave*—even to Lord Viṣṇu.

TRANSLATION

In this material world, every living entity is very much addicted to his material body. Struggling to keep his body forever, everyone tries to protect it by all means, even at the sacrifice of all his possessions. Therefore, who would be prepared to deliver his body to anyone, even if it were demanded by Lord Viṣṇu?

PURPORT

It is said, *ātmānaṁ sarvato rakṣet tato dharmaṁ tato dhanam:* one must protect his body by all means; then he may protect his religious principles and thereafter his possessions. This is the natural desire of all living entities. No one wants to give up his body unless it is forcibly given away. Even though the demigods said that they were demanding Dadhīci's body for their benefit in accordance with the order of Lord Viṣṇu, Dadhīci superficially refused to give them his body.

TEXT 5

श्रीदेवा ऊचुः
किं नु तद् दुस्त्यजं ब्रह्मन् पुंसां भूतानुकम्पिनाम् ।
भवद्विधानां महतां पुण्यश्लोकेड्यकर्मणाम् ॥ ५ ॥

śrī-devā ūcuḥ
kiṁ nu tad dustyajaṁ brahman
puṁsāṁ bhūtānukampinām
bhavad-vidhānāṁ mahatāṁ
puṇya-ślokeḍya-karmaṇām

śrī-devāḥ ūcuḥ—the demigods said; *kim*—what; *nu*—indeed; *tat*—that; *dustyajam*—difficult to give up; *brahman*—O exalted *brāhmaṇa;* *puṁsām*—of persons; *bhūta-anukampinām*—who are very sympathetic toward the suffering living entities; *bhavat-vidhānām*—like Your Lordship; *mahatām*—who are very great; *puṇya-śloka-īḍya-karmaṇām*—whose pious activities are praised by all great souls.

TRANSLATION

The demigods replied: O exalted brāhmaṇa, pious persons like you, whose activities are praiseworthy, are very kind and affectionate to people in general. What can't such pious souls give for the benefit of others? They can give everything, including their bodies.

TEXT 6

नूनं स्वार्थपरो लोको न वेद परसंकटम् ।
यदि वेद न याचेत नेति नाह यदीश्वरः ॥ ६ ॥

nūnaṁ svārtha-paro loko
na veda para-saṅkaṭam
yadi veda na yāceta
neti nāha yad īśvaraḥ

nūnam—certainly; *sva-artha-paraḥ*—interested only in sense gratification in this life or the next; *lokaḥ*—materialistic people in general; *na*—not; *veda*—know; *para-saṅkaṭam*—the pain of others; *yadi*—if; *veda*—know; *na*—not; *yāceta*—would ask; *na*—no; *iti*—thus; *na āha*—does not say; *yat*—since; *īśvaraḥ*—able to give charity.

TRANSLATION

Those who are too self-interested beg something from others, not knowing of others' pain. But if the beggar knew the difficulty of the giver, he would not ask for anything. Similarly, he who is able to give charity does not know the beggar's difficulty, for otherwise he would not refuse to give the beggar anything he might want as charity.

PURPORT

This verse describes two people—one who gives charity and one who begs for it. A beggar should not ask charity from a person who is in difficulty. Similarly, one who is able to give charity should not deny a beggar. These are the moral instructions of the *śāstra.* Cāṇakya Paṇḍita says, *san-nimitte varaṁ tyāgo vināśe niyate sati:* everything within this material world will be destroyed, and therefore one should use everything for good purposes. If one is advanced in knowledge, he must always be prepared to sacrifice anything for a better cause. At the present moment the entire world is in a dangerous position under the spell of a godless civilization. The Kṛṣṇa consciousness movement needs many exalted, learned persons who will sacrifice their lives to revive God consciousness throughout the world. We therefore invite all men and women advanced in knowledge to join the Kṛṣṇa consciousness movement and sacrifice their lives for the great cause of reviving the God consciousness of human society.

TEXT 7

श्रीऋषिरुवाच
धर्मं वः श्रोतुकामेन यूयं मे प्रत्युदाहृताः ।
एष वः प्रियमात्मानं त्यजन्तं संत्यजाम्यहम् ॥ ७ ॥

śrī-ṛṣir uvāca
dharmaṁ vaḥ śrotu-kāmena
yūyaṁ me pratyudāhṛtāḥ
eṣa vaḥ priyam ātmānaṁ
tyajantaṁ santyajāmy aham

śrī-ṛṣiḥ uvāca—the great saint Dadhīci said; *dharmam*—the principles of religion; *vaḥ*—from you; *śrotu-kāmena*—by the desire to hear; *yūyam*—you; *me*—by me; *pratyudāhṛtāḥ*—replied to the contrary; *eṣaḥ*—this; *vaḥ*—for you; *priyam*—dear; *ātmānam*—body; *tyajantam*—leaving me anyway, today or tomorrow; *santyajāmi*—give up; *aham*—I.

TRANSLATION

The great sage Dadhīci said: Just to hear from you about religious principles, I refused to offer my body at your request. Now, although my body is extremely dear to me, I must give it up for your better purposes since I know that it will leave me today or tomorrow.

TEXT 8

योऽध्रुवेणात्मना नाथा न धर्मं न यशः पुमान् ।
ईहेत भूतदयया स शोच्यः स्थावरैरपि ॥ ८ ॥

yo 'dhruveṇātmanā nāthā
na dharmaṁ na yaśaḥ pumān
īheta bhūta-dayayā
sa śocyaḥ sthāvarair api

yaḥ—anyone who; *adhruveṇa*—impermanent; *ātmanā*—by the body; *nāthāḥ*—O lords; *na*—not; *dharmam*—religious principles; *na*—not; *yaśaḥ*—fame; *pumān*—a person; *īheta*—endeavors for; *bhūta-dayayā*—by mercy for the living beings; *saḥ*—that person; *śocyaḥ*—pitiable; *sthāvaraiḥ*—by the immobile creatures; *api*—even.

TRANSLATION

O demigods, one who has no compassion for humanity in its suffering and does not sacrifice his impermanent body for the higher causes of religious principles or eternal glory is certainly pitied even by the immovable beings.

PURPORT

In this regard, a very exalted example was set by Lord Śrī Caitanya Mahāprabhu and the six Gosvāmīs of Vṛndāvana. Concerning Śrī Caitanya Mahāprabhu it is said in *Śrīmad-Bhāgavatam* (11.5.34):

tyaktvā sudustyaja-surepsita-rājya-lakṣmīṁ
dharmiṣṭha ārya-vacasā yad agād araṇyam
māyā-mṛgaṁ dayitayepsitam anvadhāvad
vande mahā-puruṣa te caraṇāravindam

"We offer our respectful obeisances unto the lotus feet of the Lord, upon whom one should always meditate. He left His householder life, leaving aside His eternal consort, whom even the denizens of heaven adore. He went into the forest to deliver the fallen souls, who are put into illusion by material energy." To accept *sannyāsa* means to commit civil suicide, but *sannyāsa* is compulsory, at least for every *brāhmaṇa*, every first-class human being. Śrī Caitanya Mahāprabhu had a very young and beautiful wife and a very affectionate mother. Indeed, the affectionate dealings of His family members were so pleasing that even the demigods could not expect such happiness at home. Nevertheless, for the deliverance of all the fallen souls of the world, Śrī Caitanya Mahāprabhu took *sannyāsa* and left home when He was only twenty-four years old. He lived a very strict life as a *sannyāsī*, refusing all bodily comforts. Similarly, His disciples the six Gosvāmīs were ministers who held exalted positions in society, but they also left everything to join the movement of Śrī Caitanya Mahāprabhu. Śrīnivāsa Ācārya says:

tyaktvā tūrṇam aśeṣa-maṇḍala-pati-śreṇīṁ sadā tucchavat
bhūtvā dīna-gaṇeśakau karuṇayā kaupīna-kanthāśritau

These Gosvāmīs left their very comfortable lives as ministers, Zamindars and learned scholars and joined Śrī Caitanya Mahāprabhu's movement, just to show mercy to the fallen souls of the world (*dīna-gaṇeśakau karuṇayā*). Accepting very humble lives as mendicants, wearing no more than loincloths and torn quilts (*kaupīna-kantha*), they lived in Vṛndāvana and followed Śrī Caitanya Mahāprabhu's order to excavate Vṛndāvana's lost glories.

Similarly, everyone else with a materially comfortable condition in this world should join the Kṛṣṇa consciousness movement to elevate the fallen souls. The words *bhūta-dayayā, māyā-mṛgaṁ dayitayepsitam* and *dīna-gaṇeśakau karuṇayā* all convey the same sense. These are very significant words for those interested in elevating human society to a proper understanding of life. One should join the Kṛṣṇa consciousness movement, following the examples of such great personalities as Śrī Caitanya Mahāprabhu, the six Gosvāmīs and, before them, the great sage Dadhīci. Instead of wasting one's life for temporary bodily comforts, one should always be prepared to give up one's life for better causes. After all, the body will be destroyed. Therefore one should sacrifice it for the glory of distributing religious principles throughout the world.

TEXT 9

एतावानव्ययो धर्मः पुण्यश्लोकैरुपासितः ।
यो भूतशोकहर्षाभ्यामात्मा शोचति हृष्यति ॥ ९ ॥

etāvān avyayo dharmaḥ
puṇya-ślokair upāsitaḥ

yo bhūta-śoka-harṣābhyām
ātmā śocati hṛṣyati

etāvān—this much; *avyayaḥ*—imperishable; *dharmaḥ*—religious principle; *puṇya-ślokaiḥ*—by famous persons who are celebrated as pious; *upāsitaḥ*—recognized; *yaḥ*—which; *bhūta*—of the living beings; *śoka*—by the distress; *harṣābhyām*—and by the happiness; *ātmā*—the mind; *śocati*—laments; *hṛṣyati*—feels happiness.

TRANSLATION

If one is unhappy to see the distress of other living beings and happy to see their happiness, his religious principles are appreciated as imperishable by exalted persons who are considered pious and benevolent.

PURPORT

One generally follows different types of religious principles or performs various occupational duties according to the body given to him by the modes of material nature. In this verse, however, real religious principles are explained. Everyone should be unhappy to see others in distress and happy to see others happy. *Ātmavat sarva-bhūteṣu:* one should feel the happiness and distress of others as his own. It is on this basis that the Buddhist religious principle of nonviolence—*ahiṁsaḥ parama-dharmaḥ*—is established. We feel pain when someone disturbs us, and therefore we should not inflict pain upon other living beings. Lord Buddha's mission was to stop unnecessary animal killing, and therefore he preached that the greatest religious principle is nonviolence.

One cannot continue killing animals and at the same time be a religious man. That is the greatest hypocrisy. Jesus Christ said, "Do not kill," but hypocrites nevertheless maintain thousands of slaughterhouses while posing as Christians. Such hypocrisy is condemned in this verse. One should be happy to see others happy, and one should be unhappy to see others unhappy. This is the principle to be followed. Unfortunately, at the present moment so-called philanthropists and humanitarians advocate the happiness of humanity at the cost of the lives of poor animals. That is not recommended herein. This verse clearly says that one should be compassionate to all living entities. Regardless of whether human, animal, tree or plant, all living entities are sons of the Supreme Personality of Godhead. Lord Kṛṣṇa says in *Bhagavad-gītā* (14.4):

sarva-yoniṣu kaunteya
mūrtayaḥ sambhavanti yāḥ
tāsāṁ brahma mahad yonir
ahaṁ bīja-pradaḥ pitā

"It should be understood that all species of life, O son of Kuntī, are made possible by birth in this material nature, and that I am the seed-giving father." The different forms of these living entities are only their external dresses. Every living being is actually a spirit soul, a part and parcel of God. Therefore one should not favor only one kind of living being. A Vaiṣṇava sees all living entities as part and parcel of God. As the Lord says in *Bhagavad-gītā* (5.18 and 18.54):

vidyā-vinaya-sampanne
brāhmaṇe gavi hastini
śuni caiva śvapāke ca
paṇḍitāḥ sama-darśinaḥ

"The humble sage, by virtue of true knowledge, sees with equal vision a learned and gentle *brāhmaṇa*, a cow, an elephant, a dog and a dog-eater [outcaste]."

brahma-bhūtaḥ prasannātmā
na śocati na kāṅkṣati
samaḥ sarveṣu bhūteṣu
mad-bhaktiṁ labhate parām

"One who is transcendentally situated at once realizes the Supreme Brahman and becomes fully joyful. He never laments nor desires to have anything; he is equally disposed to every living entity. In that state he attains pure devotional service unto Me." A Vaiṣṇava, therefore, is truly a perfect person because he laments to see others unhappy and feels joy at seeing others happy. A Vaiṣṇava is *para-duḥkha-duḥkhī;* he is always unhappy to see the conditioned souls in an unhappy state of materialism.

Therefore a Vaiṣṇava is always busy preaching Kṛṣṇa consciousness throughout the world.

TEXT 10

अहो दैन्यमहो कष्टं पारक्यैः क्षणभङ्गुरैः ।
यन्नोपकुर्यादस्वार्थैर्मर्त्यः स्वज्ञातिविग्रहैः ॥१०॥

aho dainyam aho kaṣṭaṁ
pārakyaiḥ kṣaṇa-bhaṅguraiḥ
yan nopakuryād asvārthair
martyaḥ sva-jñāti-vigrahaiḥ

aho—alas; *dainyam*—a miserable condition; *aho*—alas; *kaṣṭam*—simply tribulation; *pārakyaiḥ*—which after death are eatable by dogs and jackals; *kṣaṇa-bhaṅguraiḥ*—perishable at any moment; *yat*—because; *na*—not; *upakuryāt*—would help; *a-sva-arthaiḥ*—not meant for self-interest; *martyaḥ*—a living entity destined to die; *sva*—with his wealth; *jñāti*—relatives and friends; *vigrahaiḥ*—and his body.

TRANSLATION

This body, which is eatable by jackals and dogs after death, does not actually do any good for me, the spirit soul. It is usable only for a short time and may perish at any moment. The body and its possessions, its riches and relatives, must all be engaged for the benefit of others, or else they will be sources of tribulation and misery.

PURPORT

Similar advice is also given in *Śrīmad-Bhāgavatam* (10.22.35):

etāvaj janma-sāphalyaṁ
dehinām iha dehiṣu
prāṇair arthair dhiyā vācā
śreya ācaraṇaṁ sadā

"It is the duty of every living being to perform welfare activities for the benefit of others with his life, wealth, intelligence and words." This is the mission of life. One's own body and the bodies of his friends and relatives, as well as one's own riches and everything else one has, should be engaged for the benefit of others. This is the mission of Śrī Caitanya Mahāprabhu. As stated in *Caitanya-caritāmṛta* (*Ādi* 9.41):

bhārata-bhūmite haila manuṣya-janma yāra
janma sārthaka kari' kara para-upakāra

"One who has taken birth as a human being in the land of India [Bhārata-varṣa] should make his life successful and work for the benefit of all other people.

The word *upakuryāt* means *para-upakāra*, helping others. Of course, in human society there are many institutions to help others, but because philanthropists do not know how to help others, their propensity for philanthropy is ineffectual. They do not know the ultimate goal of life (*śreya ācaraṇam*), which is to please the Supreme Lord. If all philanthropic and humanitarian activities were directed toward achieving the ultimate goal of life—to please the Supreme Personality of Godhead—they would all be perfect. Humanitarian work without Kṛṣṇa is nothing. Kṛṣṇa must be brought to the center of all our activities; otherwise no activity will have value.

TEXT 11

श्रीबादरायणिरुवाच
एवं कृतव्यवसितो दध्यङ्ङाथर्वणस्तनुम् ।
परे भगवति ब्रह्मण्यात्मानं सन्नयञ्जहौ ॥११॥

śrī-bādarāyaṇir uvāca
evaṁ kṛta-vyavasito
dadhyaṅṅ ātharvaṇas tanum
pare bhagavati brahmaṇy
ātmānaṁ sannayañ jahau

śrī-bādarāyaṇiḥ uvāca—Śrī Śukadeva Gosvāmī said; *evam*—thus; *kṛta-vyavasitaḥ*—making certain of what to do (in giving his body to the demigods); *dadhyaṅ*—Dadhīci Muni; *ātharvaṇaḥ*—the son of Atharvā;

tanum—his body; *pare*—to the Supreme; *bhagavati*—Personality of Godhead; *brahmaṇi*—the Supreme Brahman; *ātmānam*—himself, the spirit soul; *sannayan*—offering; *jahau*—gave up.

TRANSLATION

Śrī Śukadeva Gosvāmī said: Dadhīci Muni, the son of Atharvā, thus resolved to give his body to the service of the demigods. He placed himself, the spirit soul, at the lotus feet of the Supreme Personality of Godhead and in this way gave up his gross material body made of five elements.

PURPORT

As indicated by the words *pare bhagavati brahmaṇy ātmānaṁ sannayan,* Dadhīci placed himself, as spirit soul, at the lotus feet of the Supreme Personality of Godhead. In this regard, one may refer to the incident of Dhṛtarāṣṭra's leaving his body, as described in the First Canto of *Śrīmad-Bhāgavatam* (1.13.55). Dhṛtarāṣṭra analytically divided his gross material body into the five different elements of which it was made—earth, water, fire, air and ether—and distributed them to the different reservoirs of these elements; in other words, he merged these five elements into the original *mahat-tattva.* By identifying his material conception of life, he gradually separated his spirit soul from material connections and placed himself at the lotus feet of the Supreme Personality of Godhead. The example given in this connection is that when an earthen pot is broken, the small portion of the sky within the pot is united with the large sky outside the pot. Māyāvādī philosophers misunderstand this description of *Śrīmad-Bhāgavatam.* Therefore Śrī Rāmānuja Svāmī, in his book *Vedānta-tattva-sāra,* has described that this merging of the soul means that after separating himself from the material body made of eight elements—earth, water, fire, air, ether, false ego, mind and intelligence—the individual soul engages himself in devotional service to the Supreme Personality of Godhead in His eternal form (*īśvaraḥ paramaḥ kṛṣṇaḥ sac-cid-ānanda-vigrahaḥ/ anādir ādir govindaḥ sarva-kāraṇa-kāraṇam*). The material cause of the material elements absorbs the material body, and the spiritual soul assumes its original position. As described by Śrī Caitanya Mahāprabhu, *jīvera 'svarūpa' haya——kṛṣṇera 'nitya-dāsa':* the constitutional position of the living entity is that he is the eternal servant of Kṛṣṇa. When one overcomes the material body through cultivation of spiritual knowledge and devotional service, one can revive his own position and thus engage in the service of the Lord.

TEXT 12

यताक्षासुमनोबुद्धिस्तत्त्वदृग् ध्वस्तबन्धनः ।
आस्थितः परमं योगं न देहं बुबुधे गतम् ॥१२॥

yatākṣāsu-mano-buddhis
tattva-dṛg dhvasta-bandhanaḥ
āsthitaḥ paramaṁ yogaṁ
na dehaṁ bubudhe gatam

yata—controlled; *akṣa*—senses; *asu*—the life air; *manaḥ*—the mind; *buddhiḥ*—intelligence; *tattva-dṛk*—one who knows the *tattvas*, the material and spiritual energies; *dhvasta-bandhanaḥ*—liberated from bondage; *āsthitaḥ*—being situated in; *paramam*—the supreme; *yogam*—absorption, trance; *na*—not; *deham*—the material body; *bubudhe*—perceived; *gatam*—left.

TRANSLATION

Dadhīci Muni controlled his senses, life force, mind and intelligence and became absorbed in trance. Thus he cut all his material bonds. He could not perceive how his material body became separated from his self.

PURPORT

The Lord says in *Bhagavad-gītā* (8.5):

anta-kāle ca mām eva
smaran muktvā kalevaram
yaḥ prayāti sa mad-bhāvaṁ
yāti nāsty atra saṁśayaḥ

"Whoever, at the time of death, quits his body remembering Me alone, at once attains My nature. Of this there is no doubt." Of course, one must practice before one is overcome by death, but the perfect *yogī*, namely the devotee, dies in trance, thinking of Kṛṣṇa. He does not feel his material body being separated from his soul; the soul is immediately transferred to the spiritual world. *Tyaktvā dehaṁ punar janma naiti mām eti:* the soul does not enter the womb of a material mother again, but is transferred back home, back to Godhead. This *yoga*, *bhakti-yoga*, is the highest *yoga* system, as explained by the Lord Himself in *Bhagavad-gītā* (6.47):

yoginām api sarveṣāṁ
mad-gatenāntarātmanā
śraddhāvān bhajate yo māṁ
sa me yuktatamo mataḥ

"Of all *yogīs*, he who always abides in Me with great faith, worshiping Me in transcendental loving service, is most intimately united with Me in *yoga* and is the highest of all." The *bhakti-yogī* always thinks of Kṛṣṇa, and therefore at the time of death he can very easily transfer himself to Kṛṣṇaloka, without even perceiving the pains of death.

TEXTS 13–14

अथेन्द्रो वज्रमुद्यम्य निर्मितं विश्वकर्मणा ।
मुनेः शक्तिभिरुत्सिक्तो भगवत्तेजसान्वितः ॥१३॥
वृतो देवगणैः सर्वैर्गजेन्द्रोपर्यशोभत ।
स्तूयमानो मुनिगणैस्त्रैलोक्यं हर्षयन्निव ॥१४॥

athendro vajram udyamya
nirmitaṁ viśvakarmaṇā
muneḥ śaktibhir utsikto
bhagavat-tejasānvitaḥ

vṛto deva-gaṇaiḥ sarvair
gajendropary aśobhata
stūyamāno muni-gaṇais
trailokyaṁ harṣayann iva

atha—thereafter; *indraḥ*—the King of heaven; *vajram*—the thunderbolt; *udyamya*—firmly taking up; *nirmitam*—manufactured; *viśvakarmaṇā*—by Viśvakarmā; *muneḥ*—of the great sage, Dadhīci; *śaktibhiḥ*—by the power; *utsiktaḥ*—saturated; *bhagavat*—of the Supreme Personality of Godhead; *tejasā*—with spiritual power; *anvitaḥ*—endowed; *vṛtaḥ*—encircled; *deva-gaṇaiḥ*—by the other demigods; *sarvaiḥ*—all; *gajendra*—of his elephant carrier; *upari*—upon the back; *aśobhata*—shone; *stūyamānaḥ*—being offered prayers; *muni-gaṇaiḥ*—by the saintly persons; *trai-lokyam*—to the three worlds; *harṣayan*—causing pleasure; *iva*—as it were.

TRANSLATION

Thereafter, King Indra very firmly took up the thunderbolt manufactured by Viśvakarmā from the bones of Dadhīci. Charged with the exalted power of Dadhīci Muni and enlightened by the power of the Supreme Personality of Godhead, Indra rode on the back of his carrier, Airāvata, surrounded by all the demigods, while all the great sages offered him praise. Thus he shone very beautifully, pleasing the three worlds as he rode off to kill Vṛtrāsura.

TEXT 15

वृत्रमभ्यद्रवच्छत्रुमसुरानीकयूथपैः ।
पर्यस्तमोजसा राजन् क्रुद्धो रुद्र इवान्तकम् ॥१५॥

vṛtram abhyadravac chatrum
asurānīka-yūthapaiḥ
paryastam ojasā rājan
kruddho rudra ivāntakam

vṛtram—Vṛtrāsura; *abhyadravat*—attacked; *śatrum*—the enemy; *asura-anīka-yūthapaiḥ*—by the commanders or captains of the soldiers of the *asuras; paryastam*—surrounded; *ojasā*—with great force; *rājan*—O King; *kruddhaḥ*—being angry; *rudraḥ*—an incarnation of Lord Śiva; *iva*—like; *antakam*—Antaka, or Yamarāja.

TRANSLATION

My dear King Parīkṣit, as Rudra, being very angry at Antaka [Yamarāja] had formerly run toward Antaka to kill him, Indra angrily and with great force attacked Vṛtrāsura, who was surrounded by the leaders of the demoniac armies.

TEXT 16

ततः सुराणामसुरै रणः परमदारुणः ।
त्रेतामुखे नर्मदायामभवत् प्रथमे युगे ॥१६॥

tataḥ surāṇām asurai
raṇaḥ parama-dāruṇaḥ
tretā-mukhe narmadāyām
abhavat prathame yuge

tataḥ—thereafter; *surāṇām*—of the demigods; *asuraiḥ*—with the demons; *raṇaḥ*—a great battle; *parama-dāruṇaḥ*—very fearful; *tretā-mukhe*—in the beginning of Tretā-yuga; *narmadāyām*—on the bank of the River Narmadā; *abhavat*—took place; *prathame*—in the first; *yuge*—millennium.

TRANSLATION

Thereafter, at the end of Satya-yuga and the beginning of Tretā-yuga, a fierce battle took place between the demigods and the demons on the bank of the Narmadā.

PURPORT

Herein the Narmadā does not mean the Narmadā River in India. The five sacred rivers in India—Gaṅgā, Yamunā, Narmadā, Kāverī and Kṛṣṇā—are all celestial. Like the Ganges River, the Narmadā River also flows in the higher planetary systems. The battle between the demigods and the demons took place in the higher planets.

The words *prathame yuge* mean "in the beginning of the first millennium," that is to say, in the beginning of the Vaivasvata *manvantara.* In one day of Brahmā there are fourteen Manus, who each live for seventy-one millenniums. The four *yugas*—Satya, Tretā, Dvāpara and Kali—constitute one millennium. We are presently in the *manvantara* of Vaivasvata Manu, who is mentioned in *Bhagavad-gītā* (*imaṁ vivasvate yogaṁ proktavān aham avyayam/ vivasvān manave prāha*). We are now in the twenty-eighth millennium of Vaivasvata Manu, but this fight took place in the beginning of Vaivasvata Manu's first millennium. One can historically calculate how long ago the battle took place. Since each millennium consists of 4,300,000 years and we are now in the twenty-eighth millennium, some 120,400,000 years have passed since the battle took place on the bank of the River Narmadā.

TEXTS 17–18

रुद्रैर्वसुभिरादित्यैरश्विभ्यां पितृवह्निभिः ।
मरुद्भिर्ऋभुभिः साध्यैर्विश्वेदेवैर्मरुत्पतिम् ॥१७॥
दृष्ट्वा वज्रधरं शक्रं रोचमानं स्वया श्रिया ।
नामृष्यन्नसुरा राजन् मृधे वृत्रपुरःसराः ॥१८॥

rudrair vasubhir ādityair
aśvibhyāṁ pitṛ-vahnibhiḥ
marudbhir ṛbhubhiḥ sādhyair
viśvedevair marut-patim

dṛṣṭvā vajra-dharaṁ śakraṁ
rocamānaṁ svayā śriyā
nāmṛṣyann asurā rājan
mṛdhe vṛtra-puraḥsarāḥ

rudraiḥ—by the Rudras; *vasubhiḥ*—by the Vasus; *ādityaiḥ*—by the Ādityas; *aśvibhyām*—by the Aśvinī-kumāras; *pitṛ*—by the Pitās; *vahnibhiḥ*—and the Vahnis; *marudbhiḥ*—by the Maruts; *ṛbhubhiḥ*—by the Ṛbhus; *sādhyaiḥ*—by the Sādhyas; *viśve-devaiḥ*—by the Viśvadevas; *marut-patim*—Indra, the heavenly King; *dṛṣṭvā*—seeing; *vajra-dharam*—bearing the thunderbolt; *śakram*—another name of Indra; *rocamānam*—shining; *svayā*—by his own; *śriyā*—opulence; *na*—

not; *amṛṣyan*—tolerated; *asurāḥ*—all the demons; *rājan*—O King; *mṛdhe*—in the fight; *vṛtra-puraḥsarāḥ*—headed by Vṛtrāsura.

TRANSLATION

O King, when all the asuras came onto the battlefield, headed by Vṛtrāsura, they saw King Indra carrying the thunderbolt and surrounded by the Rudras, Vasus, Ādityas, Aśvinī-kumāras, Pitās, Vahnis, Maruts, Ṛbhus, Sādhyas and Viśvadevas. Surrounded by his company, Indra shone so brightly that his effulgence was intolerable to the demons.

TEXTS 19–22

नमुचिः शम्बरोऽनर्वा द्विमूर्धा ऋषभोऽसुरः ।
हयग्रीवः शङ्कुशिरा विप्रचित्तिरयोमुखः ॥१९॥
पुलोमा वृषपर्वा च प्रहेतिर्हेतिरुत्कलः ।
दैतेया दानवा यक्षा रक्षांसि च सहस्रशः ॥२०॥
सुमालिमालिप्रमुखाः कार्तस्वरपरिच्छदाः ।
प्रतिषिध्येन्द्रसेनाग्रं मृत्योरपि दुरासदम् ॥२१॥
अभ्यर्दयन्नसंभ्रान्ताः सिंहनादेन दुर्मदाः ।
गदाभिः परिघैर्बाणैः प्रासमुद्गरतोमरैः ॥२२॥

namuciḥ śambaro 'narvā
dvimūrdhā ṛṣabho 'suraḥ
hayagrīvaḥ śaṅkuśirā
vipracittir ayomukhaḥ

pulomā vṛṣaparvā ca
prahetir hetir utkalaḥ
daiteyā dānavā yakṣā
rakṣāṁsi ca sahasraśaḥ

sumāli-māli-pramukhāḥ
kārtasvara-paricchadāḥ

pratiṣidhyendra-senāgraṁ
mṛtyor api durāsadam

abhyardayann asambhrāntāḥ
siṁha-nādena durmadāḥ
gadābhiḥ parighair bāṇaiḥ
prāsa-mudgara-tomaraiḥ

namuciḥ—Namuci; *śambaraḥ*—Śambara; *anarvā*—Anarvā; *dvimūrdhā*—Dvimūrdhā; *ṛṣabhaḥ*—Ṛṣabha; *asuraḥ*—Asura; *hayagrīvaḥ*—Hayagrīva; *śaṅkuśirāḥ*—Śaṅkuśirā; *vipracittiḥ*—Vipracitti; *ayomukhaḥ*—Ayomukha; *pulomā*—Pulomā; *vṛṣaparvā*—Vṛṣaparvā; *ca*—also; *prahetiḥ*—Praheti; *hetiḥ*—Heti; *utkalaḥ*—Utkala; *daiteyāḥ*—the Daityas; *dānavāḥ*—the Dānavas; *yakṣāḥ*—the Yakṣas; *rakṣāṁsi*—the Rākṣasas; *ca*—and; *sahasraśaḥ*—by the thousands; *sumāli-māli-pramukhāḥ*—others, headed by Sumāli and Māli; *kārtasvara*—of gold; *paricchadāḥ*—dressed in ornaments; *pratiṣidhya*—keeping back; *indra-senā-agram*—the front of Indra's army; *mṛtyoḥ*—for death; *api*—even; *durāsadam*—difficult to approach; *abhyardayan*—harassed; *asambhrāntāḥ*—without fear; *siṁha-nādena*—with a sound like a lion; *durmadāḥ*—furious; *gadābhiḥ*—with clubs; *parighaiḥ*—with iron-studded bludgeons; *bāṇaiḥ*—with arrows; *prāsa-mudgara-tomaraiḥ*—with barbed missiles, mallets and lances.

TRANSLATION

Many hundreds and thousands of demons, demi-demons, Yakṣas, Rākṣasas [man-eaters] and others, headed by Sumāli and Māli, resisted the armies of King Indra, which even death personified cannot easily overcome. Among the demons were Namuci, Śambara, Anarvā, Dvimūrdhā, Ṛṣabha, Asura, Hayagrīva, Śaṅkuśirā, Vipracitti, Ayomukha, Pulomā, Vṛṣaparvā, Praheti, Heti and Utkala. Roaring tumultuously and fearlessly like lions, these invincible demons, all dressed in golden ornaments, gave pain to the demigods with weapons like clubs, bludgeons, arrows, barbed darts, mallets and lances.

TEXT 23

शूलैः परश्वधैः खड्गैः शतघ्नीभिर्भुशुण्डिभिः ।
सर्वतोऽवाकिरन् शस्त्रैरस्त्रैश्च विबुधर्षभान् ॥२३॥

śūlaiḥ paraśvadhaiḥ khaḍgaiḥ
śataghnībhir bhuśuṇḍibhiḥ
sarvato 'vākiran śastrair
astraiś ca vibudharṣabhān

śūlaiḥ—by spears; *paraśvadhaiḥ*—by axes; *khaḍgaiḥ*—by swords; *śataghnībhiḥ*—by *śataghnīs; bhuśuṇḍibhiḥ*—by *bhuśuṇḍis; sarvataḥ*—all around; *avākiran*—scattered; *śastraiḥ*—with weapons; *astraiḥ*—with arrows; *ca*—and; *vibudha-ṛṣabhān*—the chiefs of the demigods.

TRANSLATION

Armed with lances, tridents, axes, swords and other weapons like śataghnīs and bhuśuṇḍis, the demons attacked from different directions and scattered all the chiefs of the demigod armies.

TEXT 24

न तेऽदृश्यन्त संछन्नाः शरजालैः समन्ततः ।
पुङ्खानुपुङ्खपतितैर्ज्योतींषीव नभोघनैः ॥२४॥

na te 'dṛśyanta sañchannāḥ
śara-jālaiḥ samantataḥ
puṅkhānupuṅkha-patitair
jyotīṁṣīva nabho-ghanaiḥ

na—not; *te*—they (the demigods); *adṛśyanta*—were seen; *sañchannāḥ*—being completely covered; *śara-jālaiḥ*—by networks of arrows; *samantataḥ*—all around; *puṅkha-anupuṅkha*—one arrow after another; *patitaiḥ*—falling; *jyotīṁṣi iva*—like the stars in the sky; *nabhaḥ-ghanaiḥ*—by the dense clouds.

TRANSLATION

As the stars in the sky cannot be seen when covered by dense clouds, the demigods, being completely covered by networks of arrows falling upon them one after another, could not be seen.

TEXT 25

न ते शस्त्रास्त्रवर्षौघा ह्यासेदुः सुरसैनिकान् ।
छिन्नाः सिद्धपथे देवैर्लघुहस्तैः सहस्रधा ॥२५॥

na te śastrāstra-varṣaughā
hy āseduḥ sura-sainikān
chinnāḥ siddha-pathe devair
laghu-hastaiḥ sahasradhā

na—not; *te*—those; *śastra-astra-varṣa-oghāḥ*—showers of arrows and other weapons; *hi*—indeed; *āseduḥ*—reached; *sura-sainikān*—the armies of the demigods; *chinnāḥ*—cut; *siddha-pathe*—in the sky; *devaiḥ*—by the demigods; *laghu-hastaiḥ*—quick-handed; *sahasra-dhā*—into thousands of pieces.

TRANSLATION

The showers of various weapons and arrows released to kill the soldiers of the demigods did not reach them because the demigods, acting quickly, cut the weapons into thousands of pieces in the sky.

TEXT 26

अथ क्षीणास्त्रशस्त्रौघा गिरिशृङ्गद्रुमोपलैः ।
अभ्यवर्षन् सुरबलं चिच्छिदुस्तांश्च पूर्ववत् ॥२६॥

atha kṣīṇāstra-śastraughā
giri-śṛṅga-drumopalaiḥ
abhyavarṣan sura-balaṁ
cicchidus tāṁś ca pūrvavat

atha—thereupon; *kṣīṇa*—being reduced; *astra*—of the arrows released by *mantras; śastra*—and weapons; *oghāḥ*—the multitudes;

giri—of mountains; *śṛṅga*—with the peaks; *druma*—with trees; *upalaiḥ*—and with stones; *abhyavarṣan*—showered; *sura-balam*—the soldiers of the demigods; *cicchiduḥ*—broke to pieces; *tān*—them; *ca*—and; *pūrva-vat*—as before.

TRANSLATION

As their weapons and mantras decreased, the demons began showering mountain peaks, trees and stones upon the demigod soldiers, but the demigods were so powerful and expert that they nullified all these weapons by breaking them to pieces in the sky as before.

TEXT 27

तानक्षतान् स्वस्तिमतो निशाम्य
शस्त्रास्त्रपूगैरथ वृत्रनाथाः ।
द्रुमैर्दृषद्भिर्विविधाद्रिशृङ्गै-
रविक्षतांस्तत्रसुरिन्द्रसैनिकान् ॥२७॥

tān akṣatān svastimato niśāmya
śastrāstra-pūgair atha vṛtra-nāthāḥ
drumair dṛṣadbhir vividhādri-śṛṅgair
avikṣatāṁs tatrasur indra-sainikān

tān—them (the soldiers of the demigods); *akṣatān*—not injured; *svasti-mataḥ*—being very healthy; *niśāmya*—seeing; *śastra-astra-pūgaiḥ*—by the bunches of weapons and *mantras; atha*—thereupon; *vṛtra-nāthāḥ*—the soldiers led by Vṛtrāsura; *drumaiḥ*—by the trees; *dṛṣadbhiḥ*—by the stones; *vividha*—various; *adri*—of mountains; *śṛṅgaiḥ*—by the peaks; *avikṣatān*—not injured; *tatrasuḥ*—became afraid; *indra-sainikān*—the soldiers of King Indra.

TRANSLATION

When the soldiers of the demons, commanded by Vṛtrāsura, saw that the soldiers of King Indra were quite well, having not been injured at all by their volleys of weapons, not even by the trees, stones and mountain peaks, the demons were very much afraid.

TEXT 28

सर्वे प्रयासा अभवन् विमोघाः
कृताः कृता देवगणेषु दैत्यैः ।
कृष्णानुकूलेषु यथा महत्सु
क्षुद्रैः प्रयुक्ता ऊषती रूक्षवाचः ॥२८॥

sarve prayāsā abhavan vimoghāḥ
kṛtāḥ kṛtā deva-gaṇeṣu daityaiḥ
kṛṣṇānukūleṣu yathā mahatsu
kṣudraiḥ prayuktā ūṣatī rūkṣa-vācaḥ

sarve—all; *prayāsāḥ*—endeavors; *abhavan*—were; *vimoghāḥ*—futile; *kṛtāḥ*—performed; *kṛtāḥ*—again performed; *deva-gaṇeṣu*—unto the demigods; *daityaiḥ*—by the demons; *kṛṣṇa-anukūleṣu*—who were always protected by Kṛṣṇa; *yathā*—just as; *mahatsu*—unto the Vaiṣṇavas; *kṣudraiḥ*—by insignificant persons; *prayuktāḥ*—used; *ūṣatīḥ*—unfavorable; *rūkṣa*—rough; *vācaḥ*—words.

TRANSLATION

When insignificant persons use rough words to cast false, angry accusations against saintly persons, their fruitless words do not disturb the great personalities. Similarly, all the efforts of the demons against the demigods, who were favorably situated under the protection of Kṛṣṇa, were futile.

PURPORT

There is a Bengali saying that if a vulture curses a cow to die, the curse will not be effective. Similarly, accusations made by demoniac persons against devotees of Kṛṣṇa cannot have any effect. The demigods are devotees of Lord Kṛṣṇa, and therefore the curses of the demons were futile.

TEXT 29

ते स्वप्रयासं वितथं निरीक्ष्य
हरावभक्ता हतयुद्धदर्पाः ।

पलायनायाजिमुखे विसृज्य
पतिं मनस्ते दधुरात्तसाराः ॥२९॥

te sva-prayāsaṁ vitathaṁ nirīkṣya
harāv abhaktā hata-yuddha-darpāḥ
palāyanāyāji-mukhe visṛjya
patiṁ manas te dadhur ātta-sārāḥ

te—they (the demons); *sva-prayāsam*—their own endeavors; *vitatham*—fruitless; *nirīkṣya*—seeing; *harau abhaktāḥ*—the *asuras*, those who are not devotees of the Supreme Personality of Godhead; *hata*—defeated; *yuddha-darpāḥ*—their pride in fighting; *palāyanāya*—for leaving the battlefield; *āji-mukhe*—in the very beginning of the battle; *visṛjya*—leaving aside; *patim*—their commander, Vṛtrāsura; *manaḥ*—their minds; *te*—all of them; *dadhuḥ*—gave; *ātta-sārāḥ*—whose prowess was taken away.

TRANSLATION

The asuras, who are never devotees of Lord Kṛṣṇa, the Supreme Personality of Godhead, lost their pride in fighting when they found all their endeavors futile. Leaving aside their leader even in the very beginning of the fight, they decided to flee because all their prowess had been taken away by the enemy.

TEXT 30

वृत्रोऽसुरांस्ताननुगान् मनस्वी
प्रधावतः प्रेक्ष्य बभाष एतत् ।
पलायितं प्रेक्ष्य बलं च भग्नं
भयेन तीव्रेण विहस्य वीरः ॥३०॥

vṛtro 'surāṁs tān anugān manasvī
pradhāvataḥ prekṣya babhāṣa etat
palāyitaṁ prekṣya balaṁ ca bhagnaṁ
bhayena tīvreṇa vihasya vīraḥ

vṛtraḥ—Vṛtrāsura, the commander of the demons; *asurān*—all the demons; *tān*—them; *anugān*—his followers; *manasvī*—the great-minded; *pradhāvataḥ*—fleeing; *prekṣya*—observing; *babhāṣa*—spoke; *etat*—this; *palāyitam*—fleeing; *prekṣya*—seeing; *balam*—army; *ca*—and; *bhagnam*—broken; *bhayena*—out of fear; *tīvreṇa*—intense; *vihasya*—smiling; *vīraḥ*—the great hero.

TRANSLATION

Seeing his army broken and all the asuras, even those known as great heroes, fleeing the battlefield out of intense fear, Vṛtrāsura, who was truly a great-minded hero, smiled and spoke the following words.

TEXT 31

कालोपपन्नां रुचिरां मनस्विनां
जगाद वाचं पुरुषप्रवीरः ।
हे विप्रचित्ते नमुचे पुलोमन्
मयानर्वञ्छम्बर मे शृणुध्वम् ॥३१॥

kālopapannāṁ rucirāṁ manasvināṁ
jagāda vācaṁ puruṣa-pravīraḥ
he vipracitte namuce puloman
mayānarvañ chambara me śṛṇudhvam

kāla-upapannām—suitable to the time and circumstances; *rucirām*—very beautiful; *manasvinām*—to the great, deep-minded personalities; *jagāda*—spoke; *vācam*—words; *puruṣa-pravīraḥ*—the hero among heroes, Vṛtrāsura; *he*—O; *vipracitte*—Vipracitti; *namuce*—O Namuci; *puloman*—O Pulomā; *maya*—O Maya; *anarvan*—O Anarvā; *śambara*—O Śambara; *me*—from me; *śṛṇudhvam*—please hear.

TRANSLATION

According to his position and the time and circumstances, Vṛtrāsura, the hero among heroes, spoke words that were much to be appreciated by thoughtful men. He called to the heroes of the demons, "O Vipracitti! O Namuci! O Pulomā! O Maya, Anarvā and Śambara! Please hear me and do not flee."

TEXT 32

जातस्य मृत्युर्ध्रुव एव सर्वतः
प्रतिक्रिया यस्य न चेह क्लृप्ता ।
लोको यशश्चाथ ततो यदि ह्यमुं
को नाम मृत्युं न वृणीत युक्तम् ॥३२॥

jātasya mṛtyur dhruva eva sarvataḥ
pratikriyā yasya na ceha kḷptā
loko yaśaś cātha tato yadi hy amuṁ
ko nāma mṛtyuṁ na vṛṇīta yuktam

jātasya—of one who has taken birth (all living beings); *mṛtyuḥ*—death; *dhruvaḥ*—inevitable; *eva*—indeed; *sarvataḥ*—everywhere in the universe; *pratikriyā*—counteraction; *yasya*—of which; *na*—not; *ca*—also; *iha*—in this material world; *kḷptā*—devised; *lokaḥ*—promotion to higher planets; *yaśaḥ*—reputation and glory; *ca*—and; *atha*—then; *tataḥ*—from that; *yadi*—if; *hi*—indeed; *amum*—that; *kaḥ*—who; *nāma*—indeed; *mṛtyum*—death; *na*—not; *vṛṇīta*—would accept; *yuktam*—suitable.

TRANSLATION

Vṛtrāsura said: All living entities who have taken birth in this material world must die. Surely, no one in this world has found any means to be saved from death. Even providence has not provided a means to escape it. Under the circumstances, death being inevitable, if one can gain promotion to the higher planetary systems and be always celebrated here by dying a suitable death, what man will not accept such a glorious death?

PURPORT

If by dying one can be elevated to the higher planetary systems and be ever-famous after his death, who is so foolish that he will refuse such a glorious death? Similar advice was also given by Kṛṣṇa to Arjuna. "My dear Arjuna," the Lord said, "do not desist from fighting. If you gain victory in the fight, you will enjoy a kingdom, and even if you die you will be elevated to the heavenly planets." Everyone should be ready to die while performing glorious deeds. A glorious person is not meant to meet death like cats and dogs.

TEXT 33

द्वौ संमताविह मृत्यू दुरापौ
यद् ब्रह्मसंधारणया जितासुः ।
कलेवरं योगरतो विजह्याद्
यदग्रणीर्वीरशयेऽनिवृत्तः ॥३३॥

dvau sammatāv iha mṛtyū durāpau
yad brahma-sandhāraṇayā jitāsuḥ
kalevaraṁ yoga-rato vijahyād
yad agraṇīr vīra-śaye 'nivṛttaḥ

dvau—two; *sammatau*—approved (by *śāstra* and great personalities); *iha*—in this world; *mṛtyū*—deaths; *durāpau*—extremely rare; *yat*—which; *brahma-sandhāraṇayā*—with concentration on Brahman, Paramātmā or Parabrahma, Kṛṣṇa; *jita-asuḥ*—controlling the mind and senses; *kalevaram*—the body; *yoga-rataḥ*—being engaged in the performance of *yoga; vijahyāt*—one may leave; *yat*—which; *agraṇīḥ*—taking the lead; *vīra-śaye*—on the battlefield; *anivṛttaḥ*—not turning back.

TRANSLATION

There are two ways to meet a glorious death, and both are very rare. One is to die after performing mystic yoga, especially bhakti-yoga, by which one can control the mind and living force and die absorbed in thought of the Supreme Personality of Godhead. The second is to die on the battlefield, leading the army and never showing one's back. These two kinds of death are recommended in the śāstra as glorious.

Thus end the Bhaktivedanta purports of the Sixth Canto, Tenth Chapter, of the Śrīmad-Bhāgavatam, *entitled "The Battle Between the Demigods and Vṛtrāsura."*

CHAPTER ELEVEN

The Transcendental Qualities of Vṛtrāsura

This chapter describes Vṛtrāsura's great qualities. When the prominent commanders of the demons fled, not hearing Vṛtrāsura's advice, Vṛtrāsura condemned them all as cowards. Speaking very bravely, he stood alone to face the demigods. When the demigods saw Vṛtrāsura's attitude, they were so afraid that they practically fainted, and Vṛtrāsura began trampling them down. Unable to tolerate this, Indra, the King of the demigods, threw his club at Vṛtrāsura, but Vṛtrāsura was such a great hero that he easily caught the club with his left hand and used it to beat Indra's elephant. Struck by the blow of Vṛtrāsura, the elephant was pushed back fourteen yards and fell, with Indra on its back.

King Indra had first accepted Viśvarūpa as his priest and thereafter killed him. Reminding Indra of his heinous activities, Vṛtrāsura said, "If one is a devotee of the Supreme Personality of Godhead, Lord Viṣṇu, and depends on Lord Viṣṇu in every respect, then victory, opulence and peace of mind are all inevitably available. Such a person has nothing for which to aspire in the three worlds. The Supreme Lord is so kind that He especially favors such a devotee by not giving him opulence that will hamper his devotional service. Therefore I wish to give up everything for the service of the Lord. I wish always to chant the glories of the Lord and engage in His service. Let me become unattached to my worldly family and make friendships with the devotees of the Lord. I do not desire to be promoted to the higher planetary systems, even to Dhruvaloka or Brahmaloka, nor do I desire an unconquerable position within this material world. I have no need for such things."

TEXT 1

श्रीशुक उवाच

त एवं शंसतो धर्मं वचः पत्युरचेतसः ।
नैवागृह्णन्त सम्भ्रान्ताः पलायनपरा नृप ॥ १ ॥

śrī-śuka uvāca
ta evaṁ śaṁsato dharmaṁ
vacaḥ patyur acetasaḥ
naivāgṛhṇanta sambhrāntāḥ
palāyana-parā nṛpa

śrī-śukaḥ uvāca—Śrī Śukadeva Gosvāmī said; *te*—they; *evam*—thus; *śaṁsataḥ*—praising; *dharmam*—the principles of religion; *vacaḥ*—the words; *patyuḥ*—of their master; *acetasaḥ*—their minds being very disturbed; *na*—not; *eva*—indeed; *agṛhṇanta*—accepted; *sambhrāntāḥ*—fearful; *palāyana-parāḥ*—intent upon fleeing; *nṛpa*—O King.

TRANSLATION

Śrī Śukadeva Gosvāmī said: O King, Vṛtrāsura, the commander in chief of the demons, advised his lieutenants in the principles of religion, but the cowardly demoniac commanders, intent upon fleeing the battlefield, were so disturbed by fear that they could not accept his words.

TEXTS 2–3

विशीर्यमाणां पृतनामासुरीमसुरर्षभः ।
कालानुकूलैस्त्रिदशैः काल्यमानामनाथवत् ॥ २ ॥
दृष्ट्वातप्यत संक्रुद्ध इन्द्रशत्रुरमर्षितः ।
तान् निवार्यौजसा राजन् निर्भर्त्स्येदमुवाच ह ॥ ३ ॥

viśīryamāṇāṁ pṛtanām
āsurīm asurarṣabhaḥ
kālānukūlais tridaśaiḥ
kālyamānām anāthavat

dṛṣṭvātapyata saṅkruddha
indra-śatrur amarṣitaḥ
tān nivāryaujasā rājan
nirbhartsyedam uvāca ha

viśīryamāṇām—being shattered; *pṛtanām*—the army; *āsurīm*—of the demons; *asura-ṛṣabhaḥ*—the best of the *asuras,* Vṛtrāsura; *kāla-anukūlaiḥ*—following the circumstances presented by time; *tri-daśaiḥ*—by the demigods; *kālyamānām*—being chased; *anātha-vat*—as if no one were there to protect them; *dṛṣṭvā*—seeing; *atapyata*—felt pain; *saṅkruddhaḥ*—being very angry; *indra-śatruḥ*—Vṛtrāsura, the enemy of Indra; *amarṣitaḥ*—unable to tolerate; *tān*—them (the demigods); *nivārya*—blocking; *ojasā*—with great force; *rājan*—O King Parīkṣit; *nirbhartsya*—rebuking; *idam*—this; *uvāca*—said; *ha*—indeed.

TRANSLATION

O King Parīkṣit, the demigods, taking advantage of a favorable opportunity presented by time, attacked the army of the demons from the rear and began driving away the demoniac soldiers, scattering them here and there as if their army had no leader. Seeing the pitiable condition of his soldiers, Vṛtrāsura, the best of the asuras, who was called Indraśatru, the enemy of Indra, was very much aggrieved. Unable to tolerate such reverses, he stopped and forcefully rebuked the demigods, speaking the following words in an angry mood.

TEXT 4

किं व उच्चरितैर्मातुर्धावद्भिः पृष्ठतो हतैः ।
न हि भीतवधः श्लाघ्यो न स्वर्ग्यः शूरमानिनाम् ॥४॥

kiṁ va uccaritair mātur
dhāvadbhiḥ pṛṣṭhato hataiḥ
na hi bhīta-vadhaḥ ślāghyo
na svargyaḥ śūra-māninām

kim—what is the benefit; *vaḥ*—for you; *uccaritaiḥ*—with those like the stool; *mātuḥ*—of the mother; *dhāvadbhiḥ*—running away; *pṛṣṭhataḥ*—from the back; *hataiḥ*—killed; *na*—not; *hi*—certainly; *bhīta-vadhaḥ*—the killing of a person who is afraid; *ślāghyaḥ*—

glorious; *na*—nor; *svargyaḥ*—leading to the heavenly planets; *śūra-māninām*—of persons who consider themselves heroes.

TRANSLATION

O demigods, these demoniac soldiers have taken birth uselessly. Indeed, they have come from the bodies of their mothers exactly like stool. What is the benefit of killing such enemies from behind while they are running in fear? One who considers himself a hero should not kill an enemy who is afraid of losing his life. Such killing is never glorious, nor can it promote one to the heavenly planets.

PURPORT

Vṛtrāsura rebuked both the demigods and the demoniac soldiers because the demons were running in fear of their lives and the demigods were killing them from behind. The actions of both were abominable. When a fight takes place, the opposing parties must be prepared to fight like heroes. A hero never runs from the field of battle. He always fights face to face, determined to gain victory or lay down his life in the fight. That is heroic. Killing an enemy from behind is also inglorious. When an enemy turns his back and runs in fear of his life, he should not be killed. This is the etiquette of military science.

Vṛtrāsura insulted the demoniac soldiers by comparing them to the stool of their mothers. Both stool and a cowardly son come from the abdomen of the mother, and Vṛtrāsura said that there is no difference between them. A similar comparison was given by Tulasī dāsa, who commented that a son and urine both come from the same channel. In other words, semen and urine both come from the genitals, but semen produces a child whereas urine produces nothing. Therefore if a child is neither a hero nor a devotee, he is not a son but urine. Similarly, Cāṇakya Paṇḍita also says:

ko 'rthaḥ putreṇa jātena
yo na vidvān na dhārmikaḥ
kāṇena cakṣuṣā kiṁ vā
cakṣuḥ pīḍaiva kevalam

"What is the use of a son who is neither glorious nor devoted to the Lord? Such a son is like a blind eye, which simply gives pain but cannot help one see."

TEXT 5

यदि वः प्रधने श्रद्धा सारं वा क्षुल्लका हृदि ।
अग्रे तिष्ठत मात्रं मे न चेद् ग्राम्यसुखे स्पृहा ॥ ५ ॥

yadi vaḥ pradhane śraddhā
sāraṁ vā kṣullakā hṛdi
agre tiṣṭhata mātraṁ me
na ced grāmya-sukhe spṛhā

yadi—if; *vaḥ*—of you; *pradhane*—in battle; *śraddhā*—faith; *sāram*—patience; *vā*—or; *kṣullakāḥ*—O insignificant ones; *hṛdi*—in the core of the heart; *agre*—in front; *tiṣṭhata*—just stand; *mātram*—for a moment; *me*—of me; *na*—not; *cet*—if; *grāmya-sukhe*—in sense gratification; *spṛhā*—desire.

TRANSLATION

O insignificant demigods, if you truly have faith in your heroism, if you have patience in the cores of your hearts and if you are not ambitious for sense gratification, please stand before me for a moment.

PURPORT

Rebuking the demigods, Vṛtrāsura challenged, "O demigods, if you are actually heroes, stand before me now and try to show your prowess. If you do not wish to fight, if you are afraid of losing your lives, I shall not kill you, for unlike you, I am not so evil minded as to kill persons who are neither heroic nor willing to fight. If you have faith in your heroism, please stand before me."

TEXT 6

एवं सुरगणान् क्रुद्धो भीषयन् वपुषा रिपून् ।
व्यनदत् सुमहाप्राणो येन लोका विचेतसः ॥ ६ ॥

evaṁ sura-gaṇān kruddho
bhīṣayan vapuṣā ripūn
vyanadat sumahā-prāṇo
yena lokā vicetasaḥ

evam—thus; *sura-gaṇān*—the demigods; *kruddhaḥ*—being very angry; *bhīṣayan*—terrifying; *vapuṣā*—by his body; *ripūn*—his enemies; *vyanadat*—roared; *su-mahā-prāṇaḥ*—the most powerful Vṛtrāsura; *yena*—by which; *lokāḥ*—all people; *vicetasaḥ*—unconscious.

TRANSLATION

Śukadeva Gosvāmī said: Vṛtrāsura, the angry and most powerful hero, terrified the demigods with his stout and strongly built body. When he roared with a resounding voice, nearly all living entities fainted.

TEXT 7

तेन देवगणाः सर्वे वृत्रविस्फोटनेन वै ।
निपेतुर्मूर्च्छिता भूमौ यथैवाशनिना हताः ॥ ७ ॥

tena deva-gaṇāḥ sarve
vṛtra-visphoṭanena vai
nipetur mūrcchitā bhūmau
yathaivāśaninā hatāḥ

tena—by that; *deva-gaṇāḥ*—the demigods; *sarve*—all; *vṛtra-visphoṭanena*—the tumultuous sound of Vṛtrāsura; *vai*—indeed; *nipetuḥ*—fell; *mūrcchitāḥ*—fainted; *bhūmau*—on the ground; *yathā*—just as if; *eva*—indeed; *aśaninā*—by a thunderbolt; *hatāḥ*—struck.

TRANSLATION

When all the demigods heard Vṛtrāsura's tumultuous roar, which resembled that of a lion, they fainted and fell to the ground as if struck by thunderbolts.

TEXT 8

ममर्द पद्भ्यां सुरसैन्यमातुरं
निमीलिताक्षं रणरङ्गदुर्मदः ।
गां कम्पयन्नुद्यतशूल ओजसा
नालं वनं यूथपतिर्यथोन्मदः ॥ ८ ॥

mamarda padbhyāṁ sura-sainyam āturaṁ
nimīlitākṣaṁ raṇa-raṅga-durmadaḥ
gāṁ kampayann udyata-śūla ojasā
nālaṁ vanaṁ yūtha-patir yathonmadaḥ

mamarda—trampled; *padbhyām*—by his feet; *sura-sainyam*—the army of the demigods; *āturam*—who were very afraid; *nimīlita-akṣam*—closing their eyes; *raṇa-raṅga-durmadaḥ*—arrogant on the battlefield; *gām*—the surface of the globe; *kampayan*—causing to tremble; *udyata-śūlaḥ*—taking up his trident; *ojasā*—with his strength; *nālam*—of hollow bamboo sticks; *vanam*—a forest; *yūtha-patiḥ*—an elephant; *yathā*—just as; *unmadaḥ*—maddened.

TRANSLATION

As the demigods closed their eyes in fear, Vṛtrāsura, taking up his trident and making the earth tremble with his great strength, trampled the demigods beneath his feet on the battlefield the way a mad elephant tramples hollow bamboos in the forest.

TEXT 9

विलोक्य तं वज्रधरोऽत्यमर्षितः
स्वशत्रवेऽभिद्रवते महागदाम् ।
चिक्षेप तामापततीं सुदुःसहां
जग्राह वामेन करेण लीलया ॥ ९ ॥

vilokya taṁ vajra-dharo 'tyamarṣitaḥ
sva-śatrave 'bhidravate mahā-gadām

cikṣepa tām āpatatīṁ suduḥsahāṁ
jagrāha vāmena kareṇa līlayā

vilokya—seeing; *tam*—him (Vṛtrāsura); *vajra-dharaḥ*—the carrier of the thunderbolt (King Indra); *ati*—very much; *amarṣitaḥ*—intolerant; *sva*—his own; *śatrave*—toward the enemy; *abhidravate*—running; *mahā-gadām*—a very powerful club; *cikṣepa*—threw; *tām*—that (club); *āpatatīm*—flying toward him; *su-duḥsahām*—very difficult to counteract; *jagrāha*—caught; *vāmena*—with his left; *kareṇa*—hand; *līlayā*—very easily.

TRANSLATION

Seeing Vṛtrāsura's disposition, Indra, the King of heaven, became intolerant and threw at him one of his great clubs, which are extremely difficult to counteract. However, as the club flew toward him, Vṛtrāsura easily caught it with his left hand.

TEXT 10

स इन्द्रशत्रुः कुपितो भृशं तया
महेन्द्रवाहं गदयोरुविक्रमः ।
जघान कुम्भस्थल उन्नदन् मृधे
तत्कर्म सर्वे समपूजयन्नृप ॥१०॥

sa indra-śatruḥ kupito bhṛśaṁ tayā
mahendra-vāhaṁ gadayoru-vikramaḥ
jaghāna kumbha-sthala unnadan mṛdhe
tat karma sarve samapūjayan nṛpa

saḥ—that; *indra-śatruḥ*—Vṛtrāsura; *kupitaḥ*—being angry; *bhṛśam*—very much; *tayā*—with that; *mahendra-vāham*—the elephant who is the carrier of Indra; *gadayā*—by the club; *uru-vikramaḥ*—who is famous for his great strength; *jaghāna*—struck; *kumbha-sthale*—on the head; *unnadan*—roaring loudly; *mṛdhe*—in that fight; *tat karma*—that action (striking the head of Indra's elephant with the club in his left hand); *sarve*—all the soldiers (on both sides); *samapūjayan*—glorified; *nṛpa*—O King Parīkṣit.

TRANSLATION

O King Parīkṣit, the powerful Vṛtrāsura, the enemy of King Indra, angrily struck the head of Indra's elephant with that club, making a tumultuous sound on the battlefield. For this heroic deed, the soldiers on both sides glorified him.

TEXT 11

ऐरावतो वृत्रगदाभिमृष्टो
विघूर्णितोऽद्रिः कुलिशाहतो यथा ।
अपासरद् भिन्नमुखः सहेन्द्रो
मुञ्चन्नसृक् सप्तधनुर्भृशार्तः ॥११॥

airāvato vṛtra-gadābhimṛṣṭo
vighūrṇito 'driḥ kuliśāhato yathā
apāsarad bhinna-mukhaḥ sahendro
muñcann asṛk sapta-dhanur bhṛśārtaḥ

airāvataḥ—Airāvata, the elephant of King Indra; *vṛtra-gadā-abhimṛṣṭaḥ*—struck by the club in Vṛtrāsura's hand; *vighūrṇitaḥ*—shaken; *adriḥ*—a mountain; *kuliśa*—by a thunderbolt; *āhataḥ*—struck; *yathā*—just like; *apāsarat*—was pushed back; *bhinna-mukhaḥ*—having a broken mouth; *saha-indraḥ*—with King Indra; *muñcan*—spitting; *asṛk*—blood; *sapta-dhanuḥ*—a distance measured by seven bows (approximately fourteen yards); *bhṛśa*—very severely; *ārtaḥ*—aggrieved.

TRANSLATION

Struck with the club by Vṛtrāsura like a mountain struck by a thunderbolt, the elephant Airāvata, feeling great pain and spitting blood from its broken mouth, was pushed back fourteen yards. In great distress, the elephant fell, with Indra on its back.

TEXT 12

न सन्नवाहाय विषण्णचेतसे
प्रायुङ्क्त भूयः स गदां महात्मा ।

इन्द्रोऽमृतस्यन्दिकराभिमर्श-
वीतव्यथक्षतवाहोऽवतस्थे ॥१२॥

na sanna-vāhāya viṣaṇṇa-cetase
prāyuṅkta bhūyaḥ sa gadāṁ mahātmā
indro 'mṛta-syandi-karābhimarśa-
vīta-vyatha-kṣata-vāho 'vatasthe

na—not; *sanna*—fatigued; *vāhāya*—upon him whose carrier; *viṣaṇṇa-cetase*—morose in the core of his heart; *prāyuṅkta*—used; *bhūyaḥ*—again; *saḥ*—he (Vṛtrāsura); *gadām*—the club; *mahā-ātmā*—the great soul (who refrained from striking Indra with the club when he saw Indra morose and aggrieved); *indraḥ*—Indra; *amṛta-syandi-kara*—of his hand, which produces nectar; *abhimarśa*—by the touch; *vīta*—was relieved; *vyatha*—from pains; *kṣata*—and cuts; *vāhaḥ*—whose carrier elephant; *avatasthe*—stood there.

TRANSLATION

When he saw Indra's carrier elephant thus fatigued and injured and when he saw Indra morose because his carrier had been harmed in that way, the great soul Vṛtrāsura, following religious principles, refrained from again striking Indra with the club. Taking this opportunity, Indra touched the elephant with his nectar-producing hand, thus relieving the animal's pain and curing its injuries. Then the elephant and Indra both stood silently.

TEXT 13

स तं नृपेन्द्राहवकाम्यया रिपुं
वज्रायुधं भ्रातृहणं विलोक्य ।
स्मरंश्च तत्कर्म नृशंसमंहः
शोकेन मोहेन हसञ्जगाद ॥१३॥

sa taṁ nṛpendrāhava-kāmyayā ripuṁ
vajrāyudhaṁ bhrātṛ-haṇaṁ vilokya
smaraṁś ca tat-karma nṛ-śaṁsam aṁhaḥ
śokena mohena hasañ jagāda

saḥ—he (Vṛtrāsura); *tam*—him (the King of heaven, Indra); *nṛpa-indra*—O King Parīkṣit; *āhava-kāmyayā*—with a desire to fight; *ripum*—his enemy; *vajra-āyudham*—whose weapon was the thunderbolt (made from the bones of Dadhīci); *bhrātṛ-haṇam*—who was the killer of his brother; *vilokya*—seeing; *smaran*—remembering; *ca*—and; *tat-karma*—his activities; *nṛ-śaṁsam*—cruel; *aṁhaḥ*—a great sin; *śokena*—with lamentation; *mohena*—by bewilderment; *hasan*—laughing; *jagāda*—said.

TRANSLATION

O King, when the great hero Vṛtrāsura saw Indra, his enemy, the killer of his brother, standing before him with a thunderbolt in his hand, desiring to fight, Vṛtrāsura remembered how Indra had cruelly killed his brother. Thinking of Indra's sinful activities, he became mad with lamentation and forgetfulness. Laughing sarcastically, he spoke as follows.

TEXT 14

श्रीवृत्र उवाच
दिष्ट्या भवान् मे समवस्थितो रिपु-
र्यो ब्रह्महा गुरुहा भ्रातृहा च ।
दिष्ट्यानृणोऽद्याहमसत्तम त्वया
मच्छूलनिर्भिन्नदृषद्धृदाचिरात् ॥१४॥

śrī-vṛtra uvāca
diṣṭyā bhavān me samavasthito ripur
yo brahma-hā guru-hā bhrātṛ-hā ca
diṣṭyānṛṇo 'dyāham asattama tvayā
mac-chūla-nirbhinna-dṛṣad-dhṛdācirāt

śrī-vṛtraḥ uvāca—the great hero Vṛtrāsura said; *diṣṭyā*—by good fortune; *bhavān*—Your Lordship; *me*—of me; *samavasthitaḥ*—situated (in front); *ripuḥ*—my enemy; *yaḥ*—who; *brahma-hā*—the killer of a *brāhmaṇa; guru-hā*—the killer of your *guru; bhrātṛ-hā*—the killer of my brother; *ca*—also; *diṣṭyā*—by good fortune; *anṛṇaḥ*—free from debt (to my brother); *adya*—today; *aham*—I; *asat-tama*—O most abominable one; *tvayā*—through you; *mat-śūla*—by my trident; *nirbhinna*—being pierced; *dṛṣat*—like stone; *hṛdā*—whose heart; *acirāt*—very soon.

TRANSLATION

Śrī Vṛtrāsura said: He who has killed a brāhmaṇa, he who has killed his spiritual master—indeed, he who has killed my brother—is now, by good fortune, standing before me face to face as my enemy. O most abominable one, when I pierce your stonelike heart with my trident, I shall be freed from my debt to my brother.

TEXT 15

यो नोऽग्रजस्यात्मविदो द्विजाते-
गुरोरपापस्य च दीक्षितस्य ।
विश्रभ्य खड्गेन शिरांस्यवृश्चत्
पशोरिवाकरुणः स्वर्गकामः ॥१५॥

yo no 'grajasyātma-vido dvijāter
guror apāpasya ca dīkṣitasya
viśrabhya khaḍgena śirāṁsy avṛścat
paśor ivākaruṇaḥ svarga-kāmaḥ

yaḥ—he who; *naḥ*—our; *agra-jasya*—of the elder brother; *ātma-vidaḥ*—who was fully self-realized; *dvi-jāteḥ*—a qualified *brāhmaṇa;* *guroḥ*—your spiritual master; *apāpasya*—free from all sinful activities; *ca*—also; *dīkṣitasya*—appointed as the initiator of your *yajña;* *viśrabhya*—trustfully; *khaḍgena*—by your sword; *śirāṁsi*—the heads; *avṛścat*—cut off; *paśoḥ*—of an animal; *iva*—like; *akaruṇaḥ*—merciless; *svarga-kāmaḥ*—desiring the heavenly planets.

TRANSLATION

Only for the sake of living in the heavenly planets, you killed my elder brother—a self-realized, sinless, qualified brāhmaṇa who

had been appointed your chief priest. He was your spiritual master, but although you entrusted him with the performance of your sacrifice, you later mercilessly severed his heads from his body the way one butchers an animal.

TEXT 16

श्रीह्रीदयाकीर्तिभिरुज्झितं त्वां
स्वकर्मणा पुरुषादैश्च गर्ह्यम् ।
कृच्छ्रेण मच्छूलविभिन्नदेह-
मस्पृष्टवह्निं समदन्ति गृध्राः ॥१६॥

śrī-hrī-dayā-kīrtibhir ujjhitaṁ tvāṁ
sva-karmaṇā puruṣādaiś ca garhyam
kṛcchreṇa mac-chūla-vibhinna-deham
aspṛṣṭa-vahniṁ samadanti gṛdhrāḥ

śrī—opulence or beauty; *hrī*—shame; *dayā*—mercy; *kīrtibhiḥ*—and glory; *ujjhitam*—bereft of; *tvām*—you; *sva-karmaṇā*—by your own activities; *puruṣa-adaiḥ*—by the Rākṣasas (man-eaters); *ca*—and; *garhyam*—condemnable; *kṛcchreṇa*—with great difficulty; *mat-śūla*—by my trident; *vibhinna*—pierced; *deham*—your body; *aspṛṣṭa-vahnim*—not even touched by fire; *samadanti*—will eat; *gṛdhrāḥ*—the vultures.

TRANSLATION

Indra, you are bereft of all shame, mercy, glory and good fortune. Deprived of these good qualities by the reactions of your fruitive activities, you are to be condemned even by the man-eaters [Rākṣasas]. Now I shall pierce your body with my trident, and after you die with great pain, even fire will not touch you; only the vultures will eat your body.

TEXT 17

अन्येऽनु ये त्वेह नृशंसमज्ञा
यदुद्यतास्त्राः प्रहरन्ति मह्यम् ।

तैर्भूतनाथान् सगणान् निशात-
त्रिशूलनिर्भिन्नगलैर्यजामि ॥१७॥

anye 'nu ye tveha nṛ-śaṁsam ajñā
yad udyatāstrāḥ praharanti mahyam
tair bhūta-nāthān sagaṇān niśāta-
triśūla-nirbhinna-galair yajāmi

anye—others; *anu*—follow; *ye*—who; *tvā*—you; *iha*—in this connection; *nṛ-śaṁsam*—very cruel; *ajñāḥ*—persons unaware of my prowess; *yat*—if; *udyata-astrāḥ*—with their swords raised; *praharanti*—attack; *mahyam*—me; *taiḥ*—with those; *bhūta-nāthān*—to such leaders of the ghosts as Bhairava; *sa-gaṇān*—with their hordes; *niśāta*—sharpened; *tri-śūla*—by the trident; *nirbhinna*—separated or pierced; *galaiḥ*—having their necks; *yajāmi*—I shall offer sacrifices.

TRANSLATION

You are naturally cruel. If the other demigods, unaware of my prowess, follow you by attacking me with raised weapons, I shall sever their heads with this sharp trident. With those heads I shall perform a sacrifice to Bhairava and the other leaders of the ghosts, along with their hordes.

TEXT 18

अथो हरे मे कुलिशेन वीर
हर्ता प्रमथ्यैव शिरो यदीह ।
तत्रानृणो भूतबलिं विधाय
मनस्विनां पादरजः प्रपत्स्ये ॥१८॥

atho hare me kuliśena vīra
hartā pramathyaiva śiro yadīha
tatrānṛṇo bhūta-baliṁ vidhāya
manasvināṁ pāda-rajaḥ prapatsye

atho—otherwise; *hare*—O King Indra; *me*—of me; *kuliśena*—by your thunderbolt; *vīra*—O great hero; *hartā*—you cut off; *pramathya*—

destroying my army; *eva*—certainly; *śiraḥ*—head; *yadi*—if; *iha*—in this battle; *tatra*—in that case; *anṛṇaḥ*—relieved of all debts in this material world; *bhūta-balim*—a presentation for all living entities; *vidhāya*—arranging; *manasvinām*—of great sages like Nārada Muni; *pāda-rajaḥ*—the dust of the lotus feet; *prapatsye*—I shall achieve.

TRANSLATION

But if in this battle you cut off my head with your thunderbolt and kill my soldiers, O Indra, O great hero, I shall take great pleasure in offering my body to other living entities [such as jackals and vultures]. I shall thus be relieved of my obligations to the reactions of my karma, and my fortune will be to receive the dust from the lotus feet of great devotees like Nārada Muni.

PURPORT

Śrī Narottama dāsa Ṭhākura sings:

ei chaya gosāñi yāra, mui tāra dāsa
tāṅ' sabāra pada-reṇu mora pañca-grāsa

"I am the servant of the six Gosvāmīs, and the dust of their lotus feet provides my five kinds of food." A Vaiṣṇava always desires the dust of the lotus feet of previous *ācāryas* and Vaiṣṇavas. Vṛtrāsura was certain that he would be killed in the battle with Indra, because this was the desire of Lord Viṣṇu. He was prepared for death because he knew that after his death he was destined to return home, back to Godhead. This is a great destination, and it is achieved by the grace of a Vaiṣṇava. *Chāḍiyā vaiṣṇava-sevā nistāra pāyeche kebā:* no one has ever gone back to Godhead without being favored by a Vaiṣṇava. In this verse, therefore, we find the words *manasvināṁ pāda-rajaḥ prapatsye:* "I shall receive the dust of the lotus feet of great devotees." The word *manasvinām* refers to great devotees who always think of Kṛṣṇa. They are always peaceful, thinking of Kṛṣṇa, and therefore they are called *dhīra.* The best example of such a devotee is Nārada Muni. If one receives the dust of the lotus feet of a *manasvī,* a great devotee, he certainly returns home, back to Godhead.

TEXT 19

सुरेश कस्मान्न हिनोषि वज्रं
पुरः स्थिते वैरिणि मय्यमोघम् ।
मा संशयिष्ठा न गदेव वज्रः
स्यान्निष्फलः कृपणार्थेव याच्ञा ॥१९॥

sureśa kasmān na hinoṣi vajraṁ
puraḥ sthite vairiṇi mayy amogham
mā saṁśayiṣṭhā na gadeva vajraḥ
syān niṣphalaḥ kṛpaṇārtheva yācñā

sura-īśa—O King of the demigods; *kasmāt*—why; *na*—not; *hinoṣi*—you hurl; *vajram*—the thunderbolt; *puraḥ sthite*—standing in front; *vairiṇi*—your enemy; *mayi*—at me; *amogham*—which is infallible (your thunderbolt); *mā*—do not; *saṁśayiṣṭhāḥ*—doubt; *na*—not; *gadā iva*—like the club; *vajraḥ*—the thunderbolt; *syāt*—may be; *niṣphalaḥ*—with no result; *kṛpaṇa*—from a miserly person; *arthā*—for money; *iva*—like; *yācñā*—a request.

TRANSLATION

O King of the demigods, since I, your enemy, am standing before you, why don't you hurl your thunderbolt at me? Although your attack upon me with your club was certainly useless, like a request of money from a miser, the thunderbolt you carry will not be useless. You need have no doubts about this.

PURPORT

When King Indra threw his club at Vṛtrāsura, Vṛtrāsura caught it in his left hand and retaliated by using it to strike the head of Indra's elephant. Thus Indra's attack was a disastrous failure. Indeed, Indra's elephant was injured and thrown back fourteen yards. Therefore even though Indra stood with the thunderbolt to hurl against Vṛtrāsura, he was doubtful, thinking that the thunderbolt might also fail. Vṛtrāsura, however, being a Vaiṣṇava, assured Indra that the thunderbolt would not fail, for Vṛtrāsura knew that it had been prepared in accordance with the instructions of Lord Viṣṇu. Although Indra had doubts because he could not understand that Lord Viṣṇu's order never fails, Vṛtrāsura understood Lord Viṣṇu's purpose. Vṛtrāsura was eager to be killed by the thunderbolt manufactured according to Lord Viṣṇu's instructions because he was sure that he would thus return home, back to Godhead. He was simply waiting for the opportunity of the thunderbolt's being released. In effect, therefore, Vṛtrāsura told Indra, "If you want to kill me, since I am your enemy, take this opportunity. Kill me. You will gain victory, and I shall go back to Godhead. Your deed will be equally beneficial for both of us. Do it immediately."

TEXT 20

नन्वेष वज्रस्तव शक्र तेजसा
हरेर्दधीचेस्तपसा च तेजितः ।
तेनैव शत्रुं जहि विष्णुयन्त्रितो
यतो हरिर्विजयः श्रीर्गुणास्ततः ॥२०॥

nanv eṣa vajras tava śakra tejasā
harer dadhīces tapasā ca tejitaḥ
tenaiva śatruṁ jahi viṣṇu-yantrito
yato harir vijayaḥ śrīr guṇās tataḥ

nanu—certainly; *eṣaḥ*—this; *vajraḥ*—thunderbolt; *tava*—of yours; *śakra*—O Indra; *tejasā*—by the prowess; *hareḥ*—of Lord Viṣṇu, the Supreme Personality of Godhead; *dadhīceḥ*—of Dadhīci; *tapasā*—by the austerities; *ca*—as well as; *tejitaḥ*—empowered; *tena*—with that; *eva*—certainly; *śatrum*—your enemy; *jahi*—kill; *viṣṇu-yantritaḥ*—ordered by Lord Viṣṇu; *yataḥ*—wherever; *hariḥ*—Lord Viṣṇu; *vijayaḥ*—victory; *śrīḥ*—opulences; *guṇāḥ*—and other good qualities; *tataḥ*—there.

TRANSLATION

O Indra, King of heaven, the thunderbolt you carry to kill me has been empowered by the prowess of Lord Viṣṇu and the strength of Dadhīci's austerities. Since you have come here to kill

me in accordance with Lord Viṣṇu's order, there is no doubt that I shall be killed by the release of your thunderbolt. Lord Viṣṇu has sided with you. Therefore your victory, opulence and all good qualities are assured.

PURPORT

Vṛtrāsura not only assured King Indra that the thunderbolt was invincible, but also encouraged Indra to use it against him as soon as possible. Vṛtrāsura was eager to die with the stroke of the thunderbolt sent by Lord Viṣṇu so that he could immediately return home, back to Godhead. By hurling the thunderbolt, Indra would gain victory and enjoy the heavenly planets, remaining in the material world for repeated birth and death. Indra wanted to gain victory over Vṛtrāsura and thereby become happy, but that would not at all be happiness. The heavenly planets are just below Brahmaloka, but as stated by the Supreme Lord, Kṛṣṇa, *ābrahma-bhuvanāl lokāḥ punar āvartino 'rjuna:* even if one achieves Brahmaloka, he must still fall to the lower planetary systems again and again. However, if one goes back to Godhead, he never returns to this material world. By killing Vṛtrāsura, Indra would not actually gain; he would remain in the material world. Vṛtrāsura, however, would go to the spiritual world. Therefore victory was destined for Vṛtrāsura, not for Indra.

TEXT 21

अहं समाधाय मनो यथाह नः
सङ्कर्षणस्तच्चरणारविन्दे ।
त्वद्वज्ररंहोलुलितग्राम्यपाशो
गतिं मुनेर्याम्यपविद्धलोकः ॥२१॥

ahaṁ samādhāya mano yathāha naḥ
saṅkarṣaṇas tac-caraṇāravinde
tvad-vajra-raṁho-lulita-grāmya-pāśo
gatiṁ muner yāmy apaviddha-lokaḥ

aham—I; *samādhāya*—fixing firmly; *manaḥ*—the mind; *yathā*—just as; *āha*—said; *naḥ*—our; *saṅkarṣaṇaḥ*—Lord Saṅkarṣaṇa; *tat-*

caraṇa-aravinde—at His lotus feet; *tvat-vajra*—of your thunderbolt; *raṁhaḥ*—by the force; *lulita*—torn; *grāmya*—of material attachment; *pāśaḥ*—the rope; *gatim*—the destination; *muneḥ*—of Nārada Muni and other devotees; *yāmi*—I shall achieve; *apaviddha*—giving up; *lokaḥ*—this material world (where one desires all kinds of impermanent things).

TRANSLATION

By the force of your thunderbolt, I shall be freed of material bondage and shall give up this body and this world of material desires. Fixing my mind upon the lotus feet of Lord Saṅkarṣaṇa, I shall attain the destination of such great sages as Nārada Muni, just as Lord Saṅkarṣaṇa has said.

PURPORT

The words *ahaṁ samādhāya manaḥ* indicate that the most important duty at the time of death is to concentrate one's mind. If one can fix his mind on the lotus feet of Kṛṣṇa, Viṣṇu, Saṅkarṣaṇa or any Viṣṇu *mūrti*, his life will be successful. To be killed while fixing his mind at the lotus feet of Saṅkarṣaṇa, Vṛtrāsura asked Indra to release his *vajra*, or thunderbolt. He was destined to be killed by the thunderbolt given by Lord Viṣṇu; there was no question of its being baffled. Therefore Vṛtrāsura requested Indra to release the thunderbolt immediately, and he prepared himself by fixing his mind at the lotus feet of Kṛṣṇa. A devotee is always ready to give up his material body, which is described herein as *grāmya-pāśa*, the rope of material attachment. The body is not at all good; it is simply a cause of bondage to the material world. Unfortunately, even though the body is destined for destruction, fools and rascals invest all their faith in the body and are never eager to return home, back to Godhead.

TEXT 22

पुंसां किलैकान्तधियां स्वकानां
याः सम्पदो दिवि भूमौ रसायाम् ।
न राति यद् द्वेष उद्वेग आधि-
र्मदः कलिर्व्यसनं संप्रयासः ॥२२॥

puṁsāṁ kilaikānta-dhiyāṁ svakānāṁ
yāḥ sampado divi bhūmau rasāyām
na rāti yad dveṣa udvega ādhir
madaḥ kalir vyasanaṁ samprayāsaḥ

puṁsām—unto persons; *kila*—certainly; *ekānta-dhiyām*—who are advanced in spiritual consciousness; *svakānām*—who are recognized by the Supreme Personality of Godhead as His own; *yāḥ*—which; *sampadaḥ*—opulences; *divi*—in the upper planetary systems; *bhūmau*—in the middle planetary systems; *rasāyām*—and in the lower planetary systems; *na*—not; *rāti*—bestows; *yat*—from which; *dveṣaḥ*—envy; *udvegaḥ*—anxiety; *ādhiḥ*—mental agitation; *madaḥ*—pride; *kaliḥ*—quarrel; *vyasanam*—distress due to loss; *samprayāsaḥ*—great endeavor.

TRANSLATION

Persons who fully surrender at the lotus feet of the Supreme Personality of Godhead and always think of His lotus feet are accepted and recognized by the Lord as His own personal assistants or servants. The Lord never bestows upon such servants the brilliant opulences of the upper, lower and middle planetary systems of this material world. When one possesses material opulence in any of these three divisions of the universe, his possessions naturally increase his enmity, anxiety, mental agitation, pride and belligerence. Thus one goes through much endeavor to increase and maintain his possessions, and he suffers great unhappiness when he loses them.

PURPORT

In *Bhagavad-gītā* (4.11) the Lord says:

ye yathā māṁ prapadyante
tāṁs tathaiva bhajāmy aham
mama vartmānuvartante
manuṣyāḥ pārtha sarvaśaḥ

"As devotees surrender unto Me, I reward them accordingly. Everyone follows My path in all respects, O son of Pṛthā." Both Indra and

Vṛtrāsura were certainly devotees of the Lord, although Indra took instructions from Viṣṇu to kill Vṛtrāsura. The Lord was actually more favorable to Vṛtrāsura because after being killed by Indra's thunderbolt, Vṛtrāsura would go back to Godhead, whereas the victorious Indra would rot in this material world. Because both of them were devotees, the Lord awarded them the respective benedictions they wanted. Vṛtrāsura never wanted material possessions, for he knew very well the nature of such possessions. To accumulate material possessions, one must labor very hard, and when he gets them he creates many enemies because this material world is always full of rivalry. If one becomes rich, his friends or relatives are envious. For *ekānta-bhaktas,* unalloyed devotees, Kṛṣṇa therefore never provides material possessions. A devotee sometimes needs some material possessions for preaching, but the possessions of a preacher are not like those of a *karmī.* A *karmī's* possessions are achieved as a result of *karma,* but those of a devotee are arranged by the Supreme Personality of Godhead just to facilitate his devotional activities. Because a devotee never uses material possessions for any purpose other than the service of the Lord, the possessions of a devotee are not to be compared to those of a *karmī.*

TEXT 23

त्रैवर्गिकायासविघातमस्मत्-
पतिर्विधत्ते पुरुषस्य शक्र ।
ततोऽनुमेयो भगवत्प्रसादो
यो दुर्लभोऽकिञ्चनगोचरोऽन्यैः ॥२३॥

trai-vargikāyāsa-vighātam asmat-
patir vidhatte puruṣasya śakra
tato 'numeyo bhagavat-prasādo
yo durlabho 'kiñcana-gocaro 'nyaiḥ

trai-vargika—for the three objectives, namely religiosity, economic development, and satisfaction of the senses; *āyāsa*—of endeavor; *vighātam*—the ruin; *asmat*—our; *patiḥ*—Lord; *vidhatte*—performs; *puruṣasya*—of a devotee; *śakra*—O Indra; *tataḥ*—whereby; *anumeyaḥ*—to be inferred; *bhagavat-prasādaḥ*—the special mercy of the Supreme Personality of Godhead; *yaḥ*—which; *durlabhaḥ*—very difficult to obtain; *akiñcana-gocaraḥ*—within the reach of the unalloyed devotees; *anyaiḥ*—by others, who aspire for material happiness.

TRANSLATION

Our Lord, the Supreme Personality of Godhead, forbids His devotees to endeavor uselessly for religion, economic development and sense gratification. O Indra, one can thus infer how kind the Lord is. Such mercy is obtainable only by unalloyed devotees, not by persons who aspire for material gains.

PURPORT

There are four objectives in human life—namely, religiosity (*dharma*), economic development (*artha*), sense gratification (*kāma*), and liberation (*mokṣa*) from the bondage of material existence. People generally aspire for religiosity, economic development and sense gratification, but a devotee has no other desire than to serve the Supreme Personality of Godhead both in this life and in the next. The special mercy for the unalloyed devotee is that the Lord saves him from hard labor to achieve the results of religion, economic development and sense gratification. Of course, if one wants such benefits, the Lord certainly awards them. Indra, for example, although a devotee, was not much interested in release from material bondage; instead, he desired sense gratification and a high standard of material happiness in the heavenly planets. Vṛtrāsura, however, being an unalloyed devotee, aspired only to serve the Supreme Personality of Godhead. Therefore the Lord arranged for him to go back to Godhead after his bodily bondage was destroyed by Indra. Vṛtrāsura requested Indra to release his thunderbolt against him as soon as possible so that both he and Indra would benefit according to their proportionate advancement in devotional service.

TEXT 24

अहं हरे तव पादैकमूल-
दासानुदासो भवितास्मि भूयः ।

मनः स्मरेतासुपतेर्गुणांस्ते
गृणीत वाक् कर्म करोतु कायः ॥२४॥

ahaṁ hare tava pādaika-mūla-
dāsānudāso bhavitāsmi bhūyaḥ
manaḥ smaretāsu-pater guṇāṁs te
gṛṇīta vāk karma karotu kāyaḥ

aham—I; *hare*—O my Lord; *tava*—of Your Lordship; *pāda-eka-mūla*—whose only shelter is the lotus feet; *dāsa-anudāsaḥ*—the servant of Your servant; *bhavitāsmi*—shall I become; *bhūyaḥ*—again; *manaḥ*—my mind; *smareta*—may remember; *asu-pateḥ*—of the Lord of my life; *guṇān*—the attributes; *te*—of Your Lordship; *gṛṇīta*—may chant; *vāk*—my words; *karma*—activities of service to You; *karotu*—may perform; *kāyaḥ*—my body.

TRANSLATION

O my Lord, O Supreme Personality of Godhead, will I again be able to be a servant of Your eternal servants who find shelter only at Your lotus feet? O Lord of my life, may I again become their servant so that my mind may always think of Your transcendental attributes, my words always glorify those attributes, and my body always engage in the loving service of Your Lordship?

PURPORT

This verse gives the sum and substance of devotional life. One must first become a servant of the servant of the servant of the Lord (*dāsānudāsa*). Śrī Caitanya Mahāprabhu advised, and He also showed by His own example, that a living entity should always desire to be a servant of the servant of the servant of Kṛṣṇa, the maintainer of the *gopīs* (*gopī-bhartuḥ pada-kamalayor dāsa-dāsānudāsaḥ*). This means that one must accept a spiritual master who comes in the disciplic succession and is a servant of the servant of the Lord. Under his direction, one must then engage one's three properties, namely his body, mind and words. The body should be engaged in physical activity under the order of the master, the mind should think of Kṛṣṇa incessantly, and one's words should be engaged in preaching the glories of the Lord. If one is thus engaged in the loving service of the Lord, one's life is successful.

TEXT 25

न नाकपृष्ठं न च पारमेष्ठ्यं
न सार्वभौमं न रसाधिपत्यम् ।
न योगसिद्धीरपुनर्भवं वा
समञ्जस त्वा विरहय्य काङ्क्षे ॥२५॥

na nāka-pṛṣṭhaṁ na ca pārameṣṭhyaṁ
na sārva-bhaumaṁ na rasādhipatyam
na yoga-siddhīr apunar-bhavaṁ vā
samañjasa tvā virahayya kāṅkṣe

na—not; *nāka-pṛṣṭham*—the heavenly planets or Dhruvaloka; *na*—nor; *ca*—also; *pārameṣṭhyam*—the planet on which Lord Brahmā resides; *na*—nor; *sārva-bhaumam*—sovereignty of the whole earthly planetary system; *na*—nor; *rasā-ādhipatyam*—sovereignty of the lower planetary systems; *na*—nor; *yoga-siddhīḥ*—eight kinds of mystic yogic power (*aṇimā, laghimā, mahimā,* etc.); *apunaḥ-bhavam*—liberation from rebirth in a material body; *vā*—or; *samañjasa*—O source of all opportunities; *tvā*—You; *virahayya*—being separated from; *kāṅkṣe*—I desire.

TRANSLATION

O my Lord, source of all opportunities, I do not desire to enjoy in Dhruvaloka, the heavenly planets or the planet where Lord Brahmā resides, nor do I want to be the supreme ruler of all the earthly planets or the lower planetary systems. I do not desire to be master of the powers of mystic yoga, nor do I want liberation if I have to give up Your lotus feet.

PURPORT

A pure devotee never desires to gain material opportunities by rendering transcendental loving service to the Lord. A pure devotee desires only to engage in loving service to the Lord in the constant association of the Lord and His eternal associates, as stated in the previous verse (*dāsānudāso bhavitāsmi*). As confirmed by Narottama dāsa Ṭhākura:

tāṅdera caraṇa sevi bhakta-sane vāsa
janame janame haya, ei abhilāṣa

To serve the Lord and the servants of His servants, in the association of devotees, is the only objective of a pure, unalloyed devotee.

TEXT 26

अजातपक्षा इव मातरं खगाः
स्तन्यं यथा वत्सतराः क्षुधार्ताः ।
प्रियं प्रियेव व्युषितं विषण्णा
मनोऽरविन्दाक्ष दिदृक्षते त्वाम् ॥२६॥

ajāta-pakṣā iva mātaraṁ khagāḥ
stanyaṁ yathā vatsatarāḥ kṣudh-ārtāḥ
priyaṁ priyeva vyuṣitaṁ viṣaṇṇā
mano 'ravindākṣa didṛkṣate tvām

ajāta-pakṣāḥ—who have not yet grown wings; *iva*—like; *mātaram*—the mother; *khagāḥ*—small birds; *stanyam*—the milk from the udder; *yathā*—just as; *vatsatarāḥ*—the young calves; *kṣudh-ārtāḥ*—distressed by hunger; *priyam*—the beloved or husband; *priyā*—the wife or lover; *iva*—like; *vyuṣitam*—who is away from home; *viṣaṇṇā*—morose; *manaḥ*—my mind; *aravinda-akṣa*—O lotus-eyed one; *didṛkṣate*—wants to see; *tvām*—You.

TRANSLATION

O lotus-eyed Lord, as baby birds that have not yet developed their wings always look for their mother to return and feed them, as small calves tied with ropes await anxiously the time of milking, when they will be allowed to drink the milk of their mothers, or as a morose wife whose husband is away from home always longs for

him to return and satisfy her in all respects, I always yearn for the opportunity to render direct service unto You.

PURPORT

A pure devotee always yearns to associate personally with the Lord and render service unto Him. The examples given in this regard are most appropriate. A small baby bird is practically never satisfied except when the mother bird comes to feed it, a small calf is not satisfied unless allowed to suck the milk from the mother's udder, and a chaste, devoted wife whose husband is away from home is never satisfied until she has the association of her beloved husband.

TEXT 27

ममोत्तमश्लोकजनेषु सख्यं
संसारचक्रे भ्रमतः स्वकर्मभिः ।
त्वन्माययात्मात्मजदारगेहे-
ष्वासक्तचित्तस्य न नाथ भूयात् ॥२७॥

mamottamaśloka-janeṣu sakhyaṁ
saṁsāra-cakre bhramataḥ sva-karmabhiḥ
tvan-māyayātmātmaja-dāra-geheṣv
āsakta-cittasya na nātha bhūyāt

mama—my; *uttama-śloka-janeṣu*—among devotees who are simply attached to the Supreme Personality of Godhead; *sakhyam*—friendship; *saṁsāra-cakre*—in the cycle of birth and death; *bhramataḥ*—who am wandering; *sva-karmabhiḥ*—by the results of my own fruitive activities; *tvat-māyayā*—by Your external energy; *ātma*—to the body; *ātma-ja*—children; *dāra*—wife; *geheṣu*—and home; *āsakta*—attached; *cittasya*—whose mind; *na*—not; *nātha*—O my Lord; *bhūyāt*—may there be.

TRANSLATION

O my Lord, my master, I am wandering throughout this material world as a result of my fruitive activities. Therefore I simply seek

friendship in the association of Your pious and enlightened devotees. My attachment to my body, wife, children and home is continuing by the spell of Your external energy, but I wish to be attached to them no longer. Let my mind, my consciousness and everything I have be attached only to You.

Thus end the Bhaktivedanta purports to the Sixth Canto, Eleventh Chapter, of the Śrīmad-Bhāgavatam, *entitled "The Transcendental Qualities of Vṛtrāsura."*

CHAPTER TWELVE

Vṛtrāsura's Glorious Death

This chapter describes how Indra, the King of heaven, killed Vṛtrāsura despite great reluctance.

After Vṛtrāsura finished speaking, he released his trident against King Indra with great anger, but Indra, using his thunderbolt, which was many times more powerful than the trident, broke the trident to pieces and cut off one of Vṛtrāsura's arms. Nevertheless, Vṛtrāsura used his remaining arm to strike Indra with an iron mace, making the thunderbolt fall from Indra's hand. Indra, being very ashamed of this, did not pick up the thunderbolt from the ground, but Vṛtrāsura encouraged King Indra to pick it up and fight. Vṛtrāsura then spoke to King Indra as follows, instructing him very well.

"The Supreme Personality of Godhead," he said, "is the cause of victory and defeat. Not knowing that the Supreme Lord is the cause of all causes, fools and rascals try to take credit for victory or defeat themselves, but everything is actually under the control of the Lord. No one but Him has any independence. The *puruṣa* (the enjoyer) and *prakṛti* (the enjoyed) are under the control of the Lord, for it is by His supervision that everything works systematically. Not seeing the hand of the Supreme in every action, a fool considers himself the ruler and controller of everything. When one understands, however, that the real controller is the Supreme Personality of Godhead, he is freed from the relativities of the world, such as distress, happiness, fear and impurity." Thus Indra and Vṛtrāsura not only fought, but also engaged in philosophical discourses. Then they began to fight again.

This time Indra was more powerful, and he severed Vṛtrāsura's remaining arm. Vṛtrāsura then assumed a gigantic form and swallowed King Indra, but Indra, being protected by the talisman known as Nārāyaṇa-kavaca, was able to protect himself even within Vṛtrāsura's body. Thus he emerged from Vṛtrāsura's abdomen and severed the demon's head from his body with his powerful thunderbolt. Severing the demon's head took one complete year to accomplish.

TEXT 1

श्रीऋषिरुवाच
एवं जिहासुर्नृप देहमाजौ
मृत्युं वरं विजयान्मन्यमानः ।
शूलं प्रगृह्याभ्यपतत् सुरेन्द्रं
यथा महापुरुषं कैटभोऽप्सु ॥ १ ॥

śrī-ṛṣir uvāca
evaṁ jihāsur nṛpa deham ājau
mṛtyuṁ varaṁ vijayān manyamānaḥ
śūlaṁ pragṛhyābhyapatat surendraṁ
yathā mahā-puruṣaṁ kaiṭabho 'psu

śrī-ṛṣiḥ uvāca—Śrī Śukadeva Gosvāmī said; *evam*—thus; *jihāsuḥ*—very eager to give up; *nṛpa*—O King Parīkṣit; *deham*—the body; *ājau*—in battle; *mṛtyum*—death; *varam*—better; *vijayāt*—than victory; *manyamānaḥ*—thinking; *śūlam*—trident; *pragṛhya*—taking up; *abhyapatat*—attacked; *sura-indram*—the King of heaven, Indra; *yathā*—just as; *mahā-puruṣam*—the Supreme Personality of Godhead; *kaiṭabhaḥ*—the demon Kaiṭabha; *apsu*—when the whole universe was inundated.

TRANSLATION

Śukadeva Gosvāmī said: Desiring to give up his body, Vṛtrāsura considered death in the battle preferable to victory. O King Parīkṣit, he vigorously took up his trident and with great force attacked Lord Indra, the King of heaven, just as Kaiṭabha had forcefully attacked the Supreme Personality of Godhead when the universe was inundated.

PURPORT

Although Vṛtrāsura repeatedly encouraged Indra to kill him with the thunderbolt, King Indra was morose at having to kill such a great devotee and was hesitant to throw it. Vṛtrāsura, disappointed that King Indra was reluctant despite his encouragement, took the initiative very forcefully by throwing his trident at Indra. Vṛtrāsura was not at all interested in victory; he was interested in being killed so that he could immediately return home, back to Godhead. As confirmed in *Bhagavad-gītā* (4.9), *tyaktvā dehaṁ punar janma naiti:* after giving up his body, a devotee immediately returns to Lord Kṛṣṇa and never returns to accept another body. This was Vṛtrāśura's interest.

TEXT 2

ततो युगान्ताग्निकठोरजिह्व-
माविध्य शूलं तरसासुरेन्द्रः ।
क्षिप्त्वा महेन्द्राय विनद्य वीरो
हतोऽसि पापेति रुषा जगाद ॥ २ ॥

tato yugāntāgni-kaṭhora-jihvam
āvidhya śūlaṁ tarasāsurendraḥ
kṣiptvā mahendrāya vinadya vīro
hato 'si pāpeti ruṣā jagāda

tataḥ—thereafter; *yuga-anta-agni*—like the fire at the end of every millennium; *kaṭhora*—sharp; *jihvam*—possessing points; *āvidhya*—twirling; *śūlam*—the trident; *tarasā*—with great force; *asura-indraḥ*—the great hero of the demons, Vṛtrāsura; *kṣiptvā*—throwing; *mahā-indrāya*—unto King Indra; *vinadya*—roaring; *vīraḥ*—the great hero (Vṛtrāsura); *hataḥ*—killed; *asi*—you are; *pāpa*—O sinful one; *iti*—thus; *ruṣā*—with great anger; *jagāda*—he cried out.

TRANSLATION

Then Vṛtrāsura, the great hero of the demons, whirled his trident, which had points like the flames of the blazing fire at the end of the millennium. With great force and anger he threw it at Indra, roaring and exclaiming loudly, "O sinful one, thus shall I kill you!"

TEXT 3

ख आपतत् तद् विचलद् ग्रहोल्कव-
न्निरीक्ष्य दुष्प्रेक्ष्यमजातविक्लवः ।
वज्रेण वज्री शतपर्वणाच्छिनद्
भुजं च तस्योरगराजभोगम् ॥ ३ ॥

kha āpatat tad vicalad graholkavan
nirīkṣya duṣprekṣyam ajāta-viklavaḥ
vajreṇa vajrī śata-parvaṇācchinad
bhujaṁ ca tasyoraga-rāja-bhogam

khe—in the sky; *āpatat*—flying toward him; *tat*—that trident; *vicalat*—rotating; *graha-ulka-vat*—like a falling star; *nirīkṣya*—observing; *duṣprekṣyam*—unbearable to see; *ajāta-viklavaḥ*—not afraid; *vajreṇa*—with the thunderbolt; *vajrī*—Indra, the holder of the thunderbolt; *śata-parvaṇā*—possessing one hundred joints; *ācchinat*—cut; *bhujam*—the arm; *ca*—and; *tasya*—of him (Vṛtrāsura); *uraga-rāja*—of the great serpent Vāsuki; *bhogam*—like the body.

TRANSLATION

Flying in the sky, Vṛtrāsura's trident resembled a brilliant meteor. Although the blazing weapon was difficult to look upon, King Indra, unafraid, cut it to pieces with his thunderbolt. Simultaneously, he cut off one of Vṛtrāsura's arms, which was as thick as the body of Vāsuki, the King of the serpents.

TEXT 4

छिन्नैकबाहुः परिघेण वृत्रः
संरब्ध आसाद्य गृहीतवज्रम् ।
हनौ तताडेन्द्रमथामरेभं
वज्रं च हस्तान्न्यपतन्मघोनः ॥ ४ ॥

chinnaika-bāhuḥ parigheṇa vṛtraḥ
saṁrabdha āsādya gṛhīta-vajram

hanau taṭāḍendram athāmarebhaṁ
vajraṁ ca hastān nyapatan maghonaḥ

chinna—cut off; *eka*—one; *bāhuḥ*—whose arm; *parigheṇa*—with a mace of iron; *vṛtraḥ*—Vṛtrāsura; *saṁrabdhaḥ*—being very angry; *āsādya*—reaching; *gṛhīta*—taking up; *vajram*—the thunderbolt; *hanau*—on the jaw; *tatāḍa*—struck; *indram*—Lord Indra; *atha*—also; *amara-ibham*—his elephant; *vajram*—the thunderbolt; *ca*—and; *hastāt*—from the hand; *nyapatat*—fell; *maghonaḥ*—of King Indra.

TRANSLATION

Although one of his arms was severed from his body, Vṛtrāsura angrily approached King Indra and struck him on the jaw with an iron mace. He also struck the elephant that carried Indra. Thus Indra dropped the thunderbolt from his hand.

TEXT 5

वृत्रस्य कर्मातिमहाद्भुतं तत्
सुरासुराश्चारणसिद्धसङ्घाः ।
अपूजयंस्तत् पुरुहूतसंकटं
निरीक्ष्य हा हेति विचुक्रुशुर्भृशम् ॥ ५ ॥

vṛtrasya karmāti-mahādbhutaṁ tat
surāsurāś cāraṇa-siddha-saṅghāḥ
apūjayaṁs tat puruhūta-saṅkaṭaṁ
nirīkṣya hā heti vicukruśur bhṛśam

vṛtrasya—of Vṛtrāsura; *karma*—the accomplishment; *ati*—very; *mahā*—greatly; *adbhutam*—wonderful; *tat*—that; *sura*—the demigods; *asurāḥ*—and the demons; *cāraṇa*—the Cāraṇas; *siddha-saṅghāḥ*—and the society of Siddhas; *apūjayan*—glorified; *tat*—that; *puruhūta-saṅkaṭam*—the dangerous position of Indra; *nirīkṣya*—seeing; *hā hā*—alas, alas; *iti*—thus; *vicukruśuḥ*—lamented; *bhṛśam*—very much.

TRANSLATION

The denizens of various planets, like the demigods, demons, Cāraṇas and Siddhas, praised Vṛtrāsura's deed, but when they observed that Indra was in great danger, they lamented, "Alas! Alas!"

TEXT 6

इन्द्रो न वज्रं जगृहे विलज्जित-
श्च्युतं स्वहस्तादरिसन्निधौ पुनः ।
तमाह वृत्रो हर आत्तवज्रो
जहि स्वशत्रुं न विषादकालः ॥ ६ ॥

indro na vajraṁ jagṛhe vilajjitaś
cyutaṁ sva-hastād ari-sannidhau punaḥ
tam āha vṛtro hara ātta-vajro
jahi sva-śatruṁ na viṣāda-kālaḥ

indraḥ—King Indra; *na*—not; *vajram*—the thunderbolt; *jagṛhe*—took up; *vilajjitaḥ*—being ashamed; *cyutam*—fallen; *sva-hastāt*—from his own hand; *ari-sannidhau*—in front of his enemy; *punaḥ*—again; *tam*—unto him; *āha*—said; *vṛtraḥ*—Vṛtrāsura; *hare*—O Indra; *ātta-vajraḥ*—taking up your thunderbolt; *jahi*—kill; *sva-śatrum*—your enemy; *na*—not; *viṣāda-kālaḥ*—the time for lamentation.

TRANSLATION

Having dropped the thunderbolt from his hand in the presence of his enemy, Indra was practically defeated and was very much ashamed. He dared not pick up his weapon again. Vṛtrāsura, however, encouraged him, saying, "Take up your thunderbolt and kill your enemy. This is not the time to lament your fate."

TEXT 7

युयुत्सतां कुत्रचिदाततायिनां
जयः सदैकत्र न वै परात्मनाम् ।

विनैकमुत्पत्तिलयस्थितीश्वरं
सर्वज्ञमाद्यं पुरुषं सनातनम् ॥ ७ ॥

yuyutsatāṁ kutracid ātatāyināṁ
jayaḥ sadaikatra na vai parātmanām
vinaikam utpatti-laya-sthitīśvaraṁ
sarvajñam ādyaṁ puruṣaṁ sanātanam

yuyutsatām—of those who are belligerent; *kutracit*—sometimes; *ātatāyinām*—armed with weapons; *jayaḥ*—victory; *sadā*—always; *ekatra*—in one place; *na*—not; *vai*—indeed; *para-ātmanām*—of the subordinate living entities, who work only under the direction of the Supersoul; *vinā*—except; *ekam*—one; *utpatti*—of the creation; *laya*—annihilation; *sthiti*—and maintenance; *īśvaram*—the controller; *sarva-jñam*—who knows everything (past, present and future); *ādyam*—the original; *puruṣam*—enjoyer; *sanātanam*—eternal.

TRANSLATION

Vṛtrāsura continued: O Indra, no one is guaranteed of being always victorious but the original enjoyer, the Supreme Personality of Godhead, Bhagavān. He is the cause of creation, maintenance and annihilation, and He knows everything. Being dependent and being obliged to accept material bodies, belligerent subordinates are sometimes victorious and sometimes defeated.

PURPORT

The Lord says in *Bhagavad-gītā* (15.15):

sarvasya cāhaṁ hṛdi sanniviṣṭo
mattaḥ smṛtir jñānam apohanaṁ ca

"I am seated in everyone's heart, and from Me come remembrance, knowledge and forgetfulness." When two parties fight, the fighting actually goes on under the direction of the Supreme Personality of Godhead, who is Paramātmā, the Supersoul. Elsewhere in the *Gītā* (3.27) the Lord says:

prakṛteḥ kriyamāṇāni
guṇaiḥ karmāṇi sarvaśaḥ
ahaṅkāra-vimūḍhātmā
kartāham iti manyate

"The bewildered spirit soul, under the influence of the three modes of material nature, thinks himself the doer of activities that are in actuality carried out by nature." The living entities work only under the direction of the Supreme Lord. The Lord gives orders to material nature, and she arranges facilities for the living entities. The living entities are not independent, although they foolishly think themselves the doers (*kartā*).

Victory is always with the Supreme Personality of Godhead. As for the subordinate living entities, they fight under the arrangement of the Supreme Personality of Godhead. Victory or defeat is not actually theirs; it is an arrangement by the Lord through the agency of material nature. Pride in victory, or moroseness in defeat, is useless. One should fully depend on the Supreme Personality of Godhead, who is responsible for the victory and defeat of all living entities. The Lord advises, *niyataṁ kuru karma tvaṁ karma jyāyo hy akarmaṇaḥ:* "Perform your prescribed duty, for action is better than inaction." The living entity is ordered to act according to his position. Victory or defeat depends on the Supreme Lord. *Karmaṇy evādhikāras te mā phaleṣu kadācana:* "You have a right to perform your prescribed duty, but you are not entitled to the fruits of actions." One must act sincerely, according to his position. Victory or defeat depends on the Lord.

Vṛtrāsura encouraged Indra, saying, "Don't be morose because of my victory. There is no need to stop fighting. Instead, you should go on with your duty. When Kṛṣṇa desires, you will certainly be victorious." This verse is very instructive for sincere workers in the Kṛṣṇa consciousness movement. We should not be jubilant in victory or morose in defeat. We should make a sincere effort to implement the will of Kṛṣṇa, or Śrī Caitanya Mahāprabhu, and we should not be concerned with victory and defeat. Our only duty is to work sincerely, so that our activities may be recognized by Kṛṣṇa.

TEXT 8

लोकाः सपाला यस्येमे श्वसन्ति विवशा वशे ।
द्विजा इव शिचा बद्धाः स काल इह कारणम् ॥ ८ ॥

lokāḥ sapālā yasyeme
śvasanti vivaśā vaśe
dvijā iva śicā baddhāḥ
sa kāla iha kāraṇam

lokāḥ—the worlds; *sa-pālāḥ*—with their chief deities or controllers; *yasya*—of whom; *ime*—all these; *śvasanti*—live; *vivaśāḥ*—fully dependent; *vaśe*—under the control; *dvijāḥ*—birds; *iva*—like; *śicā*—by a net; *baddhāḥ*—bound; *saḥ*—that; *kālaḥ*—time factor; *iha*—in this; *kāraṇam*—the cause.

TRANSLATION

All living beings in all the planets of this universe, including the presiding deities of all the planets, are fully under the control of the Lord. They work like birds caught in a net, who cannot move independently.

PURPORT

The difference between the *suras* and the *asuras* is that the *suras* know that nothing can happen without the desire of the Supreme Personality of Godhead, whereas the *asuras* cannot understand the supreme will of the Lord. In this fight, Vṛtrāsura is actually the *sura*, whereas Indra is the *asura.* No one can act independently; rather, everyone acts under the direction of the Supreme Personality of Godhead. Therefore victory and defeat come according to the results of one's *karma*, and the judgment is given by the Supreme Lord (*karmaṇā daiva-netreṇa*). Since we act under the control of the Supreme according to our *karma*, no one is independent, from Brahmā down to the insignificant ant. Whether we are defeated or victorious, the Supreme Lord is always victorious because everyone acts under His directions.

TEXT 9

ओजः सहो बलं प्राणममृतं मृत्युमेव च ।
तमज्ञाय जनो हेतुमात्मानं मन्यते जडम् ॥ ९ ॥

ojaḥ saho balaṁ prāṇam
amṛtaṁ mṛtyum eva ca
tam ajñāya jano hetum
ātmānaṁ manyate jaḍam

ojaḥ—the strength of the senses; *sahaḥ*—the strength of the mind; *balam*—the strength of the body; *prāṇam*—the living condition; *amṛtam*—immortality; *mṛtyum*—death; *eva*—indeed; *ca*—also; *tam*—Him (the Supreme Lord); *ajñāya*—without knowing; *janaḥ*—a foolish person; *hetum*—the cause; *ātmānam*—the body; *manyate*—considers; *jaḍam*—although as good as stone.

TRANSLATION

Our sensory prowess, mental power, bodily strength, living force, immortality and mortality are all subject to the superintendence of the Supreme Personality of Godhead. Not knowing this, foolish people think the dull material body to be the cause of their activities.

TEXT 10

यथा दारुमयी नारी यथा पत्रमयो मृगः ।
एवं भूतानि मघवन्नीशतन्त्राणि विद्धि भोः ॥१०॥

yathā dārumayī nārī
yathā patramayo mṛgaḥ
evaṁ bhūtāni maghavann
īśa-tantrāṇi viddhi bhoḥ

yathā—just as; *dāru-mayī*—made of wood; *nārī*—a woman; *yathā*—just as; *patra-mayaḥ*—made of leaves; *mṛgaḥ*—an animal; *evam*—thus; *bhūtāni*—all things; *maghavan*—O King Indra; *īśa*—the Supreme Personality of Godhead; *tantrāṇi*—depending upon; *viddhi*—please know; *bhoḥ*—O sir.

TRANSLATION

O King Indra, as a wooden doll that looks like a woman or as an animal made of grass and leaves cannot move or dance independently, but depends fully on the person who handles it, all of us dance according to the desire of the supreme controller, the Personality of Godhead. No one is independent.

PURPORT

This is confirmed in *Caitanya-caritāmṛta* (*Ādi* 5.142):

ekale īśvara kṛṣṇa, āra saba bhṛtya
yāre yaiche nācāya, se taiche kare nṛtya

"Lord Kṛṣṇa alone is the supreme controller, and all others are His servants. They dance as He makes them do so." We are all servants of Kṛṣṇa; we have no independence. We are dancing according to the desire of the Supreme Personality of Godhead, but out of ignorance and illusion we think we are independent of the supreme will. Therefore it is said:

īśvaraḥ paramaḥ kṛṣṇaḥ
sac-cid-ānanda-vigrahaḥ
anādir ādir govindaḥ
sarva-kāraṇa-kāraṇam

"Kṛṣṇa, who is known as Govinda, is the supreme controller. He has an eternal, blissful, spiritual body. He is the origin of all. He has no other origin, for He is the prime cause of all causes." (*Brahma-saṁhitā* 5.1)

TEXT 11

पुरुषः प्रकृतिर्व्यक्तमात्मा भूतेन्द्रियाशयाः ।
शक्नुवन्त्यस्य सर्गादौ न विना यदनुग्रहात् ॥११॥

puruṣaḥ prakṛtir vyaktam
ātmā bhūtendriyāśayāḥ
śaknuvanty asya sargādau
na vinā yad-anugrahāt

puruṣaḥ—the generator of the total material energy; *prakṛtiḥ*—the material energy or material nature; *vyaktam*—the principles of manifestation (*mahat-tattva*); *ātmā*—the false ego; *bhūta*—the five material elements; *indriya*—the ten senses; *āśayāḥ*—the mind, intelligence and consciousness; *śaknuvanti*—are able; *asya*—of this universe; *sarga-*

ādau—in the creation, etc.; *na*—not; *vinā*—without; *yat*—of whom; *anugrahāt*—the mercy.

TRANSLATION

The three puruṣas—Kāraṇodakaśāyī Viṣṇu, Garbhodakaśāyī Viṣṇu and Kṣīrodakaśāyī Viṣṇu—the material nature, the total material energy, the false ego, the five material elements, the material senses, the mind, the intelligence and consciousness cannot create the material manifestation without the direction of the Supreme Personality of Godhead.

PURPORT

As confirmed in the *Viṣṇu Purāṇa, parasya brahmaṇaḥ śaktis tathedam akhilaṁ jagat:* whatever manifestations we experience are nothing but various energies of the Supreme Personality of Godhead. These energies cannot create anything independently. This is also confirmed by the Lord Himself in *Bhagavad-gītā* (9.10): *mayādhyakṣeṇa prakṛtiḥ sūyate sa-carācaram.* "This material nature is working under My direction, O son of Kuntī, and it is producing all moving and unmoving living beings." Only under the direction of the Lord, the Supreme Person, can *prakṛti*, which is manifested in twenty-four elements, create different situations for the living entity. In the *Vedas* the Lord says:

madīyaṁ mahimānaṁ ca
parabrahmeti śabditam
vetsyasy anugṛhītaṁ me
sampraśnair vivṛtaṁ hṛdi

"Since everything is a manifestation of My energy, I am known as Parabrahman. Therefore everyone should hear from Me about My glorious activities." The Lord also says in *Bhagavad-gītā* (10.2), *aham ādir hi devānām:* "I am the origin of all the demigods." Therefore the Supreme Personality of Godhead is the origin of everything, and no one is independent of Him. Śrīla Madhvācārya also says, *anīśa-jīva-rūpeṇa:* the living entity is *anīśa*, never the controller, but is always controlled. Therefore when a living entity becomes proud of being an independent *īśvara*, or god, that is his foolishness. Such foolishness is described in the following verse.

TEXT 12

अविद्वानेवमात्मानं मन्यतेऽनीशमीश्वरम् ।
भूतैः सृजति भूतानि ग्रसते तानि तैः स्वयम् ॥१२॥

avidvān evam ātmānaṁ
manyate 'nīśam īśvaram
bhūtaiḥ sṛjati bhūtāni
grasate tāni taiḥ svayam

avidvān—one who is foolish, without knowledge; *evam*—thus; *ātmānam*—himself; *manyate*—considers; *anīśam*—although totally dependent on others; *īśvaram*—as the supreme controller, independent; *bhūtaiḥ*—by the living entities; *sṛjati*—He (the Lord) creates; *bhūtāni*—other living entities; *grasate*—He devours; *tāni*—them; *taiḥ*—by other living beings; *svayam*—Himself.

TRANSLATION

A foolish, senseless person cannot understand the Supreme Personality of Godhead. Although always dependent, he falsely thinks himself the Supreme. If one thinks, "According to one's previous fruitive actions, one's material body is created by the father and mother, and the same body is annihilated by another agent, as another animal is devoured by a tiger," this is not proper understanding. The Supreme Personality of Godhead Himself creates and devours the living beings through other living beings.

PURPORT

According to the conclusion of the philosophy known as *karma-mīmāṁsā*, one's *karma*, or previous fruitive activity, is the cause of everything, and therefore there is no need to work. Those who arrive at this conclusion are foolish. When a father creates a child, he does not do so independently; he is induced to do so by the Supreme Lord. As the

Lord Himself says in *Bhagavad-gītā* (15.15), *sarvasya cāhaṁ hṛdi sanniviṣṭo mattaḥ smṛtir jñānam apohanaṁ ca:* "I am in everyone's heart, and from Me come remembrance, knowledge and forgetfulness." Unless one receives dictation from the Supreme Personality of Godhead, who sits within everyone's heart, one cannot be induced to create anything. Therefore the father and mother are not the creators of the living entity. According to the living entity's *karma*, fruitive activities, he is put into the semen of the father, who injects the living entity into the womb of the mother. Then according to the body of the mother and father (*yathā-yoni yathā-bījam*), the living entity accepts a body and takes birth to suffer or enjoy. Therefore the Supreme Lord is the original cause of one's birth. Similarly, the Supreme Lord is the cause of one's being killed. No one is independent; everyone is dependent. The true conclusion is that the only independent person is the Supreme Personality of Godhead.

TEXT 13

आयुः श्रीः कीर्तिरैश्वर्यमाशिषः पुरुषस्य याः ।
भवन्त्येव हि तत्काले यथानिच्छोर्विपर्ययाः ॥१३॥

āyuḥ śrīḥ kīrtir aiśvaryam
āśiṣaḥ puruṣasya yāḥ
bhavanty eva hi tat-kāle
yathānicchor viparyayāḥ

āyuḥ—longevity; *śrīḥ*—opulence; *kīrtiḥ*—fame; *aiśvaryam*—power; *āśiṣaḥ*—benedictions; *puruṣasya*—of the living entity; *yāḥ*—which; *bhavanti*—arise; *eva*—indeed; *hi*—certainly; *tat-kāle*—at that proper time; *yathā*—just as; *anicchoḥ*—of one not desiring; *viparyayāḥ*—reverse conditions.

TRANSLATION

Just as a person not inclined to die must nonetheless give up his longevity, opulence, fame and everything else at the time of death, so, at the appointed time of victory, one can gain all these when the Supreme Lord awards them by His mercy.

PURPORT

It is not good to be falsely puffed up, saying that by one's own effort one has become opulent, learned, beautiful and so on. All such good fortune is achieved through the mercy of the Lord. From another point of view, no one wants to die, and no one wants to be poor or ugly. Therefore, why does the living entity, against his will, receive such unwanted troubles? It is due to the mercy or chastisement of the Supreme Personality of Godhead that one gains or loses everything material. No one is independent; everyone is dependent on the mercy or chastisement of the Supreme Lord. There is a common saying in Bengal that the Lord has ten hands. This means that He has control everywhere—in the eight directions and up and down. If He wants to take everything away from us with His ten hands, we cannot protect anything with our two hands. Similarly, if He wants to bestow benedictions upon us with His ten hands, we cannot factually receive them all with our two hands; in other words, the benedictions exceed our ambitions. The conclusion is that even though we do not wish to be separated from our possessions, sometimes the Lord forcibly takes them from us; and sometimes He showers such benedictions upon us that we are unable to receive them all. Therefore either in opulence or in distress we are not independent; everything is dependent on the sweet will of the Supreme Personality of Godhead.

TEXT 14

तस्मादकीर्तियशसोर्जयापजययोरपि ।
समः स्यात् सुखदुःखाभ्यां मृत्युजीवितयोस्तथा ॥१४॥

tasmād akīrti-yaśasor
jayāpajayayor api
samaḥ syāt sukha-duḥkhābhyāṁ
mṛtyu-jīvitayos tathā

tasmāt—therefore (because of being fully dependent on the pleasure of the Supreme Personality of Godhead); *akīrti*—of defamation; *yaśasoḥ*—and fame; *jaya*—of victory; *apajayayoḥ*—and defeat; *api*—even; *samaḥ*—equal; *syāt*—one should be; *sukha-duḥkhābhyām*—with the distress and happiness; *mṛtyu*—of death; *jīvitayoḥ*—or of living; *tathā*—as well as.

TRANSLATION

Since everything is dependent on the supreme will of the Personality of Godhead, one should be equipoised in fame and defamation, victory and defeat, life and death. In their effects, represented as happiness and distress, one should maintain oneself in equilibrium, without anxiety.

TEXT 15

सत्त्वं रजस्तम इति प्रकृतेर्नात्मनो गुणाः ।
तत्र साक्षिणमात्मानं यो वेद स न बध्यते ॥१५॥

sattvaṁ rajas tama iti
prakṛter nātmano guṇāḥ
tatra sākṣiṇam ātmānaṁ
yo veda sa na badhyate

sattvam—the mode of goodness; *rajaḥ*—the mode of passion; *tamaḥ*—the mode of ignorance; *iti*—thus; *prakṛteḥ*—of the material nature; *na*—not; *ātmanaḥ*—of the spirit soul; *guṇāḥ*—the qualities; *tatra*—in such a position; *sākṣiṇam*—an observer; *ātmānam*—the self; *yaḥ*—anyone who; *veda*—knows; *saḥ*—he; *na*—not; *badhyate*—is bound.

TRANSLATION

One who knows that the three qualities—goodness, passion and ignorance—are not qualities of the soul but qualities of material nature, and who knows that the pure soul is simply an observer of the actions and reactions of these qualities, should be understood to be a liberated person. He is not bound by these qualities.

PURPORT

As the Lord explains in *Bhagavad-gītā* (18.54):

brahma-bhūtaḥ prasannātmā
na śocati na kāṅkṣati
samaḥ sarveṣu bhūteṣu
mad-bhaktiṁ labhate parām

"One who is transcendentally situated at once realizes the Supreme Brahman and becomes fully joyful. He never laments or desires to have anything; he is equally disposed to every living entity. In that state he attains pure devotional service unto Me." When one attains self-realization, the *brahma-bhūta* stage, one knows that whatever happens during his life is due to the contamination of the modes of material nature. The living being, the pure soul, has nothing to do with these modes. In the midst of the hurricane of the material world, everything changes very quickly, but if one remains silent and simply observes the actions and reactions of the hurricane, he is understood to be liberated. The real qualification of the liberated soul is that he remains Kṛṣṇa conscious, undisturbed by the actions and reactions of the material energy. Such a liberated person is always jubilant. He never laments or aspires for anything. Since everything is supplied by the Supreme Lord, the living entity, being fully dependent on Him, should not protest or accept anything in terms of his personal sense gratification; rather, he should receive everything as the mercy of the Lord and remain steady in all circumstances.

TEXT 16

पश्य मां निर्जितं शत्रु वृक्णायुधभुजं मृधे ।
घटमानं यथाशक्ति तव प्राणजिहीर्षया ॥१६॥

paśya māṁ nirjitaṁ śatru
vṛkṇāyudha-bhujaṁ mṛdhe
ghaṭamānaṁ yathā-śakti
tava prāṇa-jihīrṣayā

paśya—look; *mām*—at me; *nirjitam*—already defeated; *śatru*—O enemy; *vṛkṇa*—cut off; *āyudha*—my weapon; *bhujam*—and my arm;

mṛdhe—in this fight; *ghaṭamānam*—still trying; *yathā-śakti*—according to my ability; *tava*—of you; *prāṇa*—the life; *jihīrṣayā*—with the desire to take away.

TRANSLATION

O my enemy, just look at me. I have already been defeated, for my weapon and arm have been cut to pieces. You have already overwhelmed me, but nonetheless, with a desire to kill you, I am trying my best to fight. I am not at all morose, even under such adverse conditions. Therefore you should give up your moroseness and continue fighting.

PURPORT

Vṛtrāsura was so great and powerful that in effect he was acting as the spiritual master of Indra. Although Vṛtrāsura was on the verge of defeat, he was not at all affected. He knew that he was going to be defeated by Indra, and he voluntarily accepted that, but since he was supposed to be Indra's enemy, he tried his best to kill Indra. Thus he performed his duty. One should perform his duty under all circumstances, even though one may know what the result will be.

TEXT 17

प्राणग्लहोऽयं समर इष्वक्षो वाहनासनः ।
अत्र न ज्ञायतेऽमुष्य जयोऽमुष्य पराजयः ॥१७॥

prāṇa-glaho 'yaṁ samara
iṣv-akṣo vāhanāsanaḥ
atra na jñāyate 'muṣya
jayo 'muṣya parājayaḥ

prāṇa-glahaḥ—life is the stake; *ayam*—this; *samaraḥ*—battle; *iṣu-akṣaḥ*—the arrows are the dice; *vāhana-āsanaḥ*—the carriers such as the horses and elephants are the game board; *atra*—here (in this gambling match); *na*—not; *jñāyate*—is known; *amuṣya*—of that one; *jayaḥ*—victory; *amuṣya*—of that one; *parājayaḥ*—defeat.

TRANSLATION

O my enemy, consider this battle a gambling match in which our lives are the stakes, the arrows are the dice, and the animals acting as carriers are the game board. No one can understand who will be defeated and who will be victorious. It all depends on providence.

TEXT 18

श्रीशुक उवाच
इन्द्रो वृत्रवचः श्रुत्वा गतालीकमपूजयत् ।
गृहीतवज्रः प्रहसंस्तमाह गतविस्मयः ॥१८॥

śrī-śuka uvāca
indro vṛtra-vacaḥ śrutvā
gatālīkam apūjayat
gṛhīta-vajraḥ prahasaṁs
tam āha gata-vismayaḥ

śrī-śukaḥ uvāca—Śrī Śukadeva Gosvāmī said; *indraḥ*—King Indra; *vṛtra-vacaḥ*—the words of Vṛtrāsura; *śrutvā*—hearing; *gata-alīkam*—without duplicity; *apūjayat*—worshiped; *gṛhīta-vajraḥ*—taking up the thunderbolt; *prahasan*—smiling; *tam*—unto Vṛtrāsura; *āha*—said; *gata-vismayaḥ*—giving up his wonder.

TRANSLATION

Śukadeva Gosvāmī said: Hearing the straightforward, instructive words of Vṛtrāsura, King Indra praised him and again took the thunderbolt in his hand. Without bewilderment or duplicity, he then smiled and spoke to Vṛtrāsura as follows.

PURPORT

King Indra, the greatest of the demigods, was astonished to hear the instructions of Vṛtrāsura, who was supposed to be a demon. He was struck with wonder that a demon could speak so intelligently. Then he remembered great devotees like Prahlāda Mahārāja and Bali Mahārāja, who had been born in the families of demons, and thus he came to his senses. Even so-called demons sometimes have exalted devotion for the Supreme Personality of Godhead. Therefore Indra smiled reassuringly at Vṛtrāsura.

TEXT 19

इन्द्र उवाच
अहो दानव सिद्धोऽसि यस्य ते मतिरीदृशी ।
भक्तः सर्वात्मनात्मानं सुहृदं जगदीश्वरम् ॥१९॥

indra uvāca
aho dānava siddho 'si
yasya te matir īdṛśī
bhaktaḥ sarvātmanātmānaṁ
suhṛdaṁ jagad-īśvaram

indraḥ uvāca—Indra said; *aho*—hello; *dānava*—O demon; *siddhaḥ asi*—you are now perfect; *yasya*—whose; *te*—your; *matiḥ*—consciousness; *īdṛśī*—such as this; *bhaktaḥ*—a great devotee; *sarva-ātmanā*—without diversion; *ātmānam*—to the Supersoul; *suhṛdam*—the greatest friend; *jagat-īśvaram*—to the Supreme Personality of Godhead.

TRANSLATION

Indra said: O great demon, I see by your discrimination and endurance in devotional service, despite your dangerous position, that you are a perfect devotee of the Supreme Personality of Godhead, the Supersoul and friend of everyone.

PURPORT

As stated in *Bhagavad-gītā* (6.22):

yaṁ labdhvā cāparaṁ lābhaṁ
manyate nādhikaṁ tataḥ
yasmin sthito na duḥkhena
guruṇāpi vicālyate

"Established in Kṛṣṇa consciousness, one never departs from the truth, and upon gaining this he thinks there is no greater gain. Being situated in such a position, one is never shaken, even in the midst of the greatest difficulty." An unalloyed devotee is never disturbed by any kind of trying circumstance. Indra was surprised to see that Vṛtrāsura, undisturbed, was fixed in devotional service to the Lord, for such a mentality is impossible for a demon. However, by the grace of the Supreme Personality of Godhead, anyone can become an exalted devotee (*striyo vaiśyās tathā śūdrās te 'pi yānti paraṁ gatim*). An unalloyed devotee is sure to return home, back to Godhead.

TEXT 20

भवानतार्षीन्मायां वै वैष्णवीं जनमोहिनीम् ।
यद् विहायासुरं भावं महापुरुषतां गतः ॥२०॥

bhavān atārṣīn māyāṁ vai
vaiṣṇavīṁ jana-mohinīm
yad vihāyāsuraṁ bhāvaṁ
mahā-puruṣatāṁ gataḥ

bhavān—your good self; *atārṣīt*—has surmounted; *māyām*—the illusory energy; *vai*—indeed; *vaiṣṇavīm*—of Lord Viṣṇu; *jana-mohinīm*—which deludes the mass of people; *yat*—since; *vihāya*—giving up; *āsuram*—of the demons; *bhāvam*—the mentality; *mahā-puruṣatām*—the position of an exalted devotee; *gataḥ*—obtained.

TRANSLATION

You have surmounted the illusory energy of Lord Viṣṇu, and because of this liberation, you have given up the demoniac mentality and have attained the position of an exalted devotee.

PURPORT

Lord Viṣṇu is the *mahā-puruṣa*. Therefore one who becomes a Vaiṣṇava attains the position of a *mahā-pauruṣya*. This position was attained by Mahārāja Parīkṣit. It is said in the *Padma Purāṇa* that the distinction between a demigod and a demon is that a demigod is a devotee of Lord Viṣṇu whereas a demon is just the opposite: *viṣṇu-bhaktaḥ smṛto daiva āsuras tad-viparyayaḥ.* Vṛtrāsura was considered a demon, but actually he was more than qualified as a devotee, or *mahā-pauruṣya.* If one somehow becomes a devotee of the Supreme Lord, whatever his position, he can be brought to the position of a perfect person. This is possible if an unalloyed devotee tries to serve the Lord by delivering him in this way. Therefore Śukadeva Gosvāmī says in *Śrīmad-Bhāgavatam* (2.4.18):

kirāta-hūṇāndhra-pulinda-pulkaśā
ābhīra-śumbhā yavanāḥ khasādayaḥ
ye 'nye ca pāpā yad-apāśrayāśrayāḥ
śudhyanti tasmai prabhaviṣṇave namaḥ

"Kirātas, Hūṇas, Āndhras, Pulindas, Pulkaśas, Ābhīras, Śumbhas, Yavanas and members of the Khasa races, and even others addicted to sinful acts can be purified by taking shelter of the devotees of the Lord, for He is the supreme power. I beg to offer my respectful obeisances unto Him." Anyone can be purified if he takes shelter of a pure devotee and molds his character according to the pure devotee's direction. Then, even if one is a Kirāta, Āndhra, Pulinda or whatever, he can be purified and elevated to the position of a *mahā-pauruṣya.*

TEXT 21

खल्विदं महदाश्चर्यं यद् रजःप्रकृतेस्तव ।
वासुदेवे भगवति सत्त्वात्मनि दृढा मतिः ॥२१॥

khalv idaṁ mahad āścaryaṁ
yad rajaḥ-prakṛtes tava
vāsudeve bhagavati
sattvātmani dṛḍhā matiḥ

khalu—indeed; *idam*—this; *mahat āścaryam*—great wonder; *yat*—which; *rajaḥ*—influenced by the mode of passion; *prakṛteḥ*—whose nature; *tava*—of you; *vāsudeve*—in Lord Kṛṣṇa; *bhagavati*—the Supreme Personality of Godhead; *sattva-ātmani*—who is situated in pure goodness; *dṛḍhā*—firm; *matiḥ*—consciousness.

TRANSLATION

O Vṛtrāsura, demons are generally conducted by the mode of passion. Therefore, what a great wonder it is that although you are a demon, you have adopted the mentality of a devotee and have fixed your mind on the Supreme Personality of Godhead, Vāsudeva, who is always situated in pure goodness.

PURPORT

King Indra wondered how Vṛtrāsura could have been elevated to the position of an exalted devotee. As for Prahlāda Mahārāja, he was initiated by Nārada Muni, and therefore it was possible for him to become a great devotee, although he was born in a family of demons. For Vṛtrāsura, however, Indra could not detect such causes. Therefore he was struck with wonder that Vṛtrāsura was such an exalted devotee that he could fix his mind without deviation upon the lotus feet of Lord Kṛṣṇa, Vāsudeva.

TEXT 22

यस्य भक्तिर्भगवति हरौ निःश्रेयसेश्वरे ।
विक्रीडतोऽमृताम्भोधौ किं क्षुद्रैः खातकोदकैः ॥२२॥

yasya bhaktir bhagavati
harau niḥśreyaseśvare
vikrīḍato 'mṛtāmbhodhau
kiṁ kṣudraiḥ khātakodakaiḥ

yasya—of whom; *bhaktiḥ*—devotional service; *bhagavati*—to the Supreme Personality of Godhead; *harau*—Lord Hari; *niḥśreyasa-īśvare*—the controller of the supreme perfection of life, or supreme liberation; *vikrīḍataḥ*—swimming or playing; *amṛta-ambhodhau*—in the ocean of nectar; *kim*—what is the use; *kṣudraiḥ*—with small; *khātaka-udakaiḥ*—ditches of water.

TRANSLATION

A person fixed in the devotional service of the Supreme Lord, Hari, the Lord of the highest auspiciousness, swims in the ocean of nectar. For him what is the use of the water in small ditches?

PURPORT

Vṛtrāsura has formerly prayed (*Bhāg.* 6.11.25), *na nāka-pṛṣṭhaṁ na ca pārameṣṭhyaṁ na sārva-bhaumaṁ na rasādhipatyam.* "I do not want the facilities for happiness on Brahmaloka, Svargaloka or even Dhruvaloka, not to speak of this earth or the lower planets. I simply want to return home, back to Godhead." This is the determination of a pure devotee. A pure devotee is never attracted to any exalted position within this material world. He simply wants to associate with the Supreme Personality of Godhead like the inhabitants of Vṛndāvana—Śrīmatī Rādhārāṇī, the *gopīs,* Kṛṣṇa's father and mother (Nanda Mahārāja and Yaśodā), Kṛṣṇa's friends and Kṛṣṇa's servants. He wants to associate with Kṛṣṇa's atmosphere of Vṛndāvana's beauty. These are the highest ambitions of a devotee of Kṛṣṇa. Devotees of Lord Viṣṇu may aspire for a position in Vaikuṇṭhaloka, but a devotee of Kṛṣṇa never aspires even for the facilities of Vaikuṇṭha; he wants to return to Goloka Vṛndāvana and associate with Lord Kṛṣṇa in His eternal pastimes. Any material happiness is like water in a ditch, whereas the spiritual happiness eternally enjoyed in the spiritual world is like an ocean of nectar in which a devotee wants to swim.

TEXT 23

श्रीशुक उवाच

इति ब्रुवाणावन्योन्यं धर्मजिज्ञासया नृप ।
युयुधाते महावीर्याविन्द्रवृत्रौ युधाम्पती ॥२३॥

śrī-śuka uvāca
iti bruvāṇāv anyonyaṁ
dharma-jijñāsayā nṛpa
yuyudhāte mahā-vīryāv
indra-vṛtrau yudhām patī

śrī-śukaḥ uvāca—Śrī Śukadeva Gosvāmī said; *iti*—thus; *bruvāṇau*—speaking; *anyonyam*—to one another; *dharma-jijñāsayā*—with a desire to know the supreme, ultimate religious principle (devotional service); *nṛpa*—O King; *yuyudhāte*—fought; *mahā-vīryau*—both very powerful; *indra*—King Indra; *vṛtrau*—and Vṛtrāsura; *yudhām patī*—both great military commanders.

TRANSLATION

Śrī Śukadeva Gosvāmī said: Vṛtrāsura and King Indra spoke about devotional service even on the battlefield, and then as a matter of duty they again began fighting. My dear King, both of them were great fighters and were equally powerful.

TEXT 24

आविध्य परिघं वृत्रः कार्ष्णायसमरिन्दमः ।
इन्द्राय प्राहिणोद् घोरं वामहस्तेन मारिष ॥२४॥

āvidhya parighaṁ vṛtraḥ
kārṣṇāyasam arindamaḥ
indrāya prāhiṇod ghoraṁ
vāma-hastena māriṣa

āvidhya—whirling; *parigham*—the club; *vṛtraḥ*—Vṛtrāsura; *kārṣṇa-ayasam*—made of iron; *arim-damaḥ*—who was competent to subdue his enemy; *indrāya*—at Indra; *prāhiṇot*—threw; *ghoram*—very fearful; *vāma-hastena*—with his left hand; *māriṣa*—O best of kings, Mahārāja Parīkṣit.

TRANSLATION

O Mahārāja Parīkṣit, Vṛtrāsura, who was completely able to subdue his enemy, took his iron club, whirled it around, aimed it at Indra and then threw it at him with his left hand.

TEXT 25

स तु वृत्रस्य परिघं करं च करभोपमम् ।
चिच्छेद युगपद् देवो वज्रेण शतपर्वणा ॥२५॥

sa tu vṛtrasya parighaṁ
karaṁ ca karabhopamam
ciccheda yugapad devo
vajreṇa śata-parvaṇā

saḥ—he (King Indra); *tu*—however; *vṛtrasya*—of Vṛtrāsura; *parigham*—the iron club; *karam*—his hand; *ca*—and; *karabha-upamam*—as strong as the trunk of an elephant; *ciccheda*—cut to pieces; *yugapat*—simultaneously; *devaḥ*—Lord Indra; *vajreṇa*—with the thunderbolt; *śata-parvaṇā*—having one hundred joints.

TRANSLATION

With his thunderbolt named Śataparvan, Indra simultaneously cut to pieces Vṛtrāsura's club and his remaining hand.

TEXT 26

दोर्भ्यामुत्कृत्तमूलाभ्यां बभौ रक्तस्रवोऽसुरः ।
छिन्नपक्षो यथा गोत्रः खाद् भ्रष्टो वज्रिणा हतः ॥२६॥

dorbhyām utkṛtta-mūlābhyāṁ
babhau rakta-sravo 'suraḥ
chinna-pakṣo yathā gotraḥ
khād bhraṣṭo vajriṇā hataḥ

dorbhyām—from the two arms; *utkṛtta-mūlābhyām*—cut from the very root; *babhau*—was; *rakta-sravaḥ*—profusely discharging blood; *asuraḥ*—Vṛtrāsura; *chinna-pakṣaḥ*—whose wings are cut; *yathā*—just as; *gotraḥ*—a mountain; *khāt*—from the sky; *bhraṣṭaḥ*—falling; *vajriṇā*—by Indra, the carrier of the thunderbolt; *hataḥ*—struck.

TRANSLATION

Vṛtrāsura, bleeding profusely, his two arms cut off at their roots, looked very beautiful, like a flying mountain whose wings have been cut to pieces by Indra.

PURPORT

It appears from the statement of this verse that sometimes there are flying mountains and that their wings are cut by the thunderbolt of Indra. Vṛtrāsura's huge body resembled such a mountain.

TEXTS 27–29

महाप्राणो महावीर्यो महासर्प इव द्विपम् ।
कृत्वाधरां हनुं भूमौ दैत्यो दिव्युत्तरां हनुम् ।
नभोगम्भीरवक्त्रेण लेलिहोल्बणजिह्वया ॥२७॥
दंष्ट्राभिः कालकल्पाभिर्ग्रसन्निव जगत्त्रयम् ।
अतिमात्रमहाकाय आक्षिपंस्तरसा गिरीन् ॥२८॥
गिरिराट् पादचारीव पद्भ्यां निर्जरयन् महीम् ।
जग्रास स समासाद्य वज्रिणं सहवाहनम् ॥२९॥

mahā-prāṇo mahā-vīryo
mahā-sarpa iva dvipam
kṛtvādharāṁ hanuṁ bhūmau
daityo divy uttarāṁ hanum
nabho-gambhīra-vaktreṇa
leliholbaṇa-jihvayā

daṁṣṭrābhiḥ kāla-kalpābhir
grasann iva jagat-trayam
atimātra-mahā-kāya
ākṣipaṁs tarasā girīn

giri-rāṭ pāda-cārīva
padbhyāṁ nirjarayan mahīm
jagrāsa sa samāsādya
vajriṇaṁ saha-vāhanam

mahā-prāṇaḥ—very great in bodily strength; *mahā-vīryaḥ*—showing uncommon prowess; *mahā-sarpaḥ*—the biggest snake; *iva*—like; *dvipam*—an elephant; *kṛtvā*—placing; *adharām*—the lower; *hanum*—jaw; *bhūmau*—on the ground; *daityaḥ*—the demon; *divi*—in the sky; *uttarām hanum*—the upper jaw; *nabhaḥ*—like the sky; *gambhīra*—deep; *vaktreṇa*—with his mouth; *leliha*—like a snake; *ulbaṇa*—fearful; *jihvayā*—with a tongue; *daṁṣṭrābhiḥ*—with teeth; *kāla-kalpābhiḥ*—exactly like the time factor, or death; *grasan*—devouring;

iva—as if; *jagat-trayam*—the three worlds; *ati-mātra*—very high; *mahā-kāyaḥ*—whose great body; *ākṣipan*—shaking; *tarasā*—with great force; *girīn*—the mountains; *giri-rāṭ*—the Himalaya Mountains; *pāda-cārī*—moving on foot; *iva*—as if; *padbhyām*—by his feet; *nirjarayan*—crushing; *mahīm*—the surface of the world; *jagrāsa*—swallowed; *saḥ*—he; *samāsādya*—reaching; *vajriṇam*—Indra, who carries the thunderbolt; *saha-vāhanam*—with his carrier, the elephant.

TRANSLATION

Vṛtrāsura was very powerful in physical strength and influence. He placed his lower jaw on the ground and his upper jaw in the sky. His mouth became very deep, like the sky itself, and his tongue resembled a large serpent. With his fearful, deathlike teeth, he seemed to be trying to devour the entire universe. Thus assuming a gigantic body, the great demon Vṛtrāsura shook even the mountains and began crushing the surface of the earth with his legs, as if he were the Himalayas walking about. He came before Indra and swallowed him and Airāvata, his carrier, just as a big python might swallow an elephant.

TEXT 30

वृत्रग्रस्तं तमालोक्य सप्रजापतयः सुराः ।
हा कष्टमिति निर्विण्णाश्चुक्रुशुः समहर्षयः ॥३०॥

vṛtra-grastaṁ tam ālokya
saprajāpatayaḥ surāḥ
hā kaṣṭam iti nirviṇṇāś
cukruśuḥ samaharṣayaḥ

vṛtra-grastam—swallowed by Vṛtrāsura; *tam*—him (Indra); *ālokya*—seeing; *sa-prajāpatayaḥ*—with Lord Brahmā and other *prajāpatis; surāḥ*—all the demigods; *hā*—alas; *kaṣṭam*—what a tribulation; *iti*—thus; *nirviṇṇāḥ*—being very morose; *cukruśuḥ*—lamented; *sa-mahā-ṛṣayaḥ*—with the great sages.

TRANSLATION

When the demigods, along with Brahmā, other prajāpatis and other great saintly persons, saw that Indra had been swallowed by the demon, they became very morose. "Alas," they lamented. "What a calamity! What a calamity!"

TEXT 31

निगीर्णोऽप्यसुरेन्द्रेण न ममारोदरं गतः ।
महापुरुषसन्नद्धो योगमायाबलेन च ॥३१॥

nigīrṇo 'py asurendreṇa
na mamārodaraṁ gataḥ
mahāpuruṣa-sannaddho
yogamāyā-balena ca

nigīrṇaḥ—swallowed; *api*—although; *asura-indreṇa*—by the best of the demons, Vṛtrāsura; *na*—not; *mamāra*—died; *udaram*—the abdomen; *gataḥ*—reaching; *mahā-puruṣa*—by the armor of the Supreme Lord, Nārāyaṇa; *sannaddhaḥ*—being protected; *yoga-māyā-balena*—by the mystic power that Indra himself possessed; *ca*—also.

TRANSLATION

The protective armor of Nārāyaṇa, which Indra possessed, was identical with Nārāyaṇa Himself, the Supreme Personality of Godhead. Protected by that armor and by his own mystic power, King Indra, although swallowed by Vṛtrāsura, did not die within the demon's belly.

TEXT 32

भित्त्वा वज्रेण तत्कुक्षिं निष्क्रम्य बलभिद् विभुः ।
उच्चकर्त शिरः शत्रोर्गिरिश्रृङ्गमिवौजसा ॥३२॥

bhittvā vajreṇa tat-kukṣiṁ
niṣkramya bala-bhid vibhuḥ

uccakarta śiraḥ śatror
giri-śṛṅgam ivaujasā

bhittvā—piercing; *vajreṇa*—by the thunderbolt; *tat-kukṣim*—the abdomen of Vṛtrāsura; *niṣkramya*—getting out; *bala-bhit*—the slayer of the demon Bala; *vibhuḥ*—the powerful Lord Indra; *uccakarta*—cut off; *śiraḥ*—the head; *śatroḥ*—of the enemy; *giri-śṛṅgam*—the peak of a mountain; *iva*—like; *ojasā*—with great force.

TRANSLATION

With his thunderbolt, King Indra, who was also extremely powerful, pierced through Vṛtrāsura's abdomen and came out. Indra, the killer of the demon Bala, then immediately cut off Vṛtrāsura's head, which was as high as the peak of a mountain.

TEXT 33

वज्रस्तु तत्कन्धरमाशुवेगः
कृन्तन् समन्तात् परिवर्तमानः ।
न्यपातयत् तावदहर्गणेन
यो ज्योतिषामयने वार्त्रहत्ये ॥३३॥

vajras tu tat-kandharam āśu-vegaḥ
kṛntan samantāt parivartamānaḥ
nyapātayat tāvad ahar-gaṇena
yo jyotiṣām ayane vārtra-hatye

vajraḥ—the thunderbolt; *tu*—but; *tat-kandharam*—his neck; *āśu-vegaḥ*—although very fast; *kṛntan*—cutting; *samantāt*—all around; *parivartamānaḥ*—revolving; *nyapātayat*—caused to fall; *tāvat*—so many; *ahaḥ-gaṇena*—by days; *yaḥ*—which; *jyotiṣām*—of the luminaries like the sun and moon; *ayane*—in moving to both sides of the equator; *vārtra-hatye*—at the time suitable for killing Vṛtrāsura.

TRANSLATION

Although the thunderbolt revolved around Vṛtrāsura's neck with great speed, separating his head from his body took one com-

plete year—360 days, the time in which the sun, moon and other luminaries complete a northern and southern journey. Then, at the suitable time for Vṛtrāsura to be killed, his head fell to the ground.

TEXT 34

तदा च खे दुन्दुभयो विनेदु-
गन्धर्वसिद्धाः समहर्षिसङ्घाः ।
वार्त्रघ्नलिङ्गैस्तमभिष्टुवाना
मन्त्रैर्मुदा कुसुमैरभ्यवर्षन् ॥३४॥

tadā ca khe dundubhayo vinedur
gandharva-siddhāḥ samaharṣi-saṅghāḥ
vārtra-ghna-liṅgais tam abhiṣṭuvānā
mantrair mudā kusumair abhyavarṣan

tadā—at that time; *ca*—also; *khe*—in the higher planetary systems in the sky; *dundubhayaḥ*—the kettledrums; *vineduḥ*—sounded; *gandharva*—the Gandharvas; *siddhāḥ*—and the Siddhas; *sa-maharṣi-saṅghāḥ*—with the assembly of saintly persons; *vārtra-ghna-liṅgaiḥ*—celebrating the prowess of the killer of Vṛtrāsura; *tam*—him (Indra); *abhiṣṭuvānāḥ*—praising; *mantraiḥ*—by various *mantras; mudā*—with great pleasure; *kusumaiḥ*—with flowers; *abhyavarṣan*—showered.

TRANSLATION

When Vṛtrāsura was killed, the Gandharvas and Siddhas in the heavenly planets beat kettledrums in jubilation. With Vedic hymns they celebrated the prowess of Indra, the killer of Vṛtrāsura, praising Indra and showering flowers upon him with great pleasure.

TEXT 35

वृत्रस्य देहान्निष्क्रान्तमात्मज्योतिररिन्दम ।
पश्यतां सर्वदेवानामलोकं समपद्यत ॥३५॥

vṛtrasya dehān niṣkrāntam
ātma-jyotir arindama

paśyatāṁ sarva-devānām
alokaṁ samapadyata

vṛtrasya—of Vṛtrāsura; *dehāt*—from the body; *niṣkrāntam*—coming out; *ātma-jyotiḥ*—the spirit soul, which was as brilliant as the effulgence of Brahman; *arim-dama*—O King Parīkṣit, subduer of enemies; *paśyatām*—were watching; *sarva-devānām*—while all the demigods; *alokam*—the supreme abode, filled with the Brahman effulgence; *samapadyata*—achieved.

TRANSLATION

O King Parīkṣit, subduer of enemies, the living spark then came forth from Vṛtrāsura's body and returned home, back to Godhead. While all the demigods looked on, he entered the transcendental world to become an associate of Lord Saṅkarṣaṇa.

PURPORT

Śrīla Viśvanātha Cakravartī Ṭhākura explains that Indra, not Vṛtrāsura, was actually killed. He says that when Vṛtrāsura swallowed King Indra and his carrier, the elephant, he thought, "Now I have killed Indra, and therefore there is no more need of fighting. Now let me return home, back to Godhead." Thus he stopped all his bodily activities and became situated in trance. Taking advantage of the silence of Vṛtrāsura's body, Indra pierced the demon's abdomen, and because of Vṛtrāsura's trance, Indra was able to come out. Now, Vṛtrāsura was in *yoga-samādhi*, and therefore although King Indra wanted to cut his throat, the demon's neck was so stiff that Indra's thunderbolt took 360 days to cut it to pieces. Actually it was the body left by Vṛtrāsura that was cut to pieces by Indra; Vṛtrāsura himself was not killed. In his original consciousness, Vṛtrāsura returned home, back to Godhead, to become an associate of Lord Saṅkarṣaṇa. Here the word *alokam* means the transcendental world, Vaikuṇṭhaloka, where Saṅkarṣaṇa eternally resides.

Thus end the Bhaktivedanta purports of the Sixth Canto, Twelfth Chapter, of the Śrīmad-Bhāgavatam, *entitled "Vṛtrāsura's Glorious Death."*

CHAPTER THIRTEEN

King Indra Afflicted by Sinful Reaction

This chapter describes Indra's fear at having killed a *brāhmaṇa* (Vṛtrāsura), and it also describes how he fled and was saved by the grace of Lord Viṣṇu.

When all the demigods requested Indra to kill Vṛtrāsura, he refused because Vṛtrāsura was a *brāhmaṇa.* The demigods, however, encouraged Indra not to fear killing him because Indra was protected by the Nārāyaṇa-kavaca, or the Supreme Personality of Godhead Himself, Lord Nārāyaṇa. Even by a glimpse of the chanting of Nārāyaṇa's name, one becomes free from all the sinful reactions of killing a woman, a cow or a *brāhmaṇa.* The demigods advised Indra to perform an *aśvamedha* sacrifice, by which Nārāyaṇa would be pleased, for the performer of such a sacrifice is not implicated in sinful reactions even if he kills the entire universe.

Following this instruction from the demigods, King Indra fought Vṛtrāsura, but when Vṛtrāsura was killed, everyone was satisfied but King Indra, who knew Vṛtrāsura's position. This is the nature of a great personality. Even if a great personality acquires some opulence, he is always ashamed and regretful if he acquires it illegally. Indra could understand that he was certainly entangled by sinful reactions for killing a *brāhmaṇa.* Indeed, he could see sinful reaction personified following him, and thus he fled here and there in fear, thinking of how to rid himself of his sins. He went to Mānasa-sarovara, and there, under the protection of the goddess of fortune, he meditated for one thousand years. During this time, Nahuṣa reigned over the heavenly planets as the representative of Indra. Unfortunately, however, he was attracted by the beauty of Indra's wife, Śacīdevī, and because of his sinful desire he had to accept the body of a serpent in his next life. Indra later performed a great sacrifice with the help of exalted *brāhmaṇas* and saints. In this way he was released from the reactions of his sinful killing of a *brāhmaṇa.*

TEXT 1

श्रीशुक उवाच
वृत्रे हते त्रयो लोका विना शक्रेण भूरिद ।
सपाला ह्यभवन् सद्यो विज्वरा निर्वृतेन्द्रियाः ॥ १ ॥

śrī-śuka uvāca
vṛtre hate trayo lokā
vinā śakreṇa bhūrida
sapālā hy abhavan sadyo
vijvarā nirvṛtendriyāḥ

śrī-śukaḥ uvāca—Śrī Śukadeva Gosvāmī said; *vṛtre hate*—when Vṛtrāsura was killed; *trayaḥ lokāḥ*—the three planetary systems (upper, middle and lower); *vinā*—except; *śakreṇa*—Indra, who is also called Śakra; *bhūri-da*—O Mahārāja Parīkṣit, giver of great charity; *sa-pālāḥ*—with the rulers of the various planets; *hi*—indeed; *abhavan*—became; *sadyaḥ*—immediately; *vijvarāḥ*—without fear of death; *nirvṛta*—very much pleased; *indriyāḥ*—whose senses.

TRANSLATION

Śrī Śukadeva Gosvāmī said: O King Parīkṣit, who are so charitably disposed, when Vṛtrāsura was killed, all the presiding deities and everyone else in the three planetary systems was immediately pleased and free from trouble—everyone, that is, except Indra.

TEXT 2

देवर्षिपितृभूतानि दैत्या देवानुगाः स्वयम् ।
प्रतिजग्मुः स्वधिष्ण्यानि ब्रह्मेशेन्द्रादयस्ततः ॥ २ ॥

devarṣi-pitṛ-bhūtāni
daityā devānugāḥ svayam
pratijagmuḥ sva-dhiṣṇyāni
brahmeśendrādayas tataḥ

deva—demigods; *ṛṣi*—great saintly persons; *pitṛ*—the inhabitants of Pitṛloka; *bhūtāni*—and the other living entities; *daityāḥ*—demons;

deva-anugāḥ—the inhabitants of other planets following the principles of the demigods; *svayam*—independently (without asking permission from Indra); *pratijagmuḥ*—returned; *sva-dhiṣṇyāni*—to their respective planets and homes; *brahma*—Lord Brahmā; *īśa*—Lord Śiva; *indra-ādayaḥ*—and the demigods headed by Indra; *tataḥ*—thereafter.

TRANSLATION

Thereafter, the demigods, the great saintly persons, the inhabitants of Pitṛloka and Bhūtaloka, the demons, the followers of the demigods, and also Lord Brahmā, Lord Śiva and the demigods subordinate to Indra all returned to their respective homes. While departing, however, no one spoke to Indra.

PURPORT

In this connection Śrīla Viśvanātha Cakravartī Ṭhākura comments: *brahmeśendrādaya iti. indrasya sva-dhiṣṇya-gamanaṁ nopapadyate vṛtra-vadha-kṣaṇa eva brahma-hatyopadrava-prāpteḥ. tasmāt tata ity anena mānasa-sarovarād āgatya pravartitād aśvamedhāt parata iti vyākhyeyam.*

Lord Brahmā, Lord Śiva and the other demigods returned to their respective abodes, but Indra did not, for he was disturbed at having killed Vṛtrāsura, who was actually a *brāhmaṇa.* After killing Vṛtrāsura, Indra went to the Mānasa-sarovara Lake to become free from sinful reactions. When he left the lake, he performed an *aśvamedha-yajña* and then returned to his own abode.

TEXT 3

श्रीराजोवाच

इन्द्रस्यानिर्वृतेर्हेतुं श्रोतुमिच्छामि भो मुने ।
येनासन् सुखिनो देवा हरेर्दुःखं कुतोऽभवत् ॥ ३ ॥

śrī-rājovāca
indrasyānirvṛter hetuṁ
śrotum icchāmi bho mune
yenāsan sukhino devā
harer duḥkhaṁ kuto 'bhavat

śrī-rājā uvāca—King Parīkṣit inquired; *indrasya*—of King Indra; *anirvṛteḥ*—of the moroseness; *hetum*—the reason; *śrotum*—to hear; *icchāmi*—I wish; *bhoḥ*—O my lord; *mune*—O great sage, Śukadeva Gosvāmī; *yena*—by which; *āsan*—were; *sukhinaḥ*—very happy; *devāḥ*—all the demigods; *hareḥ*—of Indra; *duḥkham*—moroseness; *kutaḥ*—from where; *abhavat*—was.

TRANSLATION

Mahārāja Parīkṣit inquired from Śukadeva Gosvāmī: O great sage, what was the reason for Indra's unhappiness? I wish to hear about this. When he killed Vṛtrāsura, all the demigods were extremely happy. Why, then, was Indra himself unhappy?

PURPORT

This, of course, is a very intelligent question. When a demon is killed, certainly all the demigods are happy. In this case, however, when all the demigods were happy because of Vṛtrāsura's having been killed, Indra was unhappy. Why? It may be suggested that Indra was unhappy because he knew that he had killed a great devotee and *brāhmaṇa*. Vṛtrāsura outwardly appeared to be a demon, but inwardly he was a great devotee and therefore a great *brāhmaṇa*.

Herein it is clearly indicated that a person who is not at all demoniac, such as Prahlāda Mahārāja and Bali Mahārāja, may outwardly be a demon or be born in a family of demons. Therefore in terms of real culture one should not be considered a demigod or demon simply according to birth. In his dealings while fighting with Indra, Vṛtrāsura proved himself a great devotee of the Supreme Personality of Godhead. Furthermore, as soon as he finished fighting with Indra and was apparently killed, Vṛtrāsura was transferred to Vaikuṇṭhaloka to become an associate of Saṅkarṣaṇa. Indra knew this, and therefore he was morose at having killed such a demon, who was actually a Vaiṣṇava or *brāhmaṇa*.

A Vaiṣṇava is already a *brāhmaṇa*, although a *brāhmaṇa* may not be a Vaiṣṇava. The *Padma Purāṇa* says:

ṣaṭ-karma-nipuṇo vipro
mantra-tantra-viśāradaḥ

avaiṣṇavo gurur na syād
vaiṣṇavaḥ śva-paco guruḥ

One may be a *brāhmaṇa* in terms of his culture and family and may be expert in Vedic knowledge (*mantra-tantra-viśāradaḥ*), but if he is not a Vaiṣṇava, he cannot be a *guru.* This means that an expert *brāhmaṇa* may not be a Vaiṣṇava, but a Vaiṣṇava is already a *brāhmaṇa.* A millionaire may very easily possess hundreds and thousands of dollars, but a person with hundreds and thousands of dollars is not necessarily a millionaire. Vṛtrāsura was a perfect Vaiṣṇava, and therefore he was also a *brāhmaṇa.*

TEXT 4

श्रीशुक उवाच
वृत्रविक्रमसंविग्नाः सर्वे देवाः सहर्षिभिः ।
तद्वधायार्थयन्निन्द्रं नैच्छद् भीतो बृहद्वधात् ॥ ४ ॥

śrī-śuka uvāca
vṛtra-vikrama-saṁvignāḥ
sarve devāḥ saharṣibhiḥ
tad-vadhāyārthayann indraṁ
naicchad bhīto bṛhad-vadhāt

śrī-śukaḥ uvāca—Śrī Śukadeva Gosvāmī said; *vṛtra*—of Vṛtrāsura; *vikrama*—by the powerful activities; *saṁvignāḥ*—being full of anxieties; *sarve*—all; *devāḥ*—the demigods; *saha ṛṣibhiḥ*—with the great sages; *tat-vadhāya*—for the killing of him; *ārthayan*—requested; *indram*—Indra; *na aicchat*—declined; *bhītaḥ*—being afraid; *bṛhat-vadhāt*—due to killing a *brāhmaṇa.*

TRANSLATION

Śrī Śukadeva Gosvāmī answered: When all the great sages and demigods were disturbed by the extraordinary power of Vṛtrāsura, they had assembled to ask Indra to kill him. Indra, however, being afraid of killing a brāhmaṇa, declined their request.

TEXT 5

इन्द्र उवाच

स्त्रीभूद्रुमजलैरेनो विश्वरूपवधोद्भवम् ।
विभक्तमनुगृह्णद्भिर्वृत्रहत्यां क्व मार्ज्म्यहम् ॥ ५ ॥

indra uvāca
strī-bhū-druma-jalair eno
viśvarūpa-vadhodbhavam
vibhaktam anugṛhṇadbhir
vṛtra-hatyāṁ kva mārjmy aham

indraḥ uvāca—King Indra replied; *strī*—by women; *bhū*—the earth; *druma*—the trees; *jalaiḥ*—and water; *enaḥ*—this (sin); *viśvarūpa*—of Viśvarūpa; *vadha*—from the killing; *udbhavam*—produced; *vibhaktam*—divided; *anugṛhṇadbhiḥ*—showing their favor (to me); *vṛtra-hatyām*—the killing of Vṛtra; *kva*—how; *mārjmi*—shall become free from; *aham*—I.

TRANSLATION

King Indra replied: When I killed Viśvarūpa, I received extensive sinful reactions, but I was favored by the women, land, trees and water, and therefore I was able to divide the sin among them. But now if I kill Vṛtrāsura, another brāhmaṇa, how shall I free myself from the sinful reactions?

TEXT 6

श्रीशुक उवाच

ऋषयस्तदुपाकर्ण्य महेन्द्रमिदमब्रुवन् ।
याजयिष्याम भद्रं ते हयमेधेन मा स्म भैः ॥ ६ ॥

śrī-śuka uvāca
ṛṣayas tad upākarṇya
mahendram idam abruvan
yājayiṣyāma bhadraṁ te
hayamedhena mā sma bhaiḥ

śrī-śukaḥ uvāca—Śrī Śukadeva Gosvāmī said; *ṛṣayaḥ*—the great sages; *tat*—that; *upākarṇya*—hearing; *mahā-indram*—unto King Indra; *idam*—this; *abruvan*—spoke; *yājayiṣyāmaḥ*—we shall perform a great sacrifice; *bhadram*—good fortune; *te*—unto you; *hayamedhena*—by the horse sacrifice; *mā sma bhaiḥ*—do not be afraid.

TRANSLATION

Śrī Śukadeva Gosvāmī said: Hearing this, the great sages replied to King Indra, "O King of heaven, all good fortune unto you. Do not fear. We shall perform an aśvamedha sacrifice to release you from any sin you may accrue by killing the brāhmaṇa."

TEXT 7

हयमेधेन पुरुषं परमात्मानमीश्वरम् ।
इष्ट्वा नारायणं देवं मोक्ष्यसेऽपि जगद्वधात् ॥ ७ ॥

hayamedhena puruṣaṁ
paramātmānam īśvaram
iṣṭvā nārāyaṇaṁ devaṁ
mokṣyase 'pi jagad-vadhāt

hayamedhena—by the sacrifice known as *aśvamedha; puruṣam*—the Supreme Person; *paramātmānam*—the Supersoul; *īśvaram*—the supreme controller; *iṣṭvā*—worshiping; *nārāyaṇam*—Lord Nārāyaṇa; *devam*—the Supreme Lord; *mokṣyase*—you will be liberated; *api*—even; *jagat-vadhāt*—from the sin for killing the whole world.

TRANSLATION

The ṛṣis continued: O King Indra, by performing an aśvamedha sacrifice and thereby pleasing the Supreme Personality of Godhead, who is the Supersoul, Lord Nārāyaṇa, the supreme controller, one can be relieved even of the sinful reactions for killing the entire world, not to speak of killing a demon like Vṛtrāsura.

TEXTS 8–9

ब्रह्महा पितृहा गोघ्नो मातृहाचार्यहाघवान् ।
श्वादः पुल्कसको वापि शुद्ध्येरन् यस्य कीर्तनात् ॥८॥
तमश्वमेधेन महामखेन
श्रद्धान्वितोऽस्माभिरनुष्ठितेन ।
हत्वापि सब्रह्मचराचरं त्वं
न लिप्यसे किं खलनिग्रहेण ॥ ९ ॥

brahma-hā pitṛ-hā go-ghno
mātṛ-hācārya-hāghavān
śvādaḥ pulkasako vāpi
śuddhyeran yasya kīrtanāt

tam aśvamedhena mahā-makhena
śraddhānvito 'smābhir anuṣṭhitena
hatvāpi sabrahma-carācaraṁ tvaṁ
na lipyase kiṁ khala-nigraheṇa

brahma-hā—a person who has killed a *brāhmaṇa; pitṛ-hā*—a person who has killed his father; *go-ghnaḥ*—a person who has killed a cow; *mātṛ-hā*—a person who has killed his mother; *ācārya-hā*—a person who has killed his spiritual master; *agha-vān*—such a sinful person; *śva-adaḥ*—a dog-eater; *pulkasakaḥ*—a *caṇḍāla,* one who is less than a *śūdra; vā*—or; *api*—even; *śuddhyeran*—may be purified; *yasya*—of whom (Lord Nārāyaṇa); *kīrtanāt*—from chanting the holy name; *tam*—Him; *aśvamedhena*—by the *aśvamedha* sacrifice; *mahā-makhena*—the topmost of all sacrifices; *śraddhā-anvitaḥ*—endowed with faith; *asmābhiḥ*—by us; *anuṣṭhitena*—conducted or managed; *hatvā*—killing; *api*—even; *sa-brahma-cara-acaram*—all the living entities, including the *brāhmaṇas; tvam*—you; *na*—not; *lipyase*—are contaminated; *kim*—what then; *khala-nigraheṇa*—by killing one disturbing demon.

TRANSLATION

One who has killed a brāhmaṇa, one who has killed a cow or one who has killed his father, mother or spiritual master can be im-

mediately freed from all sinful reactions simply by chanting the holy name of Lord Nārāyaṇa. Other sinful persons, such as dog-eaters and caṇḍālas, who are less than śūdras, can also be freed in this way. But you are a devotee, and we shall help you by performing the great horse sacrifice. If you please Lord Nārāyaṇa in that way, why should you be afraid? You will be freed even if you kill the entire universe, including the brāhmaṇas, not to speak of killing a disturbing demon like Vṛtrāsura.

PURPORT

It is said in the *Bṛhad-viṣṇu Purāṇa:*

nāmno hi yāvatī śaktiḥ
pāpa-nirharaṇe hareḥ
tāvat kartuṁ na śaknoti
pātakaṁ pātakī naraḥ

Also, in the *Prema-vivarta* by Jagadānanda Paṇḍita it is said:

eka kṛṣṇa-nāme pāpīra yata pāpa-kṣaya
bahu janme sei pāpī karite nāraya

This means that by once chanting the holy name of the Lord, one can be freed from the reactions of more sins that he can even imagine performing. The holy name is so spiritually potent that simply by chanting the holy name one can be freed from the reactions to all sinful activities. What, then, is to be said of those who chant the holy name regularly or worship the Deity regularly? For such purified devotees, freedom from sinful reaction is certainly assured. This does not mean, however, that one should intentionally commit sinful acts and think himself free from the reactions because he is chanting the holy name. Such a mentality is a most abominable offense at the lotus feet of the holy name. *Nāmno balād yasya hi pāpa-buddhiḥ:* the Lord's holy name certainly has the potency to neutralize all sinful activities, but if one repeatedly and intentionally commits sins while chanting the holy name, he is most condemned.

These verses name the performers of various sinful deeds. In the *Manu-saṁhitā* the following names are given. A son begotten by a *brāhmaṇa* and born from the womb of a *śūdra* mother is called a *pāraśava* or *niṣāda*, a hunter accustomed to stealing. A son begotten by a *niṣāda* in the womb of a *śūdra* woman is called a *pukkasa.* A child begotten by a *kṣatriya* in the womb of the daughter of a *śūdra* is called an *ugra.* A child begotten by a *śūdra* in the womb of the daughter of a *kṣatriya* is called a *kṣattā.* A child begotten by a *kṣatriya* in the womb of a lower-class woman is called a *śvāda*, or dog-eater. All such offspring are considered extremely sinful, but the holy name of the Supreme Personality of Godhead is so strong that all of them can be purified simply by chanting the Hare Kṛṣṇa *mantra.*

The Hare Kṛṣṇa movement offers everyone a chance to be purified, regardless of birth or family. As confirmed in *Śrīmad-Bhāgavatam* (2.4.18):

kirāta-hūṇāndhra-pulinda-pulkaśā
ābhīra-śumbhā yavanāḥ khasādayaḥ
ye 'nye ca pāpā yad-apāśrayāśrayāḥ
śudhyanti tasmai prabhaviṣṇave namaḥ

"Kirātas, Hūṇas, Āndhras, Pulindas, Pulkaśas, Ābhīras, Śumbhas, Yavanas, members of the Khasa races, and even others addicted to sinful acts can be purified by taking shelter of devotees of the Lord, for He is the supreme power. I beg to offer my respectful obeisances unto Him." Even such sinful persons can certainly all be purified if they chant the holy name of the Lord under the direction of a pure devotee.

Herein the sages encourage King Indra to kill Vṛtrāsura even at the risk of *brahma-hatyā*, the killing of a *brāhmaṇa*, and they guarantee to release him from sinful reactions by performing an *aśvamedha-yajña.* Such purposefully devised atonement, however, cannot relieve the performer of sinful acts. This will be seen from the following verse.

TEXT 10

श्रीशुक उवाच
एवं सञ्चोदितो विप्रैर्मरुत्वानहनद्रिपुम् ।
ब्रह्महत्या हते तस्मिन्नाससाद वृषाकपिम् ॥१०॥

śrī-śuka uvāca
evaṁ sañcodito viprair
marutvān ahanad ripum
brahma-hatyā hate tasminn
āsasāda vṛṣākapim

śrī-śukaḥ uvāca—Śrī Śukadeva Gosvāmī said; *evam*—thus; *sañcoditaḥ*—being encouraged; *vipraiḥ*—by the *brāhmaṇas; marutvān*—Indra; *ahanat*—killed; *ripum*—his enemy, Vṛtrāsura; *brahma-hatyā*—the sinful reaction for killing a *brāhmaṇa; hate*—was killed; *tasmin*—when he (Vṛtrāsura); *āsasāda*—approached; *vṛṣākapim*—Indra, who is also named Vṛṣākapi.

TRANSLATION

Śrī Śukadeva Gosvāmī said: Encouraged by the words of the sages, Indra killed Vṛtrāsura, and when he was killed the sinful reaction for killing a brāhmaṇa [brahma-hatyā] certainly took shelter of Indra.

PURPORT

After killing Vṛtrāsura, Indra could not surpass the *brahma-hatyā*, the sinful reactions for killing a *brāhmaṇa*. Formerly he had killed one *brāhmaṇa*, Viśvarūpa, out of circumstantial anger, but this time, following the advice of the sages, he killed another *brāhmaṇa* purposely. Therefore the sinful reaction was greater than before. Indra could not be relieved from the reaction simply by performing sacrifices for atonement. He had to undergo a severe series of sinful reactions, and when he was freed by such suffering, the *brāhmaṇas* allowed him to perform the horse sacrifice. The planned execution of sinful deeds on the strength of chanting the holy name of the Lord or undergoing *prāyaścitta*, atonement, cannot give relief to anyone, even to Indra or Nahuṣa. Nahuṣa was officiating for Indra while Indra, absent from heaven, was going here and there to gain release from his sinful reactions.

TEXT 11

तयेन्द्रः स्मासहत् तापं निर्वृतिर्नामुमाविशत् ।
ह्रीमन्तं वाच्यतां प्राप्तं सुखयन्त्यपि नो गुणाः ॥११॥

tayendraḥ smāsahat tāpaṁ
nirvṛtir nāmum āviśat
hrīmantaṁ vācyatāṁ prāptaṁ
sukhayanty api no guṇāḥ

tayā—by that action; *indraḥ*—King Indra; *sma*—indeed; *asahat*—suffered; *tāpam*—misery; *nirvṛtiḥ*—happiness; *na*—not; *amum*—him; *āviśat*—entered; *hrīmantam*—one who is shameful; *vācyatām*—ill fame; *prāptam*—obtaining; *sukhayanti*—give pleasure; *api*—although; *no*—not; *guṇāḥ*—good qualifications like possessing opulence.

TRANSLATION

Following the advice of the demigods, Indra killed Vṛtrāsura, and he suffered because of this sinful killing. Although the other demigods were happy, he could not derive happiness from the killing of Vṛtrāsura. Indra's other good qualities, such as tolerance and opulence, could not help him in his grief.

PURPORT

One cannot be happy by committing sinful acts, even if one is endowed with material opulence. Indra found this to be true. People began to blaspheme him, saying, "This person has killed a *brāhmaṇa* for the sake of enjoying heavenly material happiness." Therefore in spite of being King of heaven and enjoying material opulence, Indra was always unhappy because of the accusations of the populace.

TEXTS 12–13

तां ददर्शानुधावन्तीं चाण्डालीमिव रूपिणीम् ।
जरया वेपमानाङ्गीं यक्ष्मग्रस्तामसृक्पटाम् ॥१२॥
विकीर्य पलितान् केशांस्तिष्ठ तिष्ठेति भाषिणीम् ।
मीनगन्ध्यसुगन्धेन कुर्वतीं मार्गदूषणम् ॥१३॥

tāṁ dadarśānudhāvantīṁ
cāṇḍālīm iva rūpiṇīm

jarayā vepamānāṅgīṁ
yakṣma-grastām asṛk-paṭām

vikīrya palitān keśāṁs
tiṣṭha tiṣṭheti bhāṣiṇīm
mīna-gandhy-asu-gandhena
kurvatīṁ mārga-dūṣaṇam

tām—the sinful reaction; *dadarśa*—he saw; *anudhāvantīm*—chasing; *cāṇḍālīm*—a woman of the lowest class; *iva*—like; *rūpiṇīm*—taking a form; *jarayā*—because of old age; *vepamāna-aṅgīm*—whose bodily limbs were trembling; *yakṣma-grastām*—infected with tuberculosis; *asṛk-paṭām*—whose clothes were covered with blood; *vikīrya*—scattering; *palitān*—grayed; *keśān*—hair; *tiṣṭha tiṣṭha*—wait, wait; *iti*—thus; *bhāṣiṇīm*—calling; *mīna-gandhi*—the smell of fish; *asu*—whose breath; *gandhena*—by the odor; *kurvatīm*—bringing about; *mārga-dūṣaṇam*—the pollution of the whole street.

TRANSLATION

Indra saw personified sinful reaction chasing him, appearing like a caṇḍāla woman, a woman of the lowest class. She seemed very old, and all the limbs of her body trembled. Because she was afflicted with tuberculosis, her body and garments were covered with blood. Breathing an unbearable fishy odor that polluted the entire street, she called to Indra, "Wait! Wait!"

PURPORT

When a person is afflicted with tuberculosis, he often vomits blood, which makes his garments bloody.

TEXT 14

नभो गतो दिशः सर्वाः सहस्राक्षो विशाम्पते ।
प्रागुदीचीं दिशं तूर्णं प्रविष्टो नृप मानसम् ॥१४॥

nabho gato diśaḥ sarvāḥ
sahasrākṣo viśāmpate

prāg-udīcīṁ diśaṁ tūrṇaṁ
praviṣṭo nṛpa mānasam

nabhaḥ—to the sky; *gataḥ*—going; *diśaḥ*—to the directions; *sarvāḥ*—all; *sahasra-akṣaḥ*—Indra, who is endowed with one thousand eyes; *viśāmpate*—O King; *prāk-udīcīm*—to the northeast; *diśam*—direction; *tūrṇam*—very speedily; *praviṣṭaḥ*—entered; *nṛpa*—O King; *mānasam*—the lake known as Mānasa-sarovara.

TRANSLATION

O King, Indra first fled to the sky, but there also he saw the woman of personified sin chasing him. This witch followed him wherever he went. At last he very quickly went to the northeast and entered the Mānasa-sarovara Lake.

TEXT 15

स आवसत्पुष्करनालतन्तू-
नलब्धभोगो यदिहाग्निदूतः ।
वर्षाणि साहस्रमलक्षितोऽन्तः
सञ्चिन्तयन् ब्रह्मवधाद् विमोक्षम् ॥१५॥

sa āvasat puṣkara-nāla-tantūn
alabdha-bhogo yad ihāgni-dūtaḥ
varṣāṇi sāhasram alakṣito 'ntaḥ
sañcintayan brahma-vadhād vimokṣam

saḥ—he (Indra); *āvasat*—lived; *puṣkara-nāla-tantūn*—in the network of the fibers of a lotus stem; *alabdha-bhogaḥ*—not getting any material comfort (practically starving for all material needs); *yat*—which; *iha*—here; *agni-dūtaḥ*—the fire-god messenger; *varṣāṇi*—celestial years; *sāhasram*—one thousand; *alakṣitaḥ*—invisible; *antaḥ*—within his heart; *sañcintayan*—always thinking of; *brahma-vadhāt*—from the killing of a *brāhmaṇa; vimokṣam*—liberation.

TRANSLATION

Always thinking of how he could be relieved from the sinful reaction for killing a brāhmaṇa, King Indra, invisible to everyone, lived in the lake for one thousand years in the subtle fibers of the stem of a lotus. The fire-god used to bring him his share of all yajñas, but because the fire-god was afraid to enter the water, Indra was practically starving.

TEXT 16

तावत्त्रिणाकं नहुषः शशास
विद्यातपोयोगबलानुभावः ।
स सम्पदैश्वर्यमदान्धबुद्धि-
र्नीतस्तिरश्चां गतिमिन्द्रपत्न्या ॥१६॥

tāvat triṇākaṁ nahuṣaḥ śaśāsa
vidyā-tapo-yoga-balānubhāvaḥ
sa sampad-aiśvarya-madāndha-buddhir
nītas tiraścāṁ gatim indra-patnyā

tāvat—for so long; *triṇākam*—the heavenly planet; *nahuṣaḥ*—Nahuṣa; *śaśāsa*—ruled; *vidyā*—by education; *tapaḥ*—austerities; *yoga*—mystic power; *bala*—and strength; *anubhāvaḥ*—being equipped; *saḥ*—he (Nahuṣa); *sampat*—of so much wealth; *aiśvarya*—and opulence; *mada*—by the madness; *andha*—blinded; *buddhiḥ*—his intelligence; *nītaḥ*—was brought; *tiraścām*—of a snake; *gatim*—to the destination; *indra-patnyā*—by Indra's wife Śacīdevī.

TRANSLATION

As long as King Indra lived in the water, wrapped in the stem of the lotus, Nahuṣa was equipped with the ability to rule the heavenly kingdom, due to his knowledge, austerity and mystic power. Nahuṣa, however, blinded and maddened by power and opulence, made undesirable proposals to Indra's wife with a desire to enjoy her. Thus Nahuṣa was cursed by a brāhmaṇa and later became a snake.

TEXT 17

ततो गतो ब्रह्मगिरोपहूत
ऋतम्भरध्याननिवारिताघः ।
पापस्तु दिग्देवतया हतौजा-
स्तं नाभ्यभूदवितं विष्णुपत्न्या ॥१७॥

tato gato brahma-giropahūta
ṛtambhara-dhyāna-nivāritāghaḥ
pāpas tu digdevatayā hataujās
taṁ nābhyabhūd avitaṁ viṣṇu-patnyā

tataḥ—thereafter; *gataḥ*—gone; *brahma*—of the *brāhmaṇas; girā*—by the words; *upahūtaḥ*—being invited; *ṛtambhara*—on the Supreme Lord, who maintains truth; *dhyāna*—by meditation; *nivārita*—impeded; *aghaḥ*—whose sin; *pāpaḥ*—the sinful activity; *tu*—then; *dik-devatayā*—by the demigod Rudra; *hata-ojāḥ*—with all prowess diminished; *tam*—him (Indra); *na abhyabhūt*—could not overcome; *avitam*—being protected; *viṣṇu-patnyā*—by Lord Viṣṇu's wife, the goddess of fortune.

TRANSLATION

Indra's sins were diminished by the influence of Rudra, the demigod of all directions. Because Indra was protected by the goddess of fortune, Lord Viṣṇu's wife, who resides in the lotus clusters of Mānasa-sarovara Lake, Indra's sins could not affect him. Indra was ultimately relieved of all the reactions of his sinful deeds by strictly worshiping Lord Viṣṇu. Then he was called back to the heavenly planets by the brāhmaṇas and reinstated in his position.

TEXT 18

तं च ब्रह्मर्षयोऽभ्येत्य हयमेधेन भारत ।
यथावद्दीक्षयाञ्चक्रुः पुरुषाराधनेन ह ॥१८॥

taṁ ca brahmarṣayo 'bhyetya
hayamedhena bhārata

yathāvad dīkṣayāñ cakruḥ
puruṣārādhanena ha

tam—him (Lord Indra); *ca*—and; *brahma-ṛṣayaḥ*—the great saints and *brāhmaṇas; abhyetya*—approaching; *hayamedhena*—with an *aśvamedha* sacrifice; *bhārata*—O King Parīkṣit; *yathāvat*—according to the rules and regulations; *dīkṣayām cakruḥ*—initiated; *puruṣa-ārādhanena*—which consists of worship of the Supreme Person, Hari; *ha*—indeed.

TRANSLATION

O King, when Lord Indra reached the heavenly planets, the saintly brāhmaṇas approached him and properly initiated him into a horse sacrifice [aśvamedha-yajña] meant to please the Supreme Lord.

TEXTS 19–20

अथेज्यमाने पुरुषे सर्वदेवमयात्मनि ।
अश्वमेधे महेन्द्रेण वितते ब्रह्मवादिभिः ॥१९॥
स वै त्वाष्ट्रवधो भूयानपि पापचयो नृप ।
नीतस्तेनैव शून्याय नीहार इव भानुना ॥२०॥

athejyamāne puruṣe
sarva-devamayātmani
aśvamedhe mahendreṇa
vitate brahma-vādibhiḥ

sa vai tvāṣṭra-vadho bhūyān
api pāpa-cayo nṛpa
nītas tenaiva śūnyāya
nīhāra iva bhānunā

atha—therefore; *ijyamāne*—when worshiped; *puruṣe*—the Supreme Personality of Godhead; *sarva*—all; *deva-maya-ātmani*—the Supersoul and maintainer of the demigods; *aśvamedhe*—through the *aśvamedha-*

yajña; mahā-indreṇa—by King Indra; *vitate*—being administered; *brahma-vādibhiḥ*—by the saints and *brāhmaṇas* expert in Vedic knowledge; *saḥ*—that; *vai*—indeed; *tvāṣṭra-vadhaḥ*—the killing of Vṛtrāsura, the son of Tvaṣṭā; *bhūyāt*—may be; *api*—although; *pāpa-cayaḥ*—mass of sin; *nṛpa*—O King; *nītaḥ*—was brought; *tena*—by that (the horse sacrifice); *eva*—certainly; *śūnyāya*—to nothing; *nīhāraḥ*—fog; *iva*—like; *bhānunā*—by the brilliant sun.

TRANSLATION

The horse sacrifice performed by the saintly brāhmaṇas relieved Indra of the reactions to all his sins because he worshiped the Supreme Personality of Godhead in that sacrifice. O King, although he had committed a gravely sinful act, it was nullified at once by that sacrifice, just as fog is vanquished by the brilliant sunrise.

TEXT 21

स वाजिमेधेन यथोदितेन
वितायमानेन मरीचिमिश्रैः ।
इष्ट्वाधियज्ञं पुरुषं पुराण-
मिन्द्रो महानास विधूतपापः ॥२१॥

sa vājimedhena yathoditena
vitāyamānena marīci-miśraiḥ
iṣṭvādhiyajñaṁ puruṣaṁ purāṇam
indro mahān āsa vidhūta-pāpaḥ

saḥ—he (Indra); *vājimedhena*—by the *aśvamedha* sacrifice; *yathā*—just as; *uditena*—described; *vitāyamānena*—being performed; *marīci-miśraiḥ*—by the priests, headed by Marīci; *iṣṭvā*—worshiping; *adhiyajñam*—the Supreme Supersoul; *puruṣam purāṇam*—the original Personality of Godhead; *indraḥ*—King Indra; *mahān*—worshipable; *āsa*—became; *vidhūta-pāpaḥ*—being cleansed of all sinful reactions.

TRANSLATION

King Indra was favored by Marīci and the other great sages. They performed the sacrifice just according to the rules and regulations, worshiping the Supreme Personality of Godhead, the Supersoul, the original person. Thus Indra regained his exalted position and was again honored by everyone.

TEXTS 22–23

इदं महाख्यानमशेषपाप्मनां
प्रक्षालनं तीर्थपदानुकीर्तनम् ।
भक्त्युच्छ्रयं भक्तजनानुवर्णनं
महेन्द्रमोक्षं विजयं मरुत्वतः ॥२२॥
पठेयुराख्यानमिदं सदा बुधाः
शृण्वन्त्यथो पर्वणि पर्वणीन्द्रियम् ।
धन्यं यशस्यं निखिलाघमोचनं
रिपुञ्जयं स्वस्त्ययनं तथायुषम् ॥२३॥

idaṁ mahākhyānam aśeṣa-pāpmanāṁ
prakṣālanaṁ tīrthapadānukīrtanam
bhakty-ucchrayaṁ bhakta-janānuvarṇanaṁ
mahendra-mokṣaṁ vijayaṁ marutvataḥ

paṭheyur ākhyānam idaṁ sadā budhāḥ
śṛṇvanty atho parvaṇi parvaṇīndriyam
dhanyaṁ yaśasyaṁ nikhilāgha-mocanaṁ
ripuñjayaṁ svasty-ayanaṁ tathāyuṣam

idam—this; *mahā-ākhyānam*—great historical incident; *aśeṣa-pāp-manām*—of unlimited numbers of sinful acts; *prakṣālanam*—cleansing; *tīrthapada-anukīrtanam*—glorifying the Supreme Personality of Godhead, who is known as Tīrthapada; *bhakti*—of devotional service; *uc-chrayam*—in which there is an increase; *bhakta-jana*—the devotees;

anuvarṇanam—describing; *mahā-indra-mokṣam*—the liberation of the King of heaven; *vijayam*—the victory; *marutvataḥ*—of King Indra; *paṭheyuḥ*—should read; *ākhyānam*—narration; *idam*—this; *sadā*—always; *budhāḥ*—learned scholars; *śṛṇvanti*—continue to hear; *atho*—as well; *parvaṇi parvaṇi*—on the occasion of great festivals; *indriyam*—which makes the senses sharp; *dhanyam*—brings wealth; *yaśasyam*—brings fame; *nikhila*—all; *agha-mocanam*—releasing from sins; *ripum-jayam*—makes one victorious over his enemies; *svasti-ayanam*—brings good fortune for all; *tathā*—so also; *āyuṣam*—longevity.

TRANSLATION

In this very great narrative there is glorification of the Supreme Personality of Godhead, Nārāyaṇa, there are statements about the exaltedness of devotional service, there are descriptions of devotees like Indra and Vṛtrāsura, and there are statements about King Indra's release from sinful life and about his victory in fighting the demons. By understanding this incident, one is relieved of all sinful reactions. Therefore the learned are always advised to read this narration. If one does so, one will become expert in the activities of the senses, his opulence will increase, and his reputation will become widespread. One will also be relieved of all sinful reactions, he will conquer all his enemies, and the duration of his life will increase. Because this narration is auspicious in all respects, learned scholars regularly hear and repeat it on every festival day.

Thus ends the Bhaktivedanta purports of the Sixth Canto, Thirteenth Chapter, of the Śrīmad-Bhāgavatam, *entitled "King Indra Afflicted by Sinful Reaction."*

Appendixes

The Author

His Divine Grace A. C. Bhaktivedanta Swami Prabhupāda appeared in this world in 1896 in Calcutta, India. He first met his spiritual master, Śrīla Bhaktisiddhānta Sarasvatī Gosvāmī, in Calcutta in 1922. Bhaktisiddhānta Sarasvatī, a prominent devotional scholar and the founder of sixty-four Gauḍīya Maṭhas (Vedic Institutes), liked this educated young man and convinced him to dedicate his life to teaching Vedic knowledge. Śrīla Prabhupāda became his student, and eleven years later (1933) at Allahabad he became his formally initiated disciple.

At their first meeting, in 1922, Śrīla Bhaktisiddhānta Sarasvatī Ṭhākura requested Śrīla Prabhupāda to broadcast Vedic knowledge through the English language. In the years that followed, Śrīla Prabhupāda wrote a commentary on the *Bhagavad-gītā,* assisted the Gauḍīya Maṭha in its work and, in 1944, without assistance, started an English fortnightly magazine, edited it, typed the manuscripts and checked the galley proofs. He even distributed the individual copies freely and struggled to maintain the publication. Once begun, the magazine never stopped; it is now being continued by his disciples in the West.

Recognizing Śrīla Prabhupāda's philosophical learning and devotion, the Gauḍīya Vaiṣṇava Society honored him in 1947 with the title "Bhaktivedanta." In 1950, at the age of fifty-four, Śrīla Prabhupāda retired from married life, and four years later he adopted the *vānaprastha* (retired) order to devote more time to his studies and writing. Śrīla Prabhupāda traveled to the holy city of Vṛndāvana, where he lived in very humble circumstances in the historic medieval temple of Rādhā-Dāmodara. There he engaged for several years in deep study and writing. He accepted the renounced order of life (*sannyāsa*) in 1959. At Rādhā-Dāmodara, Śrīla Prabhupāda began work on his life's masterpiece: a multivolume translation and commentary on the eighteen thousand verse *Śrīmad-Bhāgavatam* (*Bhāgavata Purāṇa*). He also wrote *Easy Journey to Other Planets.*

After publishing three volumes of *Bhāgavatam,* Śrīla Prabhupāda came to the United States, in 1965, to fulfill the mission of his spiritual master. Since that time, His Divine Grace has written over forty volumes of authoritative translations, commentaries and summary studies of the philosophical and religious classics of India.

In 1965, when he first arrived by freighter in New York City, Śrīla Prabhupāda was practically penniless. It was after almost a year of great difficulty that he established the International Society for Krishna Consciousness in July of 1966. Under his careful guidance, the Society has grown within a decade to a worldwide confederation of almost one hundred *āśramas*, schools, temples, institutes and farm communities.

In 1968, Śrīla Prabhupāda created New Vṛndāvana, an experimental Vedic community in the hills of West Virginia. Inspired by the success of New Vṛndāvana, now a thriving farm community of more than one thousand acres, his students have since founded several similar communities in the United States and abroad.

In 1972, His Divine Grace introduced the Vedic system of primary and secondary education in the West by founding the Gurukula school in Dallas, Texas. The school began with 3 children in 1972, and by the beginning of 1975 the enrollment had grown to 150.

Śrīla Prabhupāda has also inspired the construction of a large international center at Śrīdhāma Māyāpur in West Bengal, India, which is also the site for a planned Institute of Vedic Studies. A similar project is the magnificent Kṛṣṇa-Balarāma Temple and International Guest House in Vṛndāvana, India. These are centers where Westerners can live to gain firsthand experience of Vedic culture.

Śrīla Prabhupāda's most significant contribution, however, is his books. Highly respected by the academic community for their authoritativeness, depth and clarity, they are used as standard textbooks in numerous college courses. His writings have been translated into eleven languages. The Bhaktivedanta Book Trust, established in 1972 exclusively to publish the works of His Divine Grace, has thus become the world's largest publisher of books in the field of Indian religion and philosophy. Its latest project is the publishing of Śrīla Prabhupāda's most recent work: a seventeen-volume translation and commentary—completed by Śrīla Prabhupāda in only eighteen months—on the Bengali religious classic *Śrī Caitanya-caritāmṛta.*

In the past ten years, in spite of his advanced age, Śrīla Prabhupāda has circled the globe twelve times on lecture tours that have taken him to six continents. In spite of such a vigorous schedule, Śrīla Prabhupāda continues to write prolifically. His writings constitute a veritable library of Vedic philosophy, religion, literature and culture.

References

The purports of *Śrīmad-Bhāgavatam* are all confirmed by standard Vedic authorities. The following authentic scriptures are specifically cited in this volume on the pages listed.

Bhagavad-gītā, 35, 38, 40, 61, 117, 120, 129, 132, 134, 141, 142, 144, 146, 152, 153, 168, 172, 173, 176, 204, 206, 217, 221, 222, 226, 228, 231, 234, 235

Brahmāṇḍa Purāṇa, 120

Brahma-saṁhitā, 127, 134, 146, 171, 225

Bṛhad-viṣṇu Purāṇa, 255

Caitanya-caritāmṛta (Kṛṣṇadāsa Kavirāja), 54, 151, 170, 225

Daśāvatāra-stotra. See: Gīta-govinda

Gīta-govinda (Jayadeva Gosvāmī), 78

Mahābhārata, 132

Manu-saṁhitā, 255–256

Nāradīya Purāṇa, 120

Padma Purāṇa, 90, 235–236

Prema-vivarta (Jagadānanda Paṇḍita), 255

Śrīmad-Bhāgavatam, 34, 39, 44, 114–115, 133, 138, 165, 169, 236, 238, 256

Viṣṇu Purāṇa, 89, 226

Glossary

A

Ācamana—purification performed by sipping water and chanting names of Viṣṇu before engaging in sacrifices.

Ācārya—a spiritual master who teaches by example.

Ādityas—the demigods who are descendants of Kaśyapa Muni's wife, Aditi.

Aṇimā—the mystic power of becoming the smallest.

Apsarās—heavenly society girls.

Ārati—a ceremony for greeting the Lord with offerings of food, lamps, fans, flowers and incense.

Arcanā—the devotional practice of Deity worship.

Āśrama—a spiritual order of life.

Asuras—atheistic demons.

Avatāra—a descent of the Supreme Lord.

B

Balarāma, Lord—Kṛṣṇa's first expansion and elder brother in Vṛndāvana.

Bhagavad-gītā—the basic directions for spiritual life spoken by the Lord Himself.

Bhakta—a devotee.

Bhakti-yoga—linking with the Supreme Lord in ecstatic devotional service.

Brahmacarya—celibate student life; the first order of Vedic spiritual life.

Brahman—the Absolute Truth; especially, the impersonal aspect of the Absolute.

Brāhmaṇa—a person in the mode of goodness; first Vedic social order.

Buddha, Lord—Kṛṣṇa's incarnation in Kali-yuga for bewildering the atheists who were misusing the *Vedas.*

D

Dāna—charity, one of the six duties of a *brāhmaṇa.*

Dānavas—a race of demons.

Daṇḍavats—respectful obeisances, falling flat like a rod.

Dāsya-rasa—affection of servitude toward the Supreme Lord.

Dhanvantari—Kṛṣṇa's incarnation as the father of the science of medicine.
Dharma—eternal occupational duty; religious principles.
Dhīra—one who is undisturbed in all circumstances.
Dhruvaloka—the polestar, which is a spiritual planet within the material universe, presided over by Dhruva Mahārāja.

E

Ekādaśī—a special fast day for increased remembrance of Kṛṣṇa, which comes on the eleventh day of both the waxing and waning moon.

G

Gandharvas—the singers among the demigods.
Garbhodakaśāyī Viṣṇu—the second Viṣṇu expansion, who enters each universe and, by His glance, creates the diverse material manifestations.
Goloka (Kṛṣṇaloka)—the highest spiritual planet, containing Kṛṣṇa's personal abodes, Dvārakā, Mathurā and Vṛndāvana.
Gopīs—Kṛṣṇa's cowherd girl friends who are His most confidential servitors.
Govinda—Kṛṣṇa, who gives pleasure to the land, the cows and the senses.
Gṛhastha—regulated householder life; the second order of Vedic spiritual life.
Guṇas—the three modes of material nature: goodness, passion and ignorance.
Guru—a spiritual master or superior person.

H

Hayagrīva, Lord—Kṛṣṇa's horse-headed incarnation, who returned the stolen *Vedas* to Brahmā.

J

Jīva-tattva—the living entities, who are small parts of the Lord.

K

Kali-yuga (Age of Kali)—the present age, which is characterized by quarrel. It is last in the cycle of four and began five thousand years ago.

Kalki, Lord—Lord Kṛṣṇa's incarnation, at the end of the last of the four ages, who annihilates all the remaining atheists.

Kapila, Lord—Lord Kṛṣṇa's incarnation to teach Sāṅkhya philosophy, a combination of devotional service and mystic realization.

Kāraṇodakaśāyī Viṣṇu—*See:* Mahā-Viṣṇu.

Karatālas—hand cymbals used in *kīrtana.*

Karma—fruitive action, for which there is always reaction, good or bad.

Karmī—a person who is satisfied with working hard for flickering sense gratification.

Kīrtana—chanting the glories of the Supreme Lord.

Kṛṣṇaloka—*See:* Goloka.

Kṣatriyas—a warrior or administrator; the second Vedic social order.

Kṣīrodakaśāyī Viṣṇu—the third Viṣṇu incarnation, who is the Supersoul living in the heart of each living entity.

Kuśa grass—a sacred grass used in Vedic sacrifices.

Kūrma, Lord—Kṛṣṇa's tortoise incarnation.

L

Laghimā—the mystic power of becoming the lightest.

M

Mādhurya-rasa—conjugal affection for the Supreme Lord.

Mahābhārata—the history of greater India compiled by Śrīla Vyāsadeva, which includes *Bhagavad-gītā.*

Mahā-mantra—the great chanting for deliverance: Hare Kṛṣṇa, Hare Kṛṣṇa, Kṛṣṇa Kṛṣṇa, Hare Hare/ Hare Rāma, Hare Rāma, Rāma Rāma, Hare Hare.

Mahā-puruṣa—the Supreme Lord, who is the supreme enjoyer.

Mahat-tattva—the total material energy before the manifestation of diverse elements.

Mahā-Viṣṇu (Kāraṇodakaśāyī Viṣṇu)—the first Viṣṇu incarnation, who lies down in the Causal Ocean and dreams the innumerable material universes.

Mantra—a sound vibration that can deliver the mind from illusion.

Maruts—the associates of King Indra.

Mathurā—Lord Kṛṣṇa's abode, surrounding Vṛndāvana, where He took birth and later returned to after performing His Vṛndāvana pastimes.

Māyā—(*mā*—not; *yā*—this), illusion; forgetfulness of one's relationship with Kṛṣṇa.

Māyāvādīs—impersonal philosophers who say that the Lord cannot have a transcendental body.

Mṛdaṅga—a clay drum used for congregational chanting.

N

Nārada Muni—Lord Brahmā's son and disciple, who travels freely all over the cosmic manifestation preaching Kṛṣṇa consciousness.

Nārāyaṇa, Lord—Kṛṣṇa's four-armed expansion who displays His full opulence as the Supreme Lord of the spiritual kingdom.

Nṛsiṁhadeva, Lord—Kṛṣṇa's half-man, half-lion incarnation.

P

Parabrahman—the Supreme Absolute Truth, Kṛṣṇa.

Paramātmā—the Supreme Lord as the Supersoul in the heart of each embodied living entity.

Paramparā—the chain of spiritual masters in disciplic succession.

Paraśurāma, Lord—Kṛṣṇa's incarnation who destroyed twenty-one consecutive generations of unlawful members of the ruling class.

Pāṣaṇḍīs—atheists.

Paṭhana—studying the scriptures, one of the six duties of a *brāhmaṇa.*

Pāṭhana—teaching, one of the six duties of a *brāhmaṇa.*

Prasāda—food spiritualized by being offered to the Lord.

Pratigraha—accepting charity, one of the six duties of a *brāhmaṇa.*

Purāṇas—Vedic supplements in the form of histories of the universe.

Puruṣa-avatāras—the three Viṣṇu incarnations, Mahā-Viṣṇu, Garbhodakaśāyī Viṣṇu and Kṣīrodakaśāyī Viṣṇu.

R

Rākṣasas—man-eating demons.

Rasa—the loving mood or mellow relished in the exchange of love with the Supreme Lord.

Ṛṣabhadeva, Lord—Kṛṣṇa's incarnation to teach religious principles as the ideal monarch.

Rudras—the expansions of Lord Śiva who rule over the material mode of ignorance.

S

Sac-cid-ānanda-vigraha—the Lord's transcendental form, which is eternal, full of knowledge and bliss.

Sakhya-rasa—fraternal affection for the Supreme Lord.

Sālokya—the liberation of gaining entrance into the Lord's own abode.

Samādhi—perfect trance in *yoga.*

Sāmīpya—the liberation of eternal association with the Lord.

Sanātana-dharma—eternal religion.

Saṅkīrtana—public chanting of the names of God, the approved *yoga* process for this age.

Sannyāsa—renounced life; the fourth order of Vedic spiritual life.

Śānta—neutral affection for the Supreme Lord.

Sārṣṭi—the liberation of achieving equal opulence with the Lord.

Sārūpya—the liberation of obtaining bodily features like the Lord's.

Śāstras—revealed scriptures.

Sāyujya—the impersonal liberation, rejected by devotees, of merging into the rays of the Lord's bodily effulgence.

Śeṣa—the expansion of Saṅkarṣaṇa who, in the form of a couch of snakes, personally serves the Supreme Personality of Godhead and holds up all the worlds on his numberless hoods.

Siddhas—a race of demigods who possess all mystic *yoga* powers.

Soma-rasa—the heavenly beverage taken by demigods for increased span of life.

Śravaṇaṁ kīrtanaṁ viṣṇoḥ—the devotional processes of hearing and chanting about Lord Viṣṇu.

Śrīvatsa—the mark of the resting place of the goddess of fortune on the chest of Lord Nārāyaṇa.

Śūdra—a laborer; the fourth of the Vedic social orders.

Svāmī—one who controls his mind and senses; title of one in the renounced order of life.

T

Tapasya—austerity; accepting some voluntary inconvenience for a higher purpose.

Tilaka—auspicious clay marks that sanctify a devotee's body as a temple of the Lord.

U

Upaniṣads—the most significant philosophical sections of the *Vedas.*

V

Vaikuṇṭha—the spiritual world, where there is no anxiety.

Vaiṣṇava—a devotee of Lord Viṣṇu, or Kṛṣṇa.

Vaiśyas—farmers and merchants; the third Vedic social order.

Vāmana, Lord—Kṛṣṇa's incarnation as a dwarf *brāhmaṇa.*

Vānaprastha—one who has retired from family life; the third order of Vedic spiritual life.

Varṇa—a social class whose members are distinguished by their quality of work and situation in the modes of nature.

Varṇāsrama—the Vedic social system of four social and four spiritual orders.

Varuṇa—the demigod who is the presiding deity of the oceans.

Vātsalya-rasa—paternal affection for the Supreme Lord.

Vedānta-sūtra—Śrīla Vyāsadeva's philosophical exposition of the Absolute Truth, written in brief codes.

Vedas—the original revealed scriptures, first spoken by the Lord Himself.

Viṣṇu, Lord—Kṛṣṇa's first expansion for the creation and maintenance of the material universes.

Vṛndāvana—Kṛṣṇa's personal abode, where He fully manifests His quality of sweetness.

Vyāsadeva—Kṛṣṇa's incarnation, at the end of Dvāpara-yuga, for compiling the *Vedas.*

Y

Yajamānas—those for whom a priest executes sacrifices.

Yajñas—sacrifice, work done for the satisfaction of Lord Viṣṇu.

Yogī—a transcendentalist who, in one way or another, is striving for union with the Supreme.

Yugas—ages in the life of a universe, occuring in a repeated cycle of four.

Z

Zamindar—in Bengal, a wealthy landowner.

GENEALOGICAL TABLE–CHART ONE

The Plenary Expansions of Godhead and Descendants of Brahmā up to the Sons and Daughters of Dakṣa

Kṛṣṇa is the source of all forms of Godhead as well as all living entities. His first expansion is Balarāma. The first part of this simplified chart portrays the different expansions of Lord Kṛṣṇa through the Puruṣa *avatāras*, or expansions for material creation, such as Mahā-Viṣṇu. From the second Puruṣa *avatāra*, Garbhodakaśāyī Viṣṇu, is born Lord Brahmā, the first created personality within the material world. Brahmā is the empowered creator of the manifested universe and everything within it. The second part of this chart depicts Brahmā's descendants as far as the sons and daughters of Dakṣa.

The daughters of Dakṣa and their descendants are shown in the second chart (pp. 282–283 following). As described in this volume, Prajāpati Dakṣa begot sixty daughters in the womb of his wife Asiknī. One should know that it is because of the union of these sixty daughters with various exalted personalities that the entire universe was filled with various kinds of living entities, such as human beings, demigods, demons, beasts, birds and serpents.

Lord Brahmā and subsequent personalities in these charts are *jīvas*, or ordinary living entities, except as noted. All expansions from Kṛṣṇa to Garbhodakaśāyī Viṣṇu are infinite forms of the Supreme Personality of Godhead, Śrī Kṛṣṇa.

References. *See also* index to this volume
From Kṛṣṇa to Garbhodakaśāyī Viṣṇu: *Śrī Caitanya-caritāmṛta, Ādi-līlā*
From Brahmā to Dakṣa and Asiknī: *Śrīmad-Bhāgavatam*, Canto Four

KṚṢṆA
- Balarāma
  - Saṅkarṣaṇa
    - Mahā-Saṅkarṣaṇa
      - Mahā-Viṣṇu
        - Garbhodakaśāyī Viṣṇu
          - Brahmā
            - Svāyambhuva Manu + Śatarūpā
              - Uttānapāda + Suruci & Sunīti
                - Uttama (son of Suruci)
                - Dhruva (son of Sunīti; Prajāpati Śiśumāra and Vāyu give daughters) + Bhrami & Ilā
                  - Vatsara + Svarvīthi
                    - Iṣa
                    - Ūrja
                    - Vasu
                    - Jaya
                    - Tigmaketu
                    - Puṣpārṇa + Doṣā & Prabhā
                      - Pradoṣa
                      - Niśitha
                      - Vyuṣṭa + Puṣkariṇī
                      - Prātaḥ
                      - Madhyandinam
                      - Sāyam
                  - Kalpa
                  - Utkala

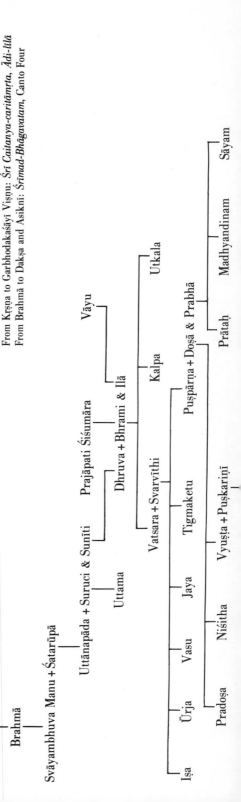

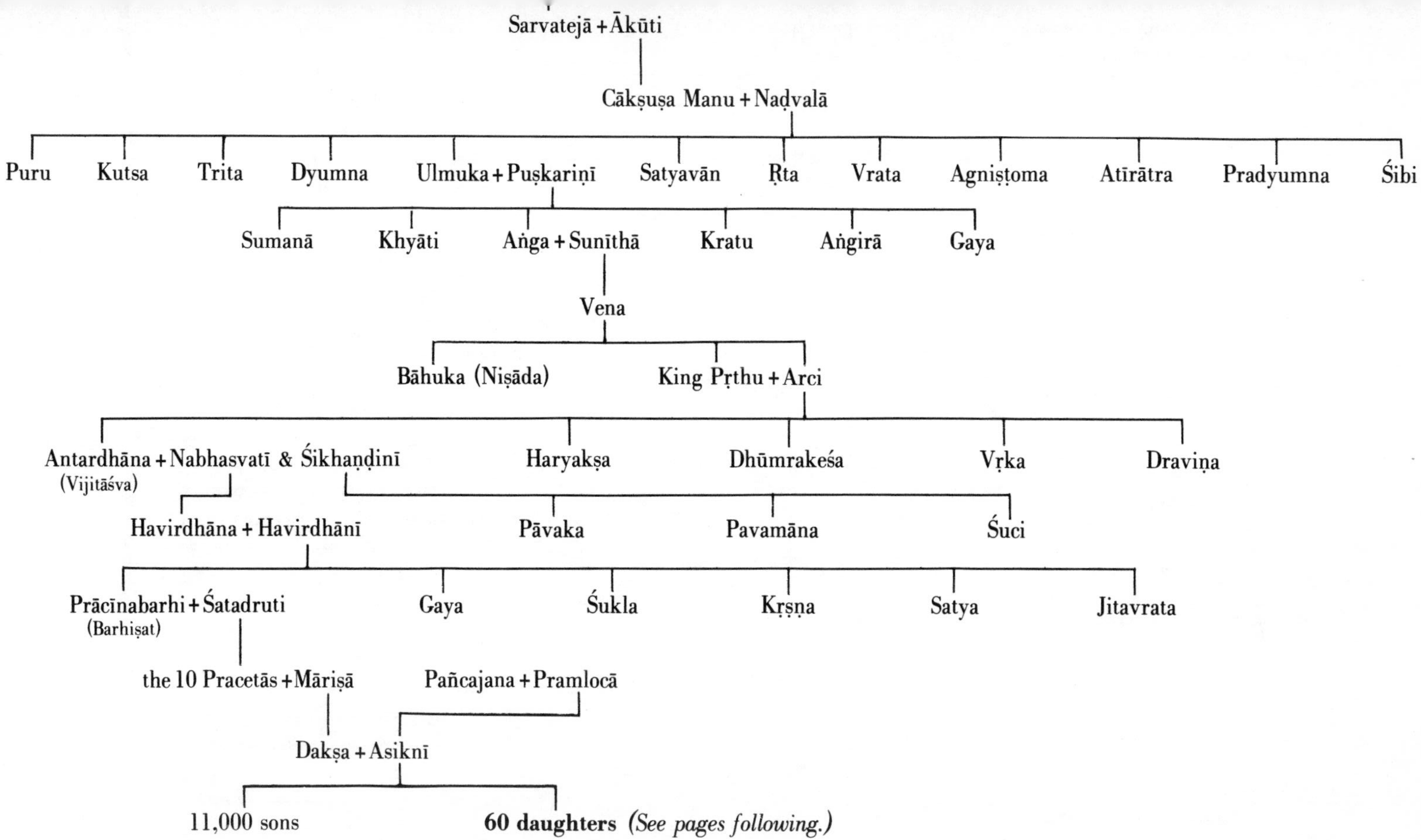
Sarvatejā + Ākūti
Cākṣuṣa Manu + Naḍvalā
Puru
Kutsa
Trita
Dyumna
Ulmuka + Puṣkariṇī
Satyavān
Ṛta
Vrata
Agniṣṭoma
Atīrātra
Pradyumna
Śibi
Sumanā
Khyāti
Aṅga + Sunīthā
Kratu
Aṅgirā
Gaya
Vena
Bāhuka (Niṣāda)
King Pṛthu + Arci
Antardhāna + Nabhasvatī & Śikhaṇḍinī
(Vijitāśva)
Haryakṣa
Dhūmrakeśa
Vṛka
Draviṇa
Havirdhāna + Havirdhānī
Pāvaka
Pavamāna
Śuci
Prācīnabarhi + Śatadruti
(Barhiṣat)
Gaya
Śukla
Kṛṣṇa
Satya
Jitavrata
the 10 Pracetās + Māriṣā
Pañcajana + Pramlocā
Dakṣa + Asiknī
11,000 sons
60 daughters (See pages following.)

+ indicates marriage ties.

GENEALOGICAL TABLE–CHART TWO

The Progeny of the Daughters of Dakṣa

Kaśyapa (received 17 wives) +

- **Timi** → aquatics
- **Vinatā** → Garuḍa, Anūru (Aruṇa)
- **Kadrū** → serpents
- **Pataṅgī** → birds
- **Yāminī** → locusts
- **Diti** → Hiraṇyākṣa, Hiraṇyakaśipu, *etc.*
- **Kāṣṭhā** → single-hooved animals
- **Ariṣṭā** → Gandharvas
- **Surasā** → Rākṣasas
- **Ilā** → creepers & trees
- **Muni** → angels
- **Krodhavaśā** → mosquitoes, serpents (dandaśūka & others)
- **Tāmrā** → large birds of prey
- **Surabhi** → cow, buffalo, *etc.*
- **Saramā** → ferocious animals
- **Danu** →
  - Aruṇa, Anutāpana, Dvimūrdhā, Śambara, Vibhāvasu, Ayomukha, Śaṅkuśirā, Kapila, Durjaya, Dhūmrakeśa, Ekacakra, Virūpākṣa,
  - Svarbhānu + NS → Suprabā + Namuci
  - Vṛṣaparvā + NS → Śarmiṣṭhā + Yayāti
  - Vipracitti + Siṁhikā → Rāhu & the one hundred Ketus
  - Hayagrīva (demon), Pulomā, Ariṣṭa,
  - Vaiśvānara + NS →
    - Upadānavī + Hiraṇyākṣa
    - Hayaśirā + Kratu
    - Pulomā, Kālakā + Kaśyapa → the Paulomas & the Kālakeyas, *headed by* Nivātakavaca

Aṅgirā (received 2 wives) +

- **Svadhā** → the Pitās
- **Satī** → Atharvāṅgirasa Veda

Bhūta (received 2 wives) +

- **NS** → ghosts & goblins
- **Sarūpā** → the ten million Rudras, *of whom eleven are prominent:* Raivata, Aja, Bhava, Bhīma, Vāma, Ugra, Ajaikapāt, Ahirbradhna, Vṛṣākapi, Mahān, Bahurūpa

Kṛśāśva (received 2 wives) +

- **Arcis** → Dhūmaketu
- **Dhiṣaṇā** → Vedaśirā, Devala, Vayuna, Manu

Moon-god (received 27 wives) + the **Kṛttikā** constellations

Aditi → Bhaga, Savitā, Vidhātā, Pūṣā, Varuṇa, Urukrama, Mitra, Dhātā,
- Tvaṣṭā + Racanā → Sanniveśa, Viśvarūpa
- Aryamā + Mātṛkā → scholars & human beings
- Śatru,
- Vivasvān + Chāyā → Śanaiścara, Sāvarṇi Muni, Tapatī + Saṁvaraṇa
- Vivasvān + Saṁjñā → Yamarāja, Śrāddhadeva, R. Yamuna (Yamī) → Aśvinī-kumāras

* Foster son. Actual father is Śiva.
+ indicates marriage ties.
→ indicates offspring.
NS not specified.
Dakṣa's daughters are indicated by boldface type.

Yamarāja (Dharmarāja) + (received 10 wives)
- **Bhānu** → Deva-ṛṣabha + NS → Indrasena
- **Lambā** → Vidyota + NS → clouds
- **Kakud** → Saṅkaṭa + NS → Kīkaṭa + NS → demigods named Durga
- **Yāmi** → Svarga + NS → Nandi
- **Saṅkalpā** → Saṅkalpa + NS → lust
- **Sādhyā** → the Sādhyas + NS → Arthasiddhi
- **Viśvā** → Viśvadevas
- **Muhūrtā** → the Mauhūrtikas (demigods)
- **Marutvatī** → Marutvān, Jayanta (Upendra, an expansion of the Supreme Lord)
- **Vasu** →
  - Dhruva + Dharaṇi → cities
  - Vāstu + Āṅgirasī → Viśvakarmā + Akṛtī
  - Droṇa + Abhimati → Harṣa, Śoka, Bhaya, *etc.*
  - Prāṇa + Ūrjasvatī → Saha, Āyus, Purojava
  - Agni + Dhārā → Draviṇaka *and others*
  - Agni + Kṛttikā → Kārttikeya (Skanda)* + NS → Viśākha *and others*
  - Doṣa + Śarvarī → Śiśumāra (an expansion of the Supreme Lord)
  - Arka + Vāsanā → Tarṣa *and others*
  - Vibhāvasu + Ūṣā → Vyuṣṭa, Rociṣa & Ātapa + NS → Pañcayāma (span of day)

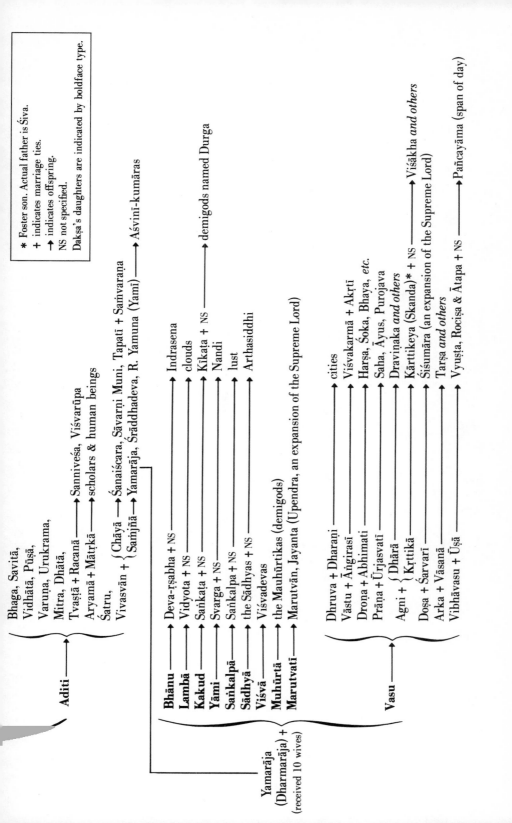

Sanskrit Pronunciation Guide

Vowels

अ a आ ā इ i ई ī उ u ऊ ū ऋ ṛ ॠ ṝ
ऌ ḷ ए e ऐ ai ओ o औ au

ं ṁ *(anusvāra)* ः ḥ *(visarga)*

Consonants

Gutturals:	क ka	ख kha	ग ga	घ gha	ङ ṅa
Palatals:	च ca	छ cha	ज ja	झ jha	ञ ña
Cerebrals:	ट ṭa	ठ ṭha	ड ḍa	ढ ḍha	ण ṇa
Dentals:	त ta	थ tha	द da	ध dha	न na
Labials:	प pa	फ pha	ब ba	भ bha	म ma
Semivowels:	य ya	र ra	ल la	व va	
Sibilants:	श śa	ष ṣa	स sa		
Aspirate:	ह ha	ऽ ' *(avagraha)* – the apostrophe			

The vowels above should be pronounced as follows:

a – like the *a* in org*a*n or the *u* in b*u*t.
ā – like the *a* in f*a*r but held twice as long as short *a*.
i – like the *i* in p*i*n.
ī – like the *i* in p*i*que but held twice as long as short *i*.
u – like the *u* in p*u*sh.
ū – like the *u* in r*u*le but held twice as long as short *u*.

ṛ – like the *ri* in *ri*m.
ṝ – like *ree* in *ree*d.
ḷ – like *l* followed by *ṛ* (*lṛ*).
e – like the *e* in th*ey*.
ai – like the *ai* in *ai*sle.
o – like the *o* in g*o*.
au – like the *ow* in h*ow*.
ṁ (*anusvāra*) – a resonant nasal like the *n* in the French word *bon.*
ḥ (*visarga*) – a final *h*-sound: *aḥ* is pronounced like *aha; iḥ* like *ihi.*

The consonants are pronounced as follows:

k – as in *k*ite
kh – as in Ec*kh*art
g – as in *g*ive
gh – as in di*g-h*ard
ṅ – as in si*ng*
c – as in *ch*air
ch – as in staun*ch-h*eart
j – as in *j*oy
jh – as in he*dgeh*og
ñ – as in ca*ny*on
ṭ – as in *t*ub
ṭh – as in ligh*t-h*eart
ḍ – as in *d*ove
ḍha- as in re*d-h*ot
ṇ – as r*na* (prepare to say the *r* and say *na*).

Cerebrals are pronounced with tongue to roof of mouth, but the following dentals are pronounced with tongue against teeth:

t – as in *t*ub but with tongue against teeth.
th – as in ligh*t-h*eart but with tongue against teeth.
d – as in *d*ove but with tongue against teeth.
dh – as in re*d-h*ot but with tongue against teeth.
n – as in *n*ut but with tongue between teeth.
p – as in *p*ine
ph – as in u*ph*ill (not *f*)
b – as in *b*ird
bh – as in ru*b-h*ard
m – as in *m*other
y – as in *y*es
r – as in *r*un
l – as in *l*ight
v – as in *v*ine
ś (palatal) – as in the *s* in the German word *sprechen*
ṣ (cerebral) – as the *sh* in *sh*ine
s – as in *s*un
h – as in *h*ome

There is no strong accentuation of syllables in Sanskrit, only a flowing of short and long (twice as long as the short) syllables.

Index of Sanskrit Verses

This index constitutes a complete listing of the first and third lines of each of the Sanskrit poetry verses and the first line of each Sanskrit prose verse of this volume of *Śrīmad-Bhāgavatam*, arranged in English alphabetical order. In the first column the Sanskrit transliteration is given, and in the second and third columns respectively the chapter-verse reference and page number for each verse are to be found.

A

B

L

M

N

U

V

Y

General Index

Numerals in boldface type indicate references to translations of the verses of *Śrīmad-Bhāgavatam.*

A

Abhaya, Kṛṣṇa as, 113
Abhimati, sons of, **8**
Ābrahma-bhuvanāl lokāḥ
quoted, 204
Absolute Truth, phases of, three described, 141–142
Ācārya. See: Spiritual master; *names of* ācāryas
Ācāryaṁ māṁ vijānīyān
quoted, 39, 44
Acintyāḥ khalu ye bhāvā
quoted, 132
Aditi, **16**
sons of, **22**
Ādityas, the, **177**
Age of Kali. *See:* Kali-yuga
Agni, **8**
personified by invited guest, **52**
wife, sons and grandsons of, **9**
Aham ādir hi devānām
quoted, 226
Aham evāsam evāgre
quoted, 120
Ahaṁ sarvasya prabhavo
verse quoted, 120
Ahaṅgrahopāsanā, 71
Ahaṅkāra-vimūḍhātmā
verse quoted, 222
Ahiṁsaḥ parama-dharmaḥ
quoted, 167
Ahirbradhna, **11**
Air, the element, **113,** 171
Airāvata, **174, 195**
Aja, **11**
Ajaikapāt, **11**
Akāma devotees, defined, 137–138
Akṛtī, **10**
son and grandsons of, **10**
America
degradation by opulence in, 34, 36
hope for, 35, 38
Āmi—vijña, ei mūrkhe 'viṣaya' kene diba?
verse quoted, 151
Anādir ādir govindaḥ
verse quoted, 171, 225
Anarvā, **178, 184**
Aṇḍāntara-stha-paramāṇu-cayāntara-sthaṁ
verse quoted, 134
Angels, **16**
Aṅgirā, **3**
wives and sons of, **12**
Āṅgirasī, **10**
son of, **10**
Animal of grass and leaves dancing, controlled living entity compared to, **224**
Animals
cloven hooved, **16**
compassion for, 167–168
ferocious, **16**
See also: specific names of animals
Animal slaughter
irreligious, 167–168
stopped by Buddha, 78
Anta-kāle ca mām eva
verse quoted, 172
Antaryāmī, 126
Antavat tu phalaṁ teṣāṁ
quoted, 153
Anupraviśya govindaḥ
verse quoted, 120
Anūru (Aruṇa, son of Vinatā), **14**
Anutāpana, **18**

B

C

D

J

L

N

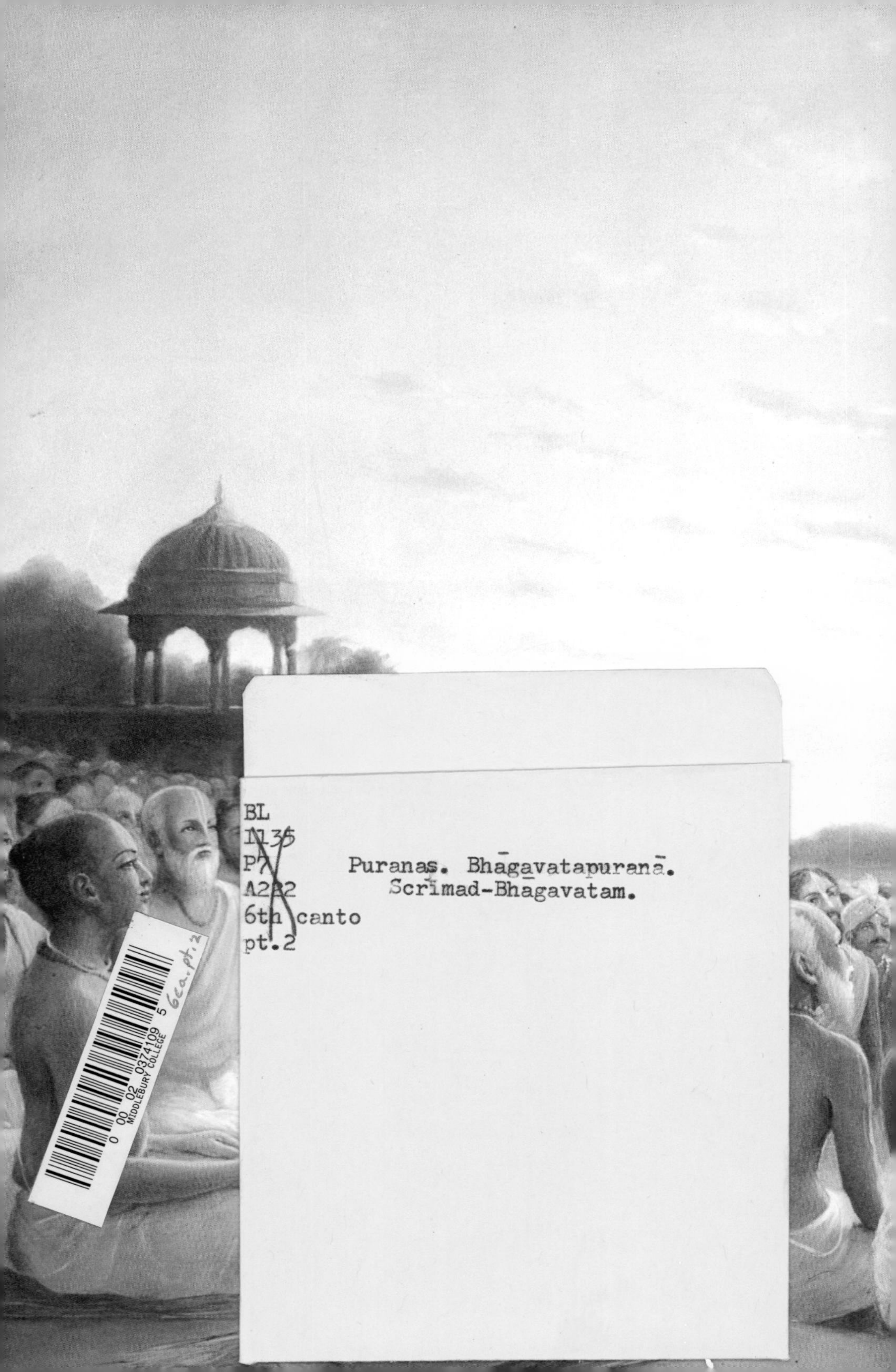